Making It Home
My year as a middle-aged runaway

Liz Moore

ISBN-13: 978-1461144120
ISBN-10: 1461144124

For Rodney and Jane Smith

CONTENTS

AUTHOR'S NOTE

I have changed the names and other identifying details of some of the businesses and individuals that I encountered on this odyssey. I am deeply grateful to all for their support, for kindness shown and lessons taught.

1 THE DAYDREAM

What have I done?

There's no one in my little Flagstaff motel room to help me with that question. Thoughts spin chaotically in my own head.

What do I do now?

Besides sweat, and tremble. Check out? Get back in my car and drive a thousand miles home?

My condo in Texas isn't home anymore. At least, not for a year. I gave it up to somebody else to be THEIR home.

MY world is now a 13-year-old Honda Civic. Three weeks ago I stuffed its trunk with clothes, a few pots and pans, a 5-inch TV, a canvas chair, and I drove away. I left one sister, two cats, many friends, a successful career and a very comfortable lifestyle.

I wanted life Elsewhere, away from roots. I said – *thought* – I wanted a home, job, new friends, new pastimes in someplace completely different from Kansas and Texas, the two states that evenly divide my first 50 years of both home and identity.

I don't have a plan or a lot of money. My idea rests on fate and whim, in a life of total freedom and reinvention, going from town to town. After a month, or two months in some small town I've never seen before, I'll move on to the next place. My loop will circle America.

I've picked Flagstaff to be the first stop, except that yesterday a housing agent dismissed me coldly. A restaurant manager told me he has no jobs. My cell phone broke and my car died.

And I'm really lonely. Without anyone or anything defining my days and setting my clock, I almost don't know who I am anymore.

Maybe there's a reason daydreams should stay daydreams – why *did I think this one would work? It was such an exciting idea.*

The boss was on his way, and that's not good.

There are seven of us this Wednesday morning, the management group of a national association. We've gathered in the board room of our office suite that takes up most of the third floor of the Chase bank tower in Arlington, Texas.

Normally, we like being in this room with its massive polished table and its walls lined with framed portraits of the organization's two dozen past presidents. The décor is blue – the carpet, the walls, and 15 upholstered chairs that rock, swivel and turn, moved by the occupants' frustration, amusement, inspiration, annoyance, conflict, camaraderie and boredom typically served up in any meeting.

We are employees of The Arc, a national organization for people who have mental retardation. For most of my 17 years here, I've managed its communications program and, forsaking all others, I basically married the job. Like a long-time but flawed marriage, there was passion in the early years, followed by a stretch of contentment and devotion. There has also been lots of struggle to "make it work," and boredom and fatigue. But always I've loved it. And now, I face divorce. We all do.

We positioned our chairs with studied casualness. We've already held the "real" meetings in numerous other places over several weeks. We've traded information in closed-door, desk-side exchanges of the latest rumors, in paranoid e-mails and whispered interoffice calls, and standing in lunch-room clusters, eyes watching the door.

"Darth Vader is here. I hear he's going to tell us something at 10:30," my colleague Jim had said early this morning.

"Darth Vader" is one of several nicknames we've tagged on the large and commanding executive director. Hired by The Arc's board of directors just weeks ago, he charged into our lives to launch "Our Future Employment" as grapevine topic No. 1. The new E.D. lives in Maryland, and it has become evident, in actions both official and alleged, that The Arc's elected leadership wants to move the headquarters to Washington, D.C. Without most of the staff. There simply isn't enough money to take us along.

This is the man who will make the severance happen.

He lumbered into the room late, distracted and nonchalant, settled into a blue chair and quickly got down to business.

"I'm looking at space in Silver Spring," he announced, and I note the language and cadence of Washington-speak. "It's on the Metro's Red Line, a 20-minute ride from the Hill, excellent space."

He added that the bank is eager to get its third floor back to accommodate its expanding operations. The Arc should have no problem getting out of the lease early.

Darth Vader was short and to the point. He invited questions, but few of the covert looks that ricocheted among us became audible communication, so he did what he usually did on his few Arlington visits – spent a few hours and got back on the plane for D.C. Sometimes he mutters an excuse for his abrupt departures, but more often he just disappears. Who can blame him? Why sit there and stare at the unsmiling faces of the past?

The evening after his office space announcement, I called my 85-year-old father in Kansas.

"How's Mr. Arc?!" he cracked, using the nickname he'd coined for the new boss. This always made me laugh and as usual, he managed to remind me in an instant not to take my job or myself too seriously.

"Looks like the move is going to happen in December, Daddy."

"Are you going to hunt for a new job?"

What he meant was, I should get started finding new employment ASAP. That's certainly what Rodney Smith would do, not that he had to in mid-20th century America. He'd been loyal to the Sinclair Pipeline Co. for 25 years, and they had been loyal to him, and that's the way employment worked in those days.

"Y-yeah, I guess so. Look for a new job. Sure."

It was true that one day in an airport bookstore, I picked up a book on job hunting. "ALL THE HELP YOU'LL EVER NEED," its cover trumpeted in vivid red and yellow graphics. I bought it even though it hurt my eyes.

Actually, it hurt my psyche. The truth was, I didn't want another job. I couldn't bear the thought of another "career position" of day-in day-out routine. In recent years, no matter what I did to stay motivated, the overall sameness of life was getting to me. Days gave way to weeks. Months fell away and seasons changed. Every year cycled the same events at the same times: January planning, quarterly newspaper production, board meetings, fund-raising letters, Summer Training, fall convention. In the non-profit world, there's never enough money, and we seemed to always be reshuffling the deck of chronic problems and thin, under-funded solutions. I was tired.

One night I was having dinner at an east Fort Worth Italian restaurant with my older sister Martha and brother-in-law Paul Gordon. Over Spaghetti Puttanesca and a beer, I decided to introduce the subject of my daydream.

"Wouldn't it be interesting…" I began, "to, uh, get in the car and leave town for a while. Say, a year. And not just drive around America, but stop here and there to spend some real time. Get little jobs and make friends and do volunteer things and otherwise, just do what there is to do there but then move on to the next place after a month or two."

There. I'd said it. This was an idea that had become stuck in my head. It had lurked there at least 30 years, ever since I'd read John Steinbeck's *Travels with Charlie* as a teenager, and Studs Terkel's *Working*.

Martha looked up without any particular expression. "Like *Blue Highways*?" she said.

I hadn't read William Least Heat Moon's book, but I made a mental note to go out and find it. So somebody has done this, meaning, it's doable. Interesting. What about female nomads?

At home, I found a space for the job hunting book high up and out of reach on the book shelves of my den.

No one needed to know that I might be crazy if I quietly polled others on my idea as a "what-if" game. After all, everybody plays it. "What if I give up my salary with my rich but heartless company and go into teaching?" "What if I go live on a beach somewhere and never again struggle through a cold winter?" "What if I just quit, period."

Usually, the game ends soon after the reverie begins. The realities of most people's lives seem to involve the needs of a spouse or close "other," feeding and educating the children, and paying insatiable bills that lure and trap one who is fattening up on growing affluence. I had no husband or children. My retirement account was healthy. I had one debt, a mortgage, which I'd been considering paying off out of my savings. In my 28-year career march, I had never taken on the latest fashions in homes, clothes, cars, furniture, or toys.

"You are an experiential kind of person," Kim Garvey pointed out. Kim, a national-level volunteer for The Arc, had just become next in a series of friends and acquaintances polled. Mild in manner, conservative in lifestyle and serious in his work, Kim's reaction – the latest in a series of excited, go-for-it responses – surprised and thrilled me.

"Tremendous! This is the most exciting thing I've ever heard. You've got to do it," he said. "When are you leaving? Where are you going first?"

Phase I, the daydream stage, had definitely ended. I launched phase II: I want to do this, and unless something stops me, I will.

Again at the Italian restaurant, my sister Martha was starting to see that the horse was leaving the barn.

"Why don't you go to London and visit your friend Karen?" she said… "(you can) get this idea out of your system."

"That's not going to do it!" I replied. I felt myself digging in my heels. Then, just as quickly, I realized the dangers of a stubborn track. Almost without exception, every listener, from best friend to total strangers, had urged me on. Excitement threatened to swamp common sense. I didn't know why my sister had become mostly silent on the subject, but I needed the grounding of her point of view.

"What about Minnie and Bigelow?" Martha said.

Minnie and Bigelow. It's not completely true to claim the freedom of childlessness. I have two cats, beloved beings who allowed me to live in their home and dote on them in the ridiculous ways of a cat lover, from catering to their finicky palates to filling photo albums with picture prints that never vary much from roll to roll.

"Take them with you!" somebody said merrily.

"HA ha HA HA haaa. That's not possible," I said, not bothering to explain why they hadn't even ridden to the vet in five years. The last time I caught Minnie to put her in the cat carrier, she panicked and flailed wildly in my grip, cat spit and pee flying about and then she slashed my arm, which got infected and I had to go to a hospital emergency room.

Clearly, I would have to find somebody to live in my condominium. I could give them a heck of a deal on the rent in exchange for simply taking care of my possessions and "the kids."

"You're going to get a new car first, aren't you?"

It's Martha again. Fair question I suppose. I am in my 13th year of driving the same Honda Civic, a four-door model purchased in "toasted almond," a light tan rarely seen in today's fashions in car design. Virtually all of the rest of the world has managed to buy new cars, their low, rounder shapes making my car look boxy and stodgy.

"I've had everything done to that car that it's possible to do; there's nothing left to fix. I want to make use of those repairs and get my money's worth. The Honda will be fine," I said. "Besides, I'll actually be putting fewer miles on my car than I do in a typical year of freeway commutes around Dallas-Fort Worth."

Part of my dream is to give up the construction-clogged, vehicle-jammed freeways and suburban streets that have become a battleground for angry drivers and the cowboys who gun their ridiculous pickups and nudge you along, grill to bumper. I want small towns again, where the commute to work is five minutes and people aren't so stressed.

There was little use trying to explain myself to my big sister. I turned to coworkers, friends and total strangers for enthusiasm and reassurance. They gave me books. They gave me ideas. They asked questions about how I planned to handle everything from personal safety ("What kind of gun do you have?" a friend's husband asked me) to on-the-road housing. Everybody offered spots Not To Be Missed.

"I have the perfect town for you," a work acquaintance exclaimed, eyes misting over in faraway thought. "Monroe, North Carolina."

"Why Monroe, Chris?"

"Because," he said, "it's where I grew up. It's my hometown. You would love it."

His whole reasoning rested on childhood memories of the 1960s. I listened for more, but that was all. Obviously, it was best to reject the idea of trying to duplicate Chris's life and experiences. I knew what he meant, though. My hometown is Independence, Kansas. I love that town, but when I try to tell others about its big park and old mansions and minor celebrities, I realize it may loom just a little bit large in my memories of its contributions to my first quarter-century of life. It's not for everyone.

I've made a decision about my itinerary. There will be none. I don't want to know where I am going until I get there. Generally, I feel my path should reach as much of the U.S. as possible, perhaps circling in a clockwise direction. And it would be lovely to be in New England by fall.

It is time to make a list of what it would take to get this trip out of the talking stage and onto the road by spring.

THINGS TO DO

1) Find a condo-and-cat caretaker.
2) Stock a year's supply of cat food and litter.
3) Make home repairs.
4) Figure a budget for both the trip and expenses remaining at home.
5) Make a packing list and buy supplies.
6) Put the Honda through a big tune-up.
7) Meet with my insurance agent.
8) Set up online banking and bill paying.
9) Rent a safe deposit box.
10) Thin out possessions.
11) Pack the car.

And then there's the whole category of communications. Martha's reticence toward the trip made me think about how to be safe, how to assure others I am safe, and how to make sure people can find me if they need me. With parents in their 80s, I have to think about the possibility of calls to hurry home to Kansas.

Not exactly a Luddite, I've been, nonetheless, a little behind the times in personal technology. My first home computer is barely a year and a half old. Now I need a laptop. Not only do I not use a cell phone, I just recently gave up my Harvest Gold rotary-dial desktop model. Yes, there's work to be done on the communications front.

Browsing books in an office supply store, I see an irresistible title: *Teach Yourself HTML in 24 Hours*. Hypertext Markup Language is the programming language of the Internet. I love books that take a difficult skill – learning Chinese, say, or building a log cabin – and make it sound not only easy, but fast and fun, too!

Euphoric from the approaching end of office life and the beginnings of my adventure as a runaway, I buy the book. The purchase isn't entirely impulsive. I want to have a Web site for family and friends. It also occurs to me that in dropping out – uh, pursuing a sabbatical (Hey, *there's* a respectable word!) – it will be useful to keep a hand in my communications career and acquire a new skill. Learning a little HTML programming will be an unexpectedly cool thing for me to do.

At The Arc, we're finally given more facts about the move and provisions for our severance. I'm retained to work four months beyond the closing of the Arlington office, which is excellent financial news for me. For a year, I've been stock-piling funds and the longer I work, the plumper the cushion. My last day is March 30. An April departure for my trip will be ideal.

I would love to pursue this dream at $1,000 a month. OK, maybe $1,200. Fifteen hundred tops.

"How can I find someone to live in my condo?" I ask my friends. "I need a cat lover who isn't a psychopathic thief, vandal or drug addict. A newspaper ad would be an engraved invitation to a ne'er do well."

"How about a visiting professor?" my friend Marsha suggests.

"How about a resident physician? Somebody from one of the nearby hospitals in our neighborhood?" my neighbor Mary says.

"Don't get a doctor. They're all crazy," my doctor friend Chuck says.

Marsha has given me the name and e-mail address of a faculty member at the University of Texas at Arlington. He responds encouragingly with an offer to circulate the opportunity among "mature grad students." Once again, I hold my breath in hope and humble prayer. The trip is really coming together. So far, it seems meant to be, and I can see my whole life building toward this adventure – every interest I've had, choice I've made, every fate, coincidence, every chunk of luck, good and bad. But finding a responsible, quiet, rent-paying, cat-loving, reliable tenant seems formidable.

By January, The Arc had left and 40 employees were scattered. Three made the move to Maryland. Most of the others started other jobs around Arlington, Fort Worth and Dallas. The half-dozen of us who stayed to support the transition are now in an Arlington warehouse space set up to contain all of the organization's publications as a new, separate, Web-based business. My colleague Jim organized it in a savvy spinoff operation called Soffar Distribution, and it has become a haven for The Arc's refugees as well as its excess furniture. I'm working at my old desk.

One morning I arrive at the office and fire up my computer to check e-mail first.

Subject: Condo
Dear Ms. Moore,
My name is Lisa Marshall and I would like to learn more about the condominium you have available. I live in Chicago now, but have an opportunity to move to Dallas to join an exciting, faith-based program for young adults. I do not have a lot of "stuff" and could take

good care of yours. I love cats and have one named Sam but he could stay with my mother while I take care of your kitties. If you would like to meet me, I will be in Dallas soon to attend a meeting…

My spirits leap. Three months to go, but if I can settle the home caretaking dilemma this early, a big problem will be solved. I also have plenty of time to check out this prospective tenant.

On a Saturday morning, Lisa arrived for a tour and a get-acquainted meeting over coffee and bagels. From initial conversation, I gathered that her "faith-based program" was for at-risk Dallas area teens, prompting one of my neighbors to grouse later, "Oh great. You're going to turn your place into a halfway house?" I chose to ignore the remark but did adopt some stereotypical ideas about the 24-year-old candidate. I fully expected her to be rough and tough, probably the product of troubled, disadvantaged years herself.

Tall and lithe, Lisa looks like Brooke Shields with short hair. She is elegant and serene. Good manners. I learn that she attended a fine college in New England, then transferred to the University of Pennsylvania where she earned a sociology degree in urban studies.

"How and why have you taken on a passion for work with street kids?" I ask.

"Let me tell you about my dad," Lisa says.

Her father, an insurance executive, was killed a few years ago in a plane crash. Lisa still grieves his loss and asked if she could bring "his chair," an oversized cocoon of comfort and memories that she takes with her everywhere.

Mr. Marshall had also been a policy advisor at the White House, and later, worked for the Illinois governor. Growing up, Lisa's adolescent rebellion took on her father's conservative politics. But instead of dismissing arguments as those of a know-nothing child, Lisa's father encouraged the debate and didn't let his daughter off the hook. He challenged her to act on her espoused beliefs. Lisa chose the most socially radical cause she could think of, and by age 16 was volunteering service to people of backgrounds and circumstances far different from her own. She became hooked on the work and chose it as a career path.

"Your opportunity is a god-send," Lisa said to me. "I found this program in Dallas and didn't know how I might be able to join it, but I just prayed and waited and the doors opened."

"I feel the same way," I said. "I don't know why, but God is making the doors fall open for me to take this trip."

Even with Lisa's pedigree and our rapport, I asked for five names I could call for references. I talked to her mother and to a long-time neighbor, a school friend and two people who knew her work and could also talk about her goals and character. Everyone was positively effusive. Soon, Lisa and I signed a contract.

By far, finding that tenant-caretaker was the most difficult aspect of trip preparations.

The second-hardest thing was loading the car.

It isn't that "loading the car" was so difficult by itself, it's also the very last thing before saying good-bye to Texas and my home. Loading the car is the final commitment to a huge risk, from life utterly predictable, to a life of unknowns. I have no plan and no expectations. What choices will I make with every sunrise and a blank canvas of a day? Beyond the desire for adventure, my only compass will be the guidance of common sense and a spiritual belief that what is meant to be will be.

April 14 dawns sunny and warm. I have slept little, awash in apprehension, excitement, fear, wonder, gratitude, guilt. The final days have been full of packing, house cleaning and repair work, and saying good-byes. I worry that I have not packed carefully, done enough to make Lisa comfortable, nor said enough good-byes and thank-yous.

"Stop worrying," Lisa said. "You're all set and I'm fine. Here..." She hands me a tissue-wrapped gift, a blue and gold scarf of frolicking cats.

I fold the scarf and place it among the over-flow of possessions that now spill from the trunk to the back seat and the passenger side of the Honda. I wanted to get everything stashed in the trunk so that my car will not display the life of a traveler so obviously, but it is time to leave and I decide I can jettison parts of the load later.

One more visit I need to make is to my 16-year neighbor Carolyn Raynes. I walk to her condo and think of the lost security of long-time friends who live "just up the sidewalk." Carolyn and her friend Vernon Walton are like a made-to-order sister and brother to me, steadfast helpers, fixers and playmates in my life.

"Are you ready? Did you say good-bye to Minnie and Bigelow?" Carolyn said.

"No. I'm not going to see them before I take off."

Carolyn's lip quivers and tears come to her eyes. Mine water too. She hands me a bag of fresh banana muffins.

We step outside and as I walk toward the Honda, a gray Volvo zips into the parking lot from the street. It is Martha, finally making an appearance. I'm shocked to see my sister, but she has no more questions and no advice.

"I wasn't sure I'd catch you before you left," she says, whipping out her camera and snapping my picture as I stand beside the Honda. Then Lisa takes our picture together.

Martha hands me a card. It contains a hundred dollar bill.

"To splurge on a better motel some night," she explains.

Ready or not it is time to go. I climb into the Honda and write into a tiny, bright orange notebook: 140,877, the odometer reading. I drive away and for once, gladly negotiate Fort Worth's suburban sprawl. I'm headed north.

2 FIRST STOP: KANSAS

The drive up I-35 through Oklahoma and into Kansas has become way too familiar. I've done it a hundred times, alone and with others. Martha and Paul and I have always traveled the route together at Christmas, and then I'm grateful that my brother-in-law drives so that I can sleep through the entire state.

"Why was Oklahoma placed in that spot?" Martha once complained. "Why couldn't it be some other state, like Rhode Island?"

The straight-up ribbon of interstate has become so monotonous to me that I measure the progress of my trip by the mere sight of the Red River, three exits for Ardmore, a brief swell of hills called the Arbuckle Mountains, Oklahoma City, Guthrie and a smattering of roadside businesses at Blackwell. Going south it's the reverse: Blackwell, Guthrie, OKC, Arbuckles, Ardmore, river.

"You've got some nerve running down my state, especially being from Kansas, like it's so much more exciting?!" my Oklahoma friend Mike once exclaimed.

"Darn right" I said. "There's the Kansas Turnpike! WICHITA! And a grain silo near Emporia painted like a Coors Beer can. And 30 years ago, when a couple of Miss Americas were from Kansas, the state's official welcome signs said, 'Kansas – Home of Beautiful Women.' That always made me feel good."

Best of all, northeast of Emporia is the 130-year-old Smith family farm, 640 acres of vast meadows, rich fields of corn and soybeans, dense woodland full of walnut trees, a shady, meandering, peaceful creek, and all the resident animals – deer, wild turkeys, pheasant….

This has been my parents' home since 1976. Rodney Smith inherited part of this paradise in the early 1960s while still employed and rearing his family in Independence. He gradually bought the rest of the property, originally the homestead of his uncle W.D. Smith, from relatives and the Lyndon Presbyterian Church. Rodney and Jane, my mother, found a two-story frame house 10 miles west of the farm and hired professional house movers to take it to their property. And then began my dad's happiest years when he retired and moved up from southeast Kansas.

He stands in the driveway as I roll in eight and a half hours after leaving Hurst.

"Park in the garage and use the zapper," he says, welcoming me and handing me one of the two garage door openers.

He surveys my car with a smile that stretches toward full-grin capacity. I'm reminded of the day I broke the news to him that I was not going to pursue another job. Waiting as long as possible to tell him about my plans to wander, I typed a long letter to him, adding color graphics as if he were a Board of Directors and this was a PowerPoint presentation demanding just the right "positioning."

Soon after getting the fancy communication, he called.

"What do you think?" I said.

He took a breath and then there was a prolonged chuckle.

"It reminds me of my Chicago trip." (Pronounced "Chicahguh.") "When I was a kid, another buddy and I decided we wanted to go to the Chicago World's Fair. I had $12 in my pocket. We hopped trains and hitch-hiked. I even came home with $2."

SO! I came by my idea quite naturally. It's genetic. I also found it interesting that as his daughter, I had never been told of the fool-hardy adventure.

Mother liked my idea instantly. I did not pause too long to wonder if she completely understood the plan. For six years, she's had a tough time, suffering small strokes and losing short-term memory to the point that she now needs 24-hour care. My father has nursed her through many mental and physical losses but insists on keeping his wife of 62 years at home. He even had a bedroom and bath built as a ground-floor addition, with doors wide enough to accommodate a wheelchair. A housekeeper looks after them on weekdays.

The trip, Mother said, "is a wonderful idea. I always wanted to do that!" And then she seemed to forget and never asked about it again.

Concern for my parents and their struggles is the reason I've started my odyssey at the farm. I want to make sure I see them just as often as ever – annually, about three or four times – so I've started the trek with a visit to Kansas and I plan to pop in a couple more times before concluding my adventure and returning to Texas.

My older brother Ed and sister-in-law Sharron, who live in Ottawa 30 miles east, also have driven to the farm and have been awaiting my arrival.

"It's about time you got here," Ed says, meaning *supper time*. "Let's go."

We push Mother in her wheelchair down the front porch ramp and Daddy helps her into their big white Oldsmobile (named "Whitey," of course).

Supper is in town at St. Patrick's Catholic Church on Osage City's lovely Sixth Street, which is tree-lined, with generous yards fronting graceful houses. The sun is setting and soon the old-fashioned, globed street lights will cast their soft glow.

Daddy and Ed are helped by some of the younger church members in getting Mother and her wheelchair down steep steps to the basement. The room is warm and teeming with townspeople and farmers. Servers scurry among the tables, joking with their friends and bringing fresh plates and bowls heaped with crispy fried fish, hot hush puppies and cold slaw. There is ice cream for dessert.

"Church dinners," I said. "I've forgotten them. I will definitely do more of these, and this one even has wine. Where do I sign up to be a Catholic?"

But I am glad to climb back into Whitey and bounce over the gravel roads back out to the farm. I am exhausted. For a week, I have worked or socialized late into the nights. My adrenaline is spent. I'm greatly relieved to see that my parents seem pretty OK and contented.

That night I slept deeply.

I stayed at the farm five more days. I cooked for my parents and chauffeured them in Whitey to help give Daddy the rest that appears hard to come by these days. At the same time, he was still my dad, wanting to take care of me. One day I noticed that a tire on the Honda might be going flat, a fact I casually mentioned since it appeared to be a fairly slow leak.

He stopped the paperwork he was doing at his desk and grabbed his jacket and hat from the wall hook in the hallway.

"Let's go into Osage," he said. "I know where we can get that fixed."

I had to jump to keep up with him. We climbed into the Honda and drove into Osage City, to a tiny garage/gas station at the east end of Market Street. It was my first car repair of the trip and cost me just $6.35. I can only hope that all repairs will be so swift, easy, cheap and conveniently timed.

I spent most of the week catching up on unfinished trip preparations: learning to use the new cell phone, getting acquainted with the new laptop computer, and organizing my stuff, trying to get it further pared down. By the time I was ready to leave, I was able to give up two large boxes of clothing, which I placed in the upstairs west bedroom to use on quick trips back. Even so, I stuffed into the Honda's trunk five dresses; four skirts; four jackets and coats; six pairs of jeans, slacks and leggings; eight T-shirts; three pairs of running shorts, four sweaters and six pairs of shoes. Plus two pairs of gloves and several scarves, purses, pieces of costume jewelry, and hats – never mind that I usually don't wear hats.

The idea, you see, is to be prepared for every occasion and every weather condition of spring, summer, fall and winter, including floods, blizzards, desert heat, tornadoes, earthquakes and locust plagues. I'm also anticipating the possibility of not being able to find any kind of clothing store at some point in America. Oh, and I'm taking coat hangers for everything.

The clothes are folded, rolled and laid in the spaces remaining from the rest of the load – "furnishings" and household goods that are essentially a microcosm of my home: chair, radio-TV, a lamp and a bed roll. I've packed a camera, an insulated cooler with a small plug-in slow cooker, a few dishes and some silverware, a cutting board and knife, dish and laundry detergent and zippered plastic storage bags.

A plastic pail contains soap, towels and sponges. I would feel insecure without paperwork, so I've packed a box and a small crate with a few notebooks, an accordion file, books to read, magazines, the big HTML book, pens, scissors, tape, a stapler, paper clips, rubber bands, a work portfolio, résumés and letters of introduction (I persuaded a few influential people in my life to write something along the lines of, "To Whom It May Concern: This lady is not crazy.") I also carry twin-framed photos of Minnie and Bigelow.

Believe it or not, most of this stuff finally fits in the trunk. But I am dismayed by it. I have over-packed, and now the baggage carries *me*.

Finally it is time to hit the road again. On the morning of April 20, I awaken as the sun rises above the dense curtain of trees east of the house, bringing light through the windows of the south bedroom. I lie in bed for a while, thinking of my first "real" day as a traveler without a destination on roads I've never driven. I've decided to go west to find my first place to settle in for a month or two. New Mexico? It is said to be a mystical, spiritual place. Arizona? I've baked in its deserts, but would like to see its mountains. California? A friend told me about Palm Springs.

"Palm Springs – that sounds like a throwback to 1950s West Coast glamour. Rich people, old people, rich old people, golf, Frank Sinatra, citrus trees, topaz swimming pools, a cheerful, la-la way of life," I said. "Kind of appealing."

"It *was* old-fashioned, but now it's being rediscovered and is becoming hip again," my friend said.

I will think about Palm Springs. Mostly, I am just excited by the idea that if I want to go off today and live in Palm Springs, California, by golly I can.

Daddy is up and working in the kitchen downstairs. I can hear him making coffee and banging pans as he starts the cooked cereal. I try to remember which day this would be. Oatmeal Day? Cream of Wheat? Malt-O-Meal? He alternates the three, assigning a day to each one and then repeating the cycle in the exact same order.

I hear him return to his bedroom to coax Mother into arising early today to see me off. That will take 45 minutes, maybe an hour to get her awake and dressed and settled into her wheelchair. *I will not worry about them. I have my cell phone. I'll never be more than a couple days away. They want to be independent. They're fine.*

Later, the three of us linger over the oatmeal. After all, not only do I not have a destination, I don't have to be wherever I am going by any particular time. I write large, "Liz's cell phone number," on a scrap of paper and stick it on the refrigerator.

"OK, well, better go," I say briskly. "I'll let you know where I wind up, but you have my number and Ed does, too."

Daddy follows me to the garage to retrieve "the zapper" to give to the next guest and to look the car over one more time. I am reminded of all the quiet ways he supports me in whatever outré thing I've wanted to do. Like the time 25 years ago when I was helping to organize a chapter of the National Organization for Women in the conservative city of Abilene, Texas. One evening I was talking to him on the phone and explained that I had to hang up to go to a N.O.W. meeting.

"You mean you're one of those 'women's libbers'?" he said.

I tensed up. "Yes, I guess you could say that."

"So am I," he said softly.

Now I have his support and confidence again and I load it into the car with me.

Over the gravel roads, taking the back way to I-35, I am speeding southwest. At Wichita, instead of turning south toward Oklahoma and Texas as I've been doing for so many years, I drive straight, crossing Wichita and settling onto Hwy. 54, brand new uncharted territory.

The trip has truly begun. It's as if the Honda has become a racy Corvette and the wind blows my hair. I feel free.

3 FREE AT LAST

Being from eastern Kansas, I've forever corrected out-of-staters in their stereotypical views that the whole state is flat. Eastern Kansas has rolling hills. Now I stare ahead at a simple geometry of the landscape of Kansas lore. A low flat horizontal line bisects my view. The bar below is green, the block above blue. The gray road is perpendicular to the green and the blue, stretching far ahead to infinity.

Sometimes a pair of tiny rectangles juts from the horizontal line. These are grain elevators. They grow as I drive, bringing more low rectangles and the boxes of a town as I get closer. And then the shapes sweep past me and my windshield view is a bare treeless vista again.

I was staring at the rectangles when, astonishingly, they started to move. They danced, actually, becoming big wide elephant legs that hopped and crossed in awkward steps. I realized the hallucination was the edge of falling asleep. I pulled into a city park at Greensburg, Kan.

Signs at the city's entrance invite one to visit the World's Largest Hand-Dug Well and Meteorite. I saw the well as a 7-year-old, and it was an awesome wonder of dark, bottomless terror. The meteorite was not there in the 1950s and I probably should have gone to see it today. Too bad the honest citizens of Greensburg can't tie the attractions together in a more intriguing way, omitting "hand-dug" from the sign and spinning tales for tourists about how the big rock drilled the well when it crashed to earth.

In the park I reclined my seat for a little nap. I am a regular nap taker, you see, and I've contemplated how that will have an impact on my wanderings: on the road, on the job, in new homes - how can I make that work? Doesn't matter. It just has to, that's all. I must have my naps. In my kindergarten class, I was the only kid who actually slept on her little braided rug. As a newspaper reporter, I always lived not more than 10 minutes from home so that I could mix lunch with a snooze. For those 18 years at The Arc, I had a couch in my office and everybody knew better than to knock on my door between 12 and 1 p.m.

I think America needs roadside nap centers - motels with tiny rooms, air conditioned in the summer, heated in the winter - that one might rent for an hour at any time of day or night. I've thought a lot about how to make nap motels a respectable, viable and vice-free enterprise and haven't come up with a plan, but it's a good mental topic that makes the miles go by.

I would listen to the radio more, but it has problems and may not last as long as the car. However, as I continue southwestward on Hwy. 54, I dial into clear reception from an AM radio station and a sprightly interview with "Miss Rodeo America." Friendly and gung-ho, she talks about her many "appearances" and the responsibility of signing autographs. This gig must be the highlight of her life; I hope she's not just an early bloomer and that it's not all downhill from here.

If my radio holds up, I'm going to love such patter of local stations all around the country.

I stop at a town called Meade to stretch my legs. Meade is a spiffy little place having as many churches as stores, with straight-shot streets that run north and south and east and west. Wandering into the courthouse, I stop to peruse a bulletin board. My eyes bore into a posted summer job announcement: A census job pays $9 an hour! *Whew, doggie, that's for me when I get to where I'm going.*

Clerk, waitress, shelf-stocker, hotel maid, babysitter, salesperson, secretary, cashier, bartender, tutor, school crossing guard, typist, bank teller...I can't wait to live my life with "just a job." I want something simple, without long-term office politics and intellectual gamesmanship and psychological gymnastics.

As soon as my job was over at The Arc, I was having coffee one morning at the faux-French bakery that I patronized alongside many other people with laptops and cell phones. Suddenly I saw my fellow customers from the outside - I'd been one of *them* - and they looked miserable, every one of them. Nobody smiled, not for real I thought. Body language was wary and self-protective. Little meeting groups always included somebody looking silent and sullen while somebody else at the table got to be the one to hold court.

Meade is the kind of town I could settle into, but it is too early – not to mention that I am still in Kansas. No, I have some more states to cross.

Like Oklahoma and Texas. Again. At least I was on the far western edges; the Oklahoma panhandle was brief and then I just had to clip the edge of the Texas panhandle before moving into a new frontier.

As the sun sank, and I was feeling the effects of the day's 400 miles, I was glad to follow my rule of No Night Driving. In Dalhart, Texas, I picked a Days Inn because of its sign claiming the newest rooms in town. It was a little pricey for my budget, but the amenities included cable TV (I don't have it at home); three phones (one in the bathroom); a refrigerator; king-size bed (non-smoking room); nice lounge chair; and a free continental breakfast. I walked over to the Sonic drive-in and picked up a burger which I took to my room and my candyland of cable TV offerings.

The next morning, Dalhart is still dark at 6:30. Dressed for a run, I head out of the motel, trot across a highway not yet busy with traffic, find the business district and a red brick street lined with beautiful homes. I love the stillness and promise of the early morning and the cool air.

A few blocks beyond downtown, there is a hospital and I enter through the emergency entrance to find a rest room. Custodians have not yet attended to the waiting room and there isn't a soul around, but it looks and smells of fear and trauma, as if the ghosts that held the reins of life and death, pain and relief, remain from the night before.

I jogged back to the motel, passing a building called the "XIT Museum."

The water tower told me Dalhart was the "XIT City."

Later I discovered KXIT radio and the XIT feed lot.

"What does 'XIT' mean?" I asked the desk clerk at the Days Inn, feeling dumb about not being able to figure out something that should be obvious. What a riddle! What could the water tower, museum, radio station and feed lot have in common?

"I don't know," the clerk said, asking the maid who was preparing for work. She didn't know either.

How could that be?! If I become a motel worker, will I be so woefully oblivious and no longer curious about things?

Eventually, via e-mail from a friend, I learned that XIT referred to a large and legendary ranch.

At 8:15 a.m. I called my aunt, the 88-year-old sister of my father, in Sun City, Ariz. She answered the phone sleepily.

"Oops," I said. "You're two hours behind me, not one. I'm sorry; I forgot about Arizona not having daylight savings time."

Aunt Lugene assured me my call was welcome. I told her I was headed west and would like to stop for a visit. She has an apartment in a fancy assisted living facility.

"I still have my house and you're welcome to use it," she said. "Stay as long as you like!"

With Sun City in mind as a short-term destination, I left Dalhart on Hwy. 54 and soon crossed into New Mexico, thrilling at the dramatic change in landscape. The flatlands yielded to rolling hills - mountains in the eyes of a Kansan - with the added flourish of many green puffs of trees.

In the small town of Logan, the only likely rest stop appears to be the school. Inside, I sneak past signs that declare "Visitors Must Check in With Office" and find a ladies' room near the gym. It is Good Friday and there are no students, but adults are working in the principal's office. Somebody might pop out at any moment!! Here I am, guilty as an eighth grader roaming without a hall pass. Nyah, nyah-nyah nyah nyaah, you can't catch me.

A middle-aged lady sneaking and hiding — well, what can I say. Cheap thrills on a dull day of driving.

Slipping out a back exit of the school, I return to the Honda and drive around town a bit. Logan looks drab and struggling, but just as I decide there is nothing left to see, a visual feast bursts upon the business district. Large and wheeled, it has rolled in and parked in front of a second-hand store. The body atop the wheels is a kaleidoscope of ornamentation - shells, beads, mirrors, statues, brick-a-brack, with Santa Claus being the dominant theme. There are dozens of Santa Claus dolls, and I eventually notice the body of a Volkswagen clinging to the roof.

"It's an 'art car,' and this is a Santa Mobile," the driver told me. He was on his way home to Reno, Nev., from Houston where he had attended an art car convention. I gawked and took a couple of pictures. Why, one must ordinarily pay admission to an art car convention to see something like this.

In Albuquerque, I find a grocery store and buy tuna and carrots to add to the milk, bread and fruit I saved from the continental breakfast at the Days Inn. I take my little lunch to an overly-built, heavily equipped park - not much green space remains after the imposition of playgrounds, driveways, fences, parking lots, tennis courts and utility buildings (you WILL have fun, Citizens of Albuquerque!)

Suddenly I am awed by the distance I've already put between myself and Hurst, Texas. It's as if I'm scaling a tower, or a mountain, and I stop to look down at the view before resuming the climb. I pull out my cell phone, this wondrous device that gives me an ample 600 minutes a month to call anywhere. I can go home with it any time.

Right now, I need to go home, just for a taste.

"Martha? Are you busy?" I am calling her at her office at Tarrant County College in Fort Worth where she's chairman of the Art Department.

"No, where are you?"

"Sitting on the trunk of my car in a park in Albuquerque having lunch."

"That sounds pleasant."

Martha's details of her week might seem mundane if I were at home, but as a stranger in a strange land today, I am enthralled. Work, pets, friends, restaurants...it's all interesting. I gave her a farm report - how Mother and Daddy seemed to be faring – and said I hope to reach Arizona by nightfall.

Rested and ready to go on, I look at my pocket atlas, which can't offer a lot of detail in its 3" by 5" pages, and choose I-25 south out of Albuquerque. An hour and a half and 78 miles later, I reach Socorro and the low point of my crossing of New Mexico.

Socorro was one of the settings for the 1975 movie, "Alice Doesn't Live Here Anymore." The wonderful actress Ellen Burstyn played Alice, married to a man with no discernibly good qualities, and she is driven to yell out the window one day, "Socorro sucks!" Fortunately, the husband's handy death at the wheel of his delivery truck allows Alice's life to roar ahead and out of their dreary town. She sells everything at a yard sale and then with her preteen son in tow, heads west to find a new life.

"Don't look back or you'll turn into a pillar of shit," she tells Tommy.

Alice's lines resonate in my mind as I turn into the squatty little town of 8,800. The afternoon sun bears down, making Socorro look even more dried up and unattractive. It's just too dang hot. Stopping at a convenience store, I rummage through the bundles of clothing in my trunk, and find a pair of cool shorts to change into from jeans that have begun to cling like a wool blanket.

People who love New Mexico speak of its legends and mystery and spiritualism. Not being into such lore, especially the Native American and UFO stuff, I smile politely and try to be patient with those who wax rhapsodic about their love of the state. When they blather on too long, I'll seize control of the conversation and talk about Kansas until *they* start backing out of the room, smiling politely.

Not being on New Mexico's wave length, I deserved to be intercepted by the flying saucer on Hwy. 60. The craft full of little space aliens hovered over my car, dipping into my path, but I refused to stop. No way was I going to allow myself to be beamed up into a space ship for study and experimentation.

OK, maybe that specific incident did not actually happen, but New Mexico did feel weird to me the rest of the day. Once I turned west and left Socorro and the interstate, the highway rose and fell and wound over forests and the Datil Mountains. There were no other cars, no people. I passed tiny towns that looked abandoned. I wanted to stop the car, step outside and shout, "IS ANYBODY HERE?!" It was a little unsettling to think that a road found in such emptiness is usually old and narrow, run-down, abandoned even, but Hwy. 60 was lovely and wide and well-maintained. For whom???

The real reason there was no flying saucer incident was the sentry-like presence of the National Radio Astronomy Observatory. Located 52 miles west of Socorro, the facility looks other-worldly with its gigantic satellite dishes turned to the sky. It is claimed that the NRAO scientists study all kinds of space objects and events through state-of-the-art telescopes. But what a good joke, I thought, looking at the mighty line of satellite dishes, if everybody inside the office is actually stretched out on La-Z-Boy recliners watching 5,000 TV channels. No one would know.

The vast, mysterious emptiness of western New Mexico seemed to go on for hundreds of miles. At last, I crossed the state line, stopped at Springerville, Arizona, and checked into the Rode Inn.

This was my second 500-mile day of driving. I must be really close to Phoenix!

"Phoenix is another 220 miles," the desk clerk informs me.

I try not to show my surprise, try not to show my dim grasp of geography – and I am bummed.

"I'll show you on the map a couple of routes you can take. One is more scenic than the other, but takes more time."

"Show me the fast way," I said. "Please."

It's time to buy a real map.

Again the next morning, I went out at 5:30 for a run on strange streets. Running is a familiar, 22-year habit, though, so I'm never afraid of getting lost, nor of being kidnapped and winding up on the evening news as a grim discovery. In fact, on my way back down a winding road, I stopped to chat with an aging hippie who was drinking coffee and enjoying the sunrise – I think I'm starved for conversation with somebody, anybody.

Spectacular scenery today! From Springerville my Honda clung to a curvy mountainous route, its beauty preserved and protected by designation as a national forest. The mountains still had little caps of snow, and at one point the Honda rolled past a patch of old snow still crusted beside the road. Several times my reward for patiently climbing the elevation was a sweeping view of deep green and smoky blue.

This was Arizona? When I worked for The Arc, I flew to Phoenix several times, and I also drove from that city to Yuma and to Tucson. The views were all-desert all the time, searing and spiked with amazing rock formations and the harsh, thorny gestures of the Saguaro cactus.

So I knew what was ahead, that I must eventually climb down from the mountains and hit the smoggy valley floor that holds the sprawl of Phoenix and the suburban home of my aunt.

After the eerie experience of crossing the Southwest and not really knowing where I was, I stopped at a Walmart and bought a large road atlas. My brother Ed had advised me during the planning stages of my trip, "Get a good map," and I thought, yeah, yeah. How many ways are there anyway to get from point A to B? So I started out inclined to sort of wing it.

Behold! A Rand McNally map. I simply had no idea of its revelations and useful information. It shows four-lane routes, Principal Highways, toll roads and scenic ways, all color-coded. There are rest areas, mountain peaks and elevations, airports, foot trails, time zone boundaries, ferries and railroads. Travel time and distance between major cities are displayed. It shows that I probably drove a hundred miles out of my way, miles that I wouldn't have chosen if I'd been aware of other options.

At 2:30 p.m. I arrived in Sun City, a place that would soon loosen my arguable grasp of sound mental health.

4 SUN CITY BLUES

Sun-baked Sun City, Arizona, is its own planet, perhaps because of spill-over effects from the forces that beam down onto New Mexico. In Sun City, I've totally lost any sense of the real world. There are no children or low-income people; there are few non-whites, and the vehicle tooling around one of its concentric circles of streets is likely to be a golf cart.

Sun City has a minimum age to be a resident; at least one person must be 55 or older and no one can be less than 18. All the houses look exactly alike, even when they are different, and every yard is the same size and shape with at least one regulation citrus tree, two palm trees (one tall, one short), a cactus plant, and a driveway so clean you could eat off it, and absolutely nothing that flaunts deed restrictions. Grass in the yards? Why have a high-maintenance thing like that when green-tinted gravel looks so beautiful and natural? There are no garbage cans beside the curb; the receptacles are actually buried, so that one merely lifts the lid and pokes the trash into the hole in the ground.

Sun City has a couple of shopping centers with a grocery store, a restaurant, a gift shop, a dress shop, a gas station and a real estate office. Much grander are the recreation centers and the medical center.

This place was one of the first "planned communities" of an Arizona contractor named Del Webb. His vision was a city designed exclusively for retired people. Over a five-month period, he created Sun City out of a cotton field, shaping a golf course, recreation center, shopping center and five model homes. On New Year's Day in 1960, Webb hoped for 10,000 visitors at the unveiling open house. More than 100,000 showed up to tour the property that weekend.

So what do I know. Most importantly, Sun City has given my aunt Lugene Roehrrman a happy and busy life for 30 years so that makes it a mighty fine place as far as I'm concerned.

Near Boswell hospital is Evergreen Villas. I step into its hotel-like lobby and look for a reception desk. Instead, Lugene herself is standing right there, just a few feet from the door, leaning on her walker and looking much smaller than the last time I saw her. She is definitely expecting me, and I wonder a little anxiously how long she's been there watching for my arrival.

How I love this aunt! She is my father's sister, not as quiet as my father and a little more controversial and lots of fun. She and my dad grew up just two miles east of my parents' present home, but her pathway off the farm took her to McPherson, Kan., Liberty, Mo., and then Sun City in retirement years with my uncle Fred, who died in 1977.

Lugene is 88 years old, with such a robust optimism that she makes light of her recent siege of problems. First she was diagnosed with Parkinson's Disease and then one day last winter, a small stroke caused her to fall in her kitchen. With the strength and focus of an inch worm determined to climb a grand staircase, she managed to reach a phone and call for help. After that, Lugene reluctantly agreed that it might be time for "assisted living." Her son and my father searched Sun City together and found this place.

I follow her down a hallway to her small, efficient apartment. The journey gives me time to see the changes: the weight loss, the stooped posture, the slowness, the maneuvering of the walker, the hair. Yes, when had her beautiful white hair straightened and grown so long and become so…well, blah? Evergreen has a beauty parlor, she said. Well there's a ruination, I thought, recalling the time I asked her why her hair always looked nice. I had asked if she used a regular stylist.

"Why, no!" she said brightly. "I cut it myself – have for years."

"How do you cut your own hair?"

"I just cut hair where I don't want hair!"

Believe me, that says SO much about my aunt.

Lugene showed me around Evergreen, its elegant furnishings and the charming way it duplicated the features of a community for gracious living. There was a room for fine dining. There was a small room with a pool table and the décor of a hunt club. There was a room with a sign saying "Ballroom" (although its heavy-script lettering made it look from a distance like "Bathroom.") The Ballroom was not large enough for a ball, of course, but adequate for group meetings and small recreational activities, like watching the big-screen TV in the corner. There was an Ice Cream Parlor. There was even a music room with sofas and a chandelier and a grand piano.

The place absolutely gave me the creeps. There was nobody in these rooms. There was no activity anywhere. A quiet, fake village devoid of villagers.

"I made a reservation for us in the dining room for supper. You'll like my table," Lugene announced, explaining that seating was reserved and she had a regular set of dinner companions. "At our table, we still have all our marbles!"

There was that bright laugh again.

She suggested driving over to the house, which is about two miles away, so that I could unpack and get settled and change clothes if I wanted.

"What time is dinner?" I asked.

"4:30."

Twenty minutes from now. Once I got over the shock of the earliness of the evening meal, I realized that my aunt had lost some sense of time and how long it takes to do things.

After dinner and some time spent with Lugene in her apartment, I drove to the house on Hidden Valley Circle, parked the Honda in the attached garage and let myself in. As I entered the family room, I was hit with a wave of sadness that her life is no longer here. The furniture and mementoes I've known for nearly 50 years have been moved out. We would not be spending evenings in side-by-side easy chairs, she with a knitting project, I prodding her for old family stories and secrets. She would not be asleep in the room across the hall from my guest room.

The emptiness was overwhelming, and with great effort and a little prayer, I resisted going out to the car to root around for the little TV I've brought along.

Television is my most wretched of time-gobbling habits. In addition to easy entertainment and cheap edification, TV is my escape from thought, anesthesia for feelings, a companion and protector. Tonight it would have stood surrogate for the soft sure presence of a beloved family member.

So I unpacked a suitcase. I leaned into the silence, survived it, and fell asleep.

The next day was Easter Sunday and the big event was church at Faith Presbyterian. I picked up Lugene to attend the 8:45 service where I was delighted by the sight of genuine, old-fashioned Easter bonnets.

This was a big church, with 1,300 members. There were that many and then some in the pews this morning. But even before entering the church, we all had to deal with the Catholics next door in an unholy war. It was metal against metal in battles ranging from sly to vicious as 1,000 cars tried to maneuver into the two church parking lots at the same time. What a traffic jam, and once we were all inside in our respective services, quite a lot of confessing of sins and praying needed to be done.

This modern cathedral of soaring space and big music made me miss the little Lyndon Presbyterian Church back in Osage County. I usually spend Easter morning there with my parents, but of course the timing did not work this year. I did join the Palm Sunday crowd last weekend. My dad drove us in Whitey and parked five feet from the wheelchair ramp at the back door. Inside, there was a grand total of 11 of us. The second-hand organ was so broken that Donna the organist was constantly having to stop and start again as our straggly voices made the arduous journey through a hymn. It was a long way from the present setting where the edifice and the appearances of "Dr." in the titles of the clergy staff rival a medical center.

On Monday, I was glad to have the early-morning hours to myself. I got up before 6 a.m., put on my running clothes and headed out for an easy 4-mile run on the flat circles of streets. I learned that if you want to see action in Sun City, and by that I mean simply the inhabitants outside doing something, that's the time, before dawn becomes brighter and hotter. People are walking, driving their carts to the golf course, and raking their gravel, or whatever they do to their yards. There were no other runners but no one seemed to object to my being an exception in the order of things.

A couple of blocks after leaving the house, I spotted a little brown rabbit. And then, of course, another. And another and another. With wide eyes bright with mischief (or is that their insatiable interest in mating?) they darted about from yard to yard. They add an unauthorized, unruly note of jocularity. I can't imagine that Del Webb considered a potential bunny problem, or he would have found a way to prevent the unsettling presence of such unmanageable lawlessness. Perhaps the rabbits will continue to multiply and even mutate and run wild in the streets and create disorder and panic in this perfect place. I will monitor this situation: This morning, I started a count. There were 12.

While Sun City is not my cup of tea, still, this is the desert Southwest and it feels foreign and exotic. When I returned to the house, I picked oranges from the trees in the backyard, then rummaged through Lugene's kitchen cabinets until I found an electric juicer and started breakfast. I felt positively exhilarated this morning, realizing I am in my fifth state and my third week on the road. Never mind that I've yet to tackle my real goal: finding an unfamiliar town in a beautiful place and creating a whole new and different "life" for myself. So far, there's been little challenge in a few days' driving and being housed by the parents and aunt who have loved me all my life.

"Lugene, thank you so much for letting me use your house. I think I would like to get back on the road, day after tomorrow."

We are in a Chinese restaurant having dinner. After two meals in the dining room at Evergreen, I've insisted on treating her (and myself) to something different.

She looks up sharply.

"So SOON??"

"I've heard a lot about Sedona. And Flagstaff," I begin, hoping the idea of remaining in the state of Arizona will appease her. For various reasons, I really have given up on the idea of Palm Springs and California in general. I also don't want any more long drives for a while.

"If I go north...," I continue, "I've never been to those places and I'm going to need to check them out, get a feel for whether I want to land there. And then it's going to be easier finding a place to live and possibly a job on a week day. My goal is to spend no more than three nights in a motel. Finding my town – a home – it's a lot to accomplish before next weekend, so I'd like to get started."

"I thought you might want to do something here," Lugene said. "There's lots to do in Sun City and the house is yours."

I'm not surprised. Ever since I first shared with her my idea of a "wandering" year off, and said I wanted to drop in for a visit on my way to my first southwestern destination, she's been dropping heavy suggestions that Sun City is just the place.

"Lugene, it would be so easy to stay here. The house is wonderful and I just love having all this time with you. But the trip has been almost too easy so far, and I'm getting antsy to find out if my idea will work."

My diplomacy is met with a non-committal silence.

My precious aunt. Her fragility is a new, unexpected wrinkle. This morning, I drove her to the Hallmark store to pick out greeting cards in the luxury of time – the driver for Evergreen would have allowed one hour – and she seemed to appreciate all the little things I was trying to do for her – the dinner out, the errands, a breakfast at the house, the Easter service on Sunday, and now, Moo Goo Gai Kow, all on *her* timetable. Finally, I agreed to stay through the week and not leave until next Monday.

So I've settled into the house and unpacked more of the car and, yes, the TV came out and got plugged into a kitchen wall socket.

On Tuesday I had to chalk one up for Evergreen. Just as I was getting used to Lugene's institutional way of life – I don't care how pretty the wallpaper is, it's still an institution – something a little more spirited popped up. Lugene asked if I would like to go on "a hot dog run."

At 11 o'clock, a dozen of us gathered at the front door and boarded the facility's purple, handicapped-accessible van. Susie the driver took us to a place that felt "over the border," out of Sun City, into the real world and the parking lot of a Home Depot store. There, a hot dog vendor had opened his lunch-time business. We all lined up, bought hot dogs and ate them in the shade provided by a few umbrellas. Susie had also brought chips, soda pop, and BEER! I was a little afraid we would then have to actually go inside Home Depot, but we didn't. We briskly reboarded the bus and toddled back home. It was just a simple, quick little excursion.

"Lugene, how can I help you this week?" I pose the question as we spend the evening in her apartment. She is doing some reading and writing and I'm toiling away on my laptop, trying to launch my new Web site, "Travels with Liz."

"We might take a look at the sewing closet" at the house, she says.

Now that she is fully moved and established in her apartment, she wants to get her house cleaned out, with nobody having to inherit or otherwise find themselves responsible for a messy garage or hopeless closets. She definitely has the overall house effort under control. There is little clutter, few stashes, nothing that looks forgotten and shoved aside. We agree to get started on the sewing closet the next day.

I started the morning with a run. There were 30 bunnies.

My aunt's agenda began with an audiology appointment, but after that, I brought her back to the house for a lunch of leftovers from the Chinese restaurant, and then we went to work. In a small room containing a twin bed, a cabinet sewing machine and an ironing board, the closet is short and narrow, closed with a set of bi-fold doors. How much could be in there?

The truth is that Lugene was an extraordinary seamstress, both skilled and prolific. She always made her own clothes – not those little "make-it-in-an-hour" kinds of frocks, mind you – but entire Vogue-pattern ensembles. She also made clothes for others, and I still remember my favorite dress as a 6-year-old. It had puffed sleeves and a full skirt that twirled out flat when I spun around.

We opened the closet and I stared at boxes, bags and a small chest of drawers. I couldn't see the back wall, and yet the closet can't be more than a foot and a half deep. We removed one drawer from the chest, and Lugene picked up a tiny bundle of blue fabric, slowly unrolled it and examined it carefully. This is why, three hours later, we had cleared only one drawer and one bag and the back wall was still not in sight. She wanted to hold every single scrap and recall what it had "become" – a skirt, blouse, suit…I tried to imagine the nostalgia and sadness she must have felt for the pattern pieces for granddaughters' nightgowns and the few unfinished projects that now, really should be abandoned.

I went through a similar "purge" of sewing projects and other kinds of possessions as I worked on my home to get ready for my trip. It was difficult. But I had done it, and she can, too. Enough of the sweet nostalgia. Let's make a bonfire.

"I finally realized that somebody else might make better use of things that I didn't want to deal with any more," I said with great hope, summoning all my powers of persuasion. "I'll bet somebody can use some of these patterns and fabric pieces. How about taking it all to Goodwill?"

Lugene finally agreed to start a pile for recycling. But she also retrieved projects, pledging to "finish them up," and so much of it wound up right back in the drawer.

We moved from a creep to a crawl the next day. By the third day, in about the tenth hour of the project, I hit The Wall. The Goodwill pile sat in the middle of the floor, and I stared at it, morose. Plus, I was tired and cranky and hot and bored. I couldn't imagine how I was going to hunt down a store and get these remnants delivered. I just wanted to leave this neighborhood, this town, before it somehow swallowed me up and imprisoned me through my own rapidly-approaching golden years, choking the life out of me.

Suddenly, I heard the rumble of a truck outside, up the street. Peering out the window, I could see the garbage collectors making their way toward our driveway. I gathered an armload of the tattered remnants, announced that I was getting them out of our way, ran at break-neck speed through the house, out the garage, and then I poked the whole lot into the hole in the ground. The garbage truck made it vanish from my sight forever.

What have I done?! What if she decides she wants something back?

She didn't. Eventually, the pace of the sewing closet project did pick up, but it still took five days. We did take a donation to Goodwill. At the end, the closet was nice and neat and largely empty. Lugene thanked me and said it couldn't have happened without me. (*I'll* say!)

On Friday evening, at the end of good deeds and bunny counts, I get to leave Sun City, destined for a surprise: wacky adventure.

I've met Neili Asbury only once. She is the daughter of Texas neighbors Diane and Dwayne Wilcox and happens to live and teach high school math in Glendale, which is next to Sun City. Before I left Hurst to start my trip, Diane urged me to look Neili up. So I did and called her mid-week. It could have been one of those slightly pleasant, call So-and-So kinds of favors, but I was truly ready for conversation with a 30-year-old, somebody way younger than the age of admittance to Sun City. Neili suggested meeting at a Mexican restaurant for Happy Hour on Friday night.

Oh boy! I get there early.

The door of cool, dark Macayo's opens, bringing a blinding flash of sunshine and Neili. She is 10 minutes late and out of breath.

"I'm so sorry, and I'm afraid I have to leave by 7." That's less than an hour from now.

"Oh." I am disappointed.

She is rehearsing with other faculty members for a skit to be performed during Centennial High School's annual spring dance recital. The dance students will be showing off the results of their hard work; the teachers will provide a little comic relief.

"Do you know about 'Riverdance'?" Neili asked.

"Of course – the Irish step dancing show."

The teachers have organized their own spoof of "Riverdance."

"We had a rehearsal last night and people say it's really funny. If you want, you can join us and be in it too. The show's tonight," Neili said.

"Say what?"

"Really! There's a bunch of us. We don't know what we're doing, but it doesn't matter."

Suddenly, I'm wide awake from my somnambulant days in a geriatric world that has scared and depressed me. I'm young – not old anyway. I'm silly. I'm capable of madcap adventure. Still, I had to get my mind around the idea of being IN a show, as a DANCER no less – something I do very little of without the aid of alcohol.

We raced back to Lugene's house so that I could assemble a costume. I had black leggings, shirt and shoes, just what I needed. One of the teachers had made red-sequined stretchy bands that we could wear any way we pleased, so I used mine as a headband. Voila.

Soon I found myself on a sprawling high school campus. It's fun already!

In the school's rehearsal hall, Neili and I were only the third and fourth people to show up. She had said that some of the teachers who were supposed to be there last night weren't. They actually *needed* me.

Patty, the choreographer, began working with our motley few. Gradually, others trickled in until there were 14.

I was a little alarmed that the performance had some real planning around it. It went something like this: Line up, half of us facing forward, the other half back. Clasp arms and march around from horizontal line to vertical formation. Solo, we staggered our shuffle-ball-change hop-hop steps until we'd all moved into an "X" formation. Miscellaneous dancing into a big square. Join hands, fly around in a circle. Then we got to stand and clap (16 counts) and there's another Rockettes-style line with more hopping. And then finally, mercifully, the end, as we fell to our knees with outstretched arms.

The rehearsal was chaotic, with most of us occasionally whispering, "Do you know what we're doing? I'm lost." Finally, we decided we were close enough to looking like Riverdance, albeit for laughs. We took some pictures for my Web site and for souvenirs, and suddenly it was time to face the audience. The act scheduled before ours was ending. We moved from the rehearsal hall to a very dark back stage.

And now, it's show time!

In the glare of the stage lights, we cannot see the crowd but we definitely hear it. We pour onto the stage, find our marks, and the Irish music begins. I do my best to dance in approximately the same way everybody else is dancing. (I just hope I don't stand out – I hear there's videotaping.) We do the jumps and kicks. We hop. We run, bumping into each other but trying not to crash. Then comes the clapping in sync as we circle two Michael Flatley-type protagonists (who are wildly popular teachers) then drop to our knees, jubilantly raising out-stretched arms.

A roar goes up. There's laughing and hooting and pounding applause.

Joining the audience afterward, I am stunned to see a thousand kids and adults in a hall that's standing-room-only. I am glad to be totally, utterly anonymous.

Afterward, I went out with the group for dinner and camaraderie at a different Mexican restaurant. What great, good fun, and the dismal social aspect of my week in Sun City is obliterated.

On Sunday, I rejoiced over the details of my last day in Sun City. I beat the sunrise for one more 4-mile run and bunny count. I picked up my aunt early to return to the house for breakfast with orange juice from the fruit of her trees. We went to church where I was pleased to still see Easter hats. We had one more dinner in Evergreen's dining room and that afternoon, one more treat in the Ice Cream Parlor. I cleaned Lugene's house. I packed my suitcases and loaded the trunk.

And on the eve of my departure for the "real" start of the trip – venturing into lands unknown – I discovered big glistening spots of oil on the clean floor of the garage underneath the Honda.

5 ARIZONA HIGHWAYS

"Since it's Monday, we're pretty busy as you can see," the repairman at the service station tells me, barely looking up. "If you want, you can park your car over there and we'll take a look at it."

Outside the garage, cars are parked helter-skelter.

"Any idea when that might be?"

"Going to be late this afternoon."

I want to shout. *DO SOMETHING NOW! HELP ME!* But making a scene probably will not help. Especially if I have a mortally wounded car, I need to conserve my reserves of forbearance.

I left and drove to a Texaco station. The scene was similarly busy, but at least the station was close enough to Lugene's house that if I needed to, I could walk to the house and have a nice quiet breakdown.

God wears a star. A Great Big Texaco Star.

First, a mechanic who seemed to be coordinating traffic flow actually acknowledged my existence. Furthermore, it was as if my car was the first of the day and business was slow. He listened to my description of the oil leak and looked concerned.

"Let's get it up on the rack and check things out." AND HE DID. Right then and there ahead of the 50 other cars, including an official U.S. Postal Service truck. He also called a mechanic over to get a description of the problem from me.

The real problem, I said, trying not to let my voice quiver, is that I've been in Sun City 10 days and really need to leave town. Now. Today.

He burst out laughing.

"Hey, you don't have to tell me...I don't live here, but I've worked here 14 years. It gets to me too sometimes."

The news only got better. The oil leak was not real. The repairman "tightened things up a bit" but otherwise "couldn't find anything really wrong." Charge: $7 to put the car up on the rack.

Free as a bird, I left Sun City, found I-17 and flew northward out of the flat, baking, glaring desert of the Valley. I soared – mentally, for sure, and in fact, climbing about 4,000 feet into the Coconino National Forest. During the week, I had settled on two destinations: Sedona and Flagstaff. I would arrive in Sedona first, look around and see if the place spoke to me, and if not, drive the short distance to Flag.

Sedona itself rambles haphazardly, its motels, art galleries and gift shops coexisting with new commercial and condo developments and expensive houses. But it's the natural beauty of its setting that is vivid and captivating. Huge, red rock formations jut from the hills, ever-changing in color and character throughout the day as the sun slowly travels its course across a deep blue sky. People who love Sedona speak of it in mystical, spiritual terms.

I looked for mystical. Tried to feel the spiritual. But I couldn't get around the coarseness of its own little urban sprawl and the tacky efforts of some of its entrepreneurs who sell crystals and other forms of fortune telling to tourists. The Chamber of Commerce touts the area as "the second most visited site in the state after the Grand Canyon." Still, I'm wanting to give it a shot. I park the car and wander into an "information center."

I missed seeing the name "Fairfield" on the sign.

The man inside is a little too briskly helpful, producing a large map and using a pen to mark all sorts of points of interest without my asking for them. I pretend to be interested, but my mind is edging toward Flagstaff. He seems to read this thought.

"Would you stay one night if you had a free hotel room?" he said. That's the wind-up. And now the pitch: His company (Fairfield) would pay for a free night for me in the Quality Inn IF I would attend a 90-minute orientation and tour of "a wonderful new property development."

I take 5 seconds to weigh the opportunity of getting a free night in a hotel in exchange for submitting myself to a 90-minute sales spiel. What else do I have to do tomorrow but drive 30 miles to Flag? I accept.

With the next 24 hours settled, I found a Safeway store and bought a four-pack of mini-bottles of wine, some Havarti cheese and crackers and set out to find a place for a picnic among the red rocks. I stopped on an unpaved road off the highway, climbed a short way up a mountain side, and enjoyed the sunset and God's benediction on the day.

Promptly at 9 o'clock the next morning, I cheerfully presented myself at the office of Fairfield, a lovely lodge-like building on the highway near the Safeway store. There were 15 of us. I don't know why the others were there, but I think we were all trying not to look apprehensive. My hope was that the sales presentation would involve us en masse.

Alas, we were called, one by one, by our assigned sales person.

"Elizabeth?" he said. "I'm Carl. Come on back."

He escorts me to a big room with many tables. Other little clusters of salespeople and prospects are spaced apart and talking low.

"Thanks, Carl! It's so nice to meet you. Call me Liz."

You poor devil. You're pudgy and red-faced and moist. High blood pressure maybe? And why such fussing with the hair, so coiffed. I try not to stare at an elaborate, curling, villain-style moustache.

Sure enough, Carl is nice as he can be. Having no intention of even listening to what he has to say, I tell him the truth, that I've lost my job and have hit the road for a year or so, and as soon as I arrived in Sedona, I was offered this free night at the Quality Inn in exchange for my presence here. I'm writing about my travels, I said; perhaps he'd like to check out my Web site?

Why, he said, I'm a writer, too! He's a poet AND he's written a novel about international intrigue and off we go on a long conversation about books.

So the first 45 minutes were easy. I was hoping the chit-chat was simply a front for Carl to look busy. Clearly, pressuring and locking people into a huge financial commitment to another home (actually, even the simplest floor plan was bigger than my condo) was not nearest and dearest to his heart and mind. But rather suddenly, the conversation turned to my preferred choices of "travel destinations." And wouldn't you know, all my travel destinations are within a very few hundred miles of a Fairfield property. I also can not derail him by rhapsodizing over European capitals.

Soon, my brain simply shuts down. The scene might remind you of that Gary Larson "Far Side" cartoon about what people say to their dogs and what dogs hear: Our human commands and admonishments sound like a lot of gibberish, except when the dog hears its name. And so it is at Fairfield this morning: "blah blah Liz blah blah blah blah Liz blah blah blah." Sometimes the blah-blahs end with a question mark and I have to figure out some kind of response that halfway makes sense. Like, "Say that again?" Or, "You know, Carl, I'm afraid I'm not hearing anything that makes good sense for me right now."

Nothing deters Carl from plowing onward. He produces a piece of paper and starts writing a lot of numbers and drawing boxes around them and crossing numbers out, then writing new numbers and scratching arrows and stars and exclamation points. This part of the pitch reminds me of my Uncle Fred's clever routine when I was a child: He "drew" a story on a piece of paper about a large oval pond and a small round pond and flying fish and when he was finished, he'd actually drawn a chicken.

Three hours later, Carl has run out of ways to convince me to commit, TODAY, to make the largest financial commitment of my life. It is time to concede defeat and call his supervisor over to "verify" my decision. At last, my release is imminent!

The supervisor asks me if all the information presented was explained clearly. Was there anything I didn't understand?

"Carl did an excellent job," I said. "What a terrific place - and an excellent opportunity! I'm afraid it's just not for me."

Carl and the supervisor both look wounded. *Betrayed* even, and they actually ask me why in the world I would visit Fairfield and hear the "presentation" if I had no intention of buying. Were they not aware of the deal going on at the information center? The free room at the Quality Inn?

Perhaps Carl didn't hear me any better than I'd listened to him.

In addition to the free lodging in Sedona, the information center guy gave me a wonderful tip related to driving on to Flagstaff. Instead of going back to I-17, he suggested, take Hwy. 89A, one of the most beautiful scenic routes in the country. For 28 miles, I drove on a road that clung to mountain sides, gradually climbing from 4,000 feet to Flagstaff's 7,000 ft. elevation, rising from the red rocks and desert terrain to ground that was still dry, but forested with towering pines.

Even though I was driving, my thoughts, if audible, would sound like huffing and puffing and sighing as if I were walking the route with a back pack. Either the slow switchbacks and hairpin turns were stressful, or I was empathizing with a car – I hope it was the former.

Twelve miles south of Flagstaff, I stopped at a splendid overlook and official rest area. I got out of the Honda and walked toward the edge of the promontory point, passing through a gauntlet of Navajo and Hopi Indians set up to sell jewelry on side-by-side portable tables. Eventually, I sought out a picnic table for my lunch of remaining edible leftovers, which had not improved in transport all the way from Sun City. There were no empty picnic tables, but a couple let me perch at the other end of theirs. We chatted, without asking a lot of personal questions, but I wondered about them because they were deeply tanned Scottish citizens living in the United Arab Emirate of Dubai and now traveling the U.S. for unspecified reasons.

I drove into Flagstaff through a string of strip shopping centers and motels and a big Barnes & Noble bookstore. But once I crossed railroad tracks, I liked what I saw: a well-preserved western town bordered by Route 66 - now touted as "Historic" Route 66 - and a handsome Amtrak train station. The whole scene was framed by the snow-capped San Francisco mountains to the north with Arizona's highest elevation, Humphreys Peak at 12,643 ft.

This is my place. This must be Stop No. 1. I will have a life here for the next month - a home and a job and I will do something to help my humankind of Flagstaff and leave it a better place, I've decided.

I passed the nicer lodging coming into town, but I want to commune with Route 66, which is lined with low-end motels, relics of the mid-20th century when the fabled highway was not only a key artery in the national road system, but an icon of American life. Ahhh, the old TV show "Route 66," Tod Stiles and Linc Case tooling cross-country in their red Corvette. Actually, since my family's TV set and most shows in 1960 were in black and white, I don't know that the Corvette was red, but who can forget that theme song, cool to this day...do Do Do DO Do Do do doooo, do do d-d-do duh, d-do do duh do...

Parallel to the highway are railroad tracks. I love trains, but among the many motels right on the highway and so close to both vehicle and train traffic, I've wisely picked the Travelodge, which is set back a ways and has a sort of mini park with trees to absorb noise.

I was flying high on this Tuesday afternoon, having checked in and dropped off my bags. I'm in my first strange town. The experiment begins. No more soft stays with relatives.

I drove to the Amtrak station, which has a visitors' center, and I'm given a list of real estate offices that handle rental properties. I scanned the list of offices for familiar addresses based on the limited tour I'd already made of the city. Near the central business district, I found an office that looked like a cozy middle-class house itself on a leafy neighborhood street.

"May I help you?" the woman asked in a tone that barely leaned into the pleasant side of neutral.

Well, I said, I'm doing something kind of interesting. I have just begun a tour of America, picking out nice small towns and cities - like Flagstaff! - where I'd like to live and work and get acquainted in the span of a month or so. As you might imagine, a hotel for that length of time would deplete my savings, so I am looking for a small, affordable house or apartment.

Suddenly, the temperature in that room dropped a good 20 degrees.

"Our properties start at fifteen hundred dollars," she said, her thin smile going away completely. She said nothing further.

I overlooked the brevity of her assistance and chattered on, making eye contact with the few other agents in the room.

"Perhaps you know of owners of vacation homes who might like to have someone mature and responsible, someone who would give them a little rental income before the summer vacation season arrives…" I said.

"I'm afraid I don't," she said. "You might try another office but I doubt if you can find anything."

Suddenly, a tall young man named Jason, not far out of college, stood up at his desk and walked over.

"My family has a cabin with a kitchenette available for $395," he said. "We have somebody there until May 15th, but I can check and see if he would be able to leave earlier."

The temperature dropped another 30 degrees and now carried a cold wind. The agent who thought she was about to see me turn on my heel and head out the door shot Jason a look. Bless his handsome, gray-eyed self. But oh the pain. What was that moment like for him? Did he see his short career life flash before his eyes?

"I don't care," he told me later that night on the phone, confirming that his stepping forward had put him in hot water with the agency. His offer had been personal and was not only completely unrelated, but in conflict with agency business.

"I've been there a year and they aren't following through on things they promised me," Jason said.

The tenant occupying Jason's parents' property did not wish to leave two weeks early, but it was the first – and only -- encouragement on my first days in a town with an extremely tight housing market. I tried other real estate offices and a couple of Route 66 motels advertising weekly and monthly rates and by late afternoon of my second day, I was getting scared.

The gliding rhythms of the "Route 66" theme song went out of my head like a phonograph needle skipping across a vinyl record to a stop.

With logic and focus breaking down, I stopped to inquire about rates at a Residence Inn just because it looked cool and beautiful and I apparently needed a break from the harshness of reality.

I stepped out of the car, eager to rush in and learn that this wonderful place full of well-dressed business guests might be affordable after all.

My phone, which had been resting on top of my purse, dropped to the pavement. It broke in two. My lifeline! The breakage of my fancy, expensive gadgets was simply the worst thing that could happen. I might as well turn around and go home.

Except that the car won't start.

I finally stopped the whirl of thought and emotion. I took a breath. The car started again. That's one step forward again.

At the Travelodge I sought to further re-group. For an hour, I alternated between trying to put my phone back together and looking feverishly in the phone book for Telephone Repair - Wireless – Nokia (I've lost the owner's manual). I could find nothing, but suddenly, miraculously, the two phone halves suddenly slid back together and snapped into place. It was just the battery panel that had popped.

Two steps forward. The trip is still on. I was able to sleep that night.

"Well, I know of an apartment where somebody is leaving and they're probably looking for a roommate - if you don't mind living with party animals."

This was the Travelodge desk clerk speaking the next morning. I decided early to hit the ground running - both literally with a 7 a.m. jog, and in aggressive pursuit of housing. My new plan is to talk to absolutely everybody in my path, and so I've stopped by to the motel's office to reserve an additional night on my way to find breakfast.

The desk clerk is a student at Northern Arizona University. After suggesting the fearsome idea about the "party animals," he tells me about bulletin boards on the campus where I should find "tons" of roommate notices.

I am a church goer, and so church is on my general list of help and support in practical matters as well as the spiritual. On my way to the campus, I find the beautiful building of one of the Protestant denominations and stop to introduce myself to the minister.

"He's not here this week," the secretary tells me. Her name is Ruth, and in my fevered, talk-to-anybody approach, I decide to try her for leads on a place to rent. This will not be easy. Ruth is very pleasant, but also quiet and shy and wary from having to deal with transient strangers who hit up church offices for "Christian help."

I asked her about the history of the building and so began a real conversation as she escorted me on a little tour. Gradually, her timidity gave way as our visit about the church ranged into other issues, from general things about Flagstaff to personal details of her own life. It became a female bonding sort of thing – you know, put any two female strangers together and within five minutes, whole life stories are being shared. We had worries over aging parents in common.

"My mother is in a nursing home, and today is her birthday," Ruth said.

In fact, she was going to see her shortly and on the way, planned to stop and buy ice cream and flowers.

"I'm going to get some peonies, because they're big and bright enough that she can see them," Ruth said. And then she began to cry.

I abandoned the idea of asking Ruth for help in my efforts to settle into Flagstaff. I told her that her mother was going to have a wonderful day because of her and then we hugged and I thanked her for the tour.

The morning was wearing on. I drove to the NAU campus and walked among its stately buildings until I found the student center. Wow, the Travelodge kid was right. A bulletin board offered dozens of notices and I started copying names and phone numbers. One problem I had was that my timing was off; I needed someplace now, and most people were looking for roommates for the summer session two, three and four weeks from now. Finally, one of the roommate appeals said, "Need Immediately." I dialed the number but had to leave a message.

An hour later, I sat on the edge of the bed again, staring off, having sent several e-mails and made numerous calls, all going to voice mail. In short, I'd made 17 inquiries. Prospects for making a home here looked dim. It's time to move on...*oh, it's so unfair* – I like Flagstaff; why doesn't Flagstaff like me?

Suddenly, the bedside phone rings LOUD.

Heather Blair was returning my call. She explained that with another woman, she recently moved into a three-bedroom house. Heather had a 3 ½-year-old daughter, and there were also two big dogs. Now normally, I have been reassured by a belief of the late W. C. Fields: "Anybody who doesn't like dogs and children can't be all bad." I've never had either in my life. But at that moment, EVERYTHING about the house on Philomena Drive sounded perfect.

Coincidentally, Heather said, one other person needing a home for just the month of May was coming over at 1 p.m.

"When would you like to see the house?" Heather said.

"How about now?"

It was noon and I knew I'd better get a jump on the other roommate candidate.

By 12:45 p.m., I was writing Heather a check and accepting a key. I had a home in Flagstaff!

Life is good. God is good.

6 FINDING WORK

My bedroom was small, beige, completely unfurnished and utterly beautiful. How lovely it was, after three weeks on the road, to unload everything from the Honda and transform the room to be mine! The only thing I needed was a bed, so I found a Target store and an air bed. I made up the bed on the carpeted floor with sheets, pillow and comforter, set up my camp chair and a lamp in one corner, created a "desk" made of two cardboard boxes, and I stacked suitcases to make a stand to hold the TV. My overly-complete wardrobe nearly filled the closet. I propped the small framed pictures of Minnie and Bigelow on the window ledge.

My view is of a fence and the side of the house next door. However, our house sits on the north end of town, at the edge of a forest, and from the backyard, we can see a snow-streaked mountain peak.

"Katie and I are going to the park," Heather announced as I was settling in. "Would you like to go with us?"

I spent the afternoon getting acquainted with mother and daughter, the first tot I've ever shared a house with. Heather and I sat in the grass, watching Katie play on her bike and the playground equipment with the energy and antics of a monkey.

Heather seems able to keep up with her daughter completely. She is fit, vivacious, 45 years old and in the midst of enormous change. She was a registered nurse until Katie's birth, and then felt inspired to change her priorities. It had become unacceptable to work nights and weekends in a career that no longer felt right. Heather wanted to devote her life to rearing Katie, and with a long-time love of history, she decided to quit nursing and go back to college. She would like to be a teacher but is open to other history-based job ideas.

Heather's decisions have created hardship for her. There's no money, of course, with all of her time consumed by motherhood and classes. Worst of all is a legal battle over visitation rights with Katie's father Bill. Soon after Heather became pregnant, he announced he wanted no part of parenthood. Yet sometime after the baby was born, when Heather had moved several states away, Bill launched a well-funded legal battle to see Katie more often. Strong and willful, Heather chose to fight back, but every legal maneuver takes resources for her side that she doesn't have. Lawyer friends and subsidized legal services have barely been enough to keep her in the game.

Heather spoke of these things a mile a minute, indulging in a few cigarettes, which she won't smoke in the house, and occasionally using language that hasn't singed my ears since I worked in newsrooms. She alternated between withering attacks on Bill and raucous observations on the ironies of her life that kept me in stitches. Her evolution as a person, from wild girl to doting mother and straight-A student, fascinates me.

When we returned from the park, I met Stella, another independent soul of 30. She works on the NAU campus and is studiously avoiding any career that would cut into her passion for travel and a love of the outdoors. Stella studied sociology, but found her work creeping into high technology as she showed an aptitude for computers. Sometimes she helps the business office of an outdoors store called Peace Surplus. Katie loves Stella, who is wild about Katie. No wonder this little girl is so bright-eyed and happy. I hope Katie will merely like me, despite the fact I have no idea how to interact with a 3-year-old. I mean, what do we *talk* about?

Rounding out the household are the dogs, Stella's Misha and Heather's Aimee, two large, gentle Labrador mixes. I don't think they'll jump up on me nor bark much so we should get along fine.

In the evening, Heather, Katie and Stella took the dogs out for a walk. I decided to surprise the girls with a fully-cooked dinner. This was great fun for me, especially with the challenges: tiny kitchen and no table-and-chairs for "dining." The kitchen opens onto a room, probably designed to be a family room because of a fireplace, but a sofa is the only piece of furniture and the big empty space of hardwood floor is better suited for dog romping. It's the front "living room" that draws everybody. There is a television that gets only NBC because cable service is an unnecessary luxury. There is a computer station where Heather does her studying. There are two upholstered chairs.

The rest of the room definitely belongs to Katie, with a playhouse, tot-sized tables and chairs and many toys merrily strewn about.

"Surprise!" I said when they walked in the door. I had made chicken and salad and set places at Katie's little play tables, which were placed together and covered with the colorful vinyl tablecloth from my possessions. I'd picked flowers from the yard and used a vase from the mantel top.

I reveled in the companionship and the idea of being at home in Flagstaff.

"Would you like to go hiking tomorrow?" Stella asked. "There are a couple of options on the mountains, depending on the weather. This time of year it's fun to walk under the ski lifts because the snow has melted and you find really cool stuff that skiers have dropped – once I found a watch."

After dinner, I retired to my room and connected with the world. One reason I picked a town the size of Flagstaff is that it has an America Online access number. All I had to do was plug my computer's phone line into the jack in my room and I had Internet service. I also spent some time on the phone with friends at home, having subscribed to a national one-rate call-anywhere-anytime plan. Again, Flagstaff, unlike many remote reaches in this mountainous state, generally keeps my connections open through a phone tower or something. Trite but true, the world has become smaller than ever.

The next morning, the weather was unsettled, so Stella and I canceled the walk up the mountain. We lounged around drinking hot tea instead, and later, I helped Heather with her garage sale, which turned into yet another irresistible gab fest when our next-door neighbor Catherine strolled over. Catherine is a psychotherapist, with a daughter Katie's age, and we all sat around on the driveway swapping outrageous stories and no-holds-barred observations. (This happened only after I believed Catherine wouldn't psychoanalyze me, or at least say anything out loud that would indicate that.)

"Y'all," I said, "where can I find a job? That would make my life complete."

Catherine looked at me closely.

"What kind of job?" she said.

I explained that in my few days in town, I've started looking. At the drug store down the street, I filled out an application after seeing a sign for a part-time position in the photo department. I stopped by the census office, but the process of just clearing my application to become a census taker would take nearly as long as I planned to be in Flag. I also filled out an application at The Diner, where I'd settled into having breakfast nearly every morning.

"I really want to be a waitress," I said, "while I still have the energy. I might not feel this way later in the trip."

Heather has waited tables and Catherine's older daughter works at a funky little café called "Morning Glory" so they were full of advice and encouragement.

"Don't tell people you're only here for a few weeks," Heather said. "People quit restaurants all the time; a few weeks is a long-term commitment."

I resolved to pound the pavement first thing Monday morning.

Early Sunday morning, with directions from Stella, I headed out on an early-morning run in beautiful Buffalo Park, which is just a few blocks from the house but feels miles out of town. The view is of majestic mountain vistas, and there is a two-mile trail that winds over woodsy hillsides and broad, open spaces.

En route back to the house, I noticed the flock gathering at the small, pretty Shepherd of the Hills Lutheran Church. After a shower and dressing up, I went back to the church. Pastor Dick Hamlin virtually opened the door, greeting me and everybody else in the warmest way, and later he introduced me as "Liz from Texas, who found us while she went on a run through the park. Doesn't she clean up good!"

Church with a friendly congregation was a wonderful way to start this day because later, my cell phone delivered family worries from Kansas. Daddy is admitting to feeling overwhelmed, said my brother Ed. The physical and mental demands of caring for our mother at the farm are wearing him down. Now, he's owning up to a persistent stomach ache that began, oh, maybe last January. January! He'd said nary a word about it all this time. The reluctant confessions were occurring in Ottawa, where my parents were spending the day with Ed and Sharron.

Don't alter your trip plans, Ed said. By late afternoon, he called again to say that he and our dad had returned from their regular Sunday trip to McDonald's for a Coke break while Mother napped at the house. Daddy was in better spirits and made it clear that he did not want to discuss issues further.

I felt the first serious pangs of homesickness today. I was worried by the Kansas developments, of course. This was also the first day that I felt aimless, at loose ends, not wanting to work or write or sight-see or meet new people or have adventures.

"Monday, May 8 - *I will leave this house and not return until I have a job.*"

So began my diary entry. Dreary Sunday was behind me and, being of a minority who actually like Mondays, in the same way that we like mornings – the first "work day" of the week offers a fresh start, new hope – I looked forward to this day and to fulfilling my resolve. Dressed for job interviews, I practically *marched* out of the house to go off and find the employer that would reestablish the pleasures of Monday as the start of a work week for me.

I coasted the Honda down the sharp slope of Beaver Street into the old town center of restaurants, offices and stores, the picture of their whole looking part Old West, large part college town, with disciplined appeal to tourists. There is a look of rugged, youthful enjoyment of northern Arizona's abundance of outdoor pursuits, especially hiking, camping and skiing. Flagstaff accommodates tourists, but doesn't go overboard in trying to snare their dollar.

My first stop was The Diner to have breakfast and try, for the third time, to talk to somebody in authority who would let me be a waitress. Excuse me, I mean "server," which I've learned is the politically correct word. I filled out an application for a "serving position." The Diner is an unadorned, comfortable, basic sort of place, busy but not frantic, where most of the customers appear to be regulars and the employees seem like waiters and waitresses.

"Andy," the manager, walked over to my booth. Against everyone's advice, I had confessed to being a short-timer. Andy said he couldn't hire me if I'm here for just a few weeks. He was nice in the way he said no. So were the two guys running an Italian deli around the corner on San Francisco Street.

"Have you had restaurant experience," one of them asked pleasantly.

"Oh yes! I've done it all," I said, filling in with a wave of the hand whatever I meant by "done it all." Eaten in restaurants mostly. The pure truth was that I'd waited tables and worked behind a buffet line at Sherwood's Restaurant for six weeks, part time, as a 16-year-old high school student in Independence, Kansas.

At least it was a beautiful day to walk in the cool, dry air. Yep, walk and get turned down. "No" came in a nice way at Morning Glory, the Amtrak station's visitors' center, a flower shop, an office supply store, two book stores, a bakery and a grocery store. My cell phone didn't ring back from the inquiry I'd made about a caretaker's position for a mildly disabled woman.

I had worried about rejection and what it would do to my ego, but you know, it wasn't bad at all. Everybody who would talk to me tried to be helpful with suggestions of other places to try. It became no big deal to get a turn-down; I simply moved on to the next suggested employer, even making another cold call or two on the way.

"You should try a temp agency; we have several," a woman advised me at the Chamber of Commerce office. Again, *nice*.

And so that's how I've found myself at Staffing Solutions talking to Adam Davis, who cannot understand how I picked FLAGSTAFF for my sojourn. He seems fascinated by my whole story about leaving home to spend a year living elsewhere in America.

"Why Flagstaff," he asks. "You could go anywhere."

This seems predictable as the viewpoint of a young guy on the cusp between school teen and free adult, when limitless choices open before you. Suddenly, the old hometown becomes a dead-end Hicksville in his eyes.

Adam gave me tests in spelling, arithmetic and filing. They were a breeze; to my great relief I aced 'em all.

"There is a job at Flagstaff Cablevision – they weren't happy with today's temp. She couldn't even turn ON a calculator. Are you interested and do you think you can..."

At that moment, Adam's head is bathed in a golden light. Angels are singing the "Halleluia Chorus" to full orchestral accompaniment on Handel's "Messiah." White doves flutter, bells peal, balloons soar, the skies shower confetti.

"Yes! Send me!!!!"

I start tomorrow.

Before returning to the house, I indulged in financial extravagance – a bottle of wine at the grocery store – to bring home to my little household. Stella and I made the celebration dinner, including our group's favorite dessert: Sara Lee Pound Cake slathered with cherry pie filling and real whipped cream.

At 8:15 a.m. on Tuesday, I was a happy part of Flagstaff's "rush hour" traffic, cruising down Beaver Street, jogging west and over the railroad tracks, and finally finding the office of Flagstaff Cablevision on South Plaza Way. The commute is 10 minutes, a lovely change from my old 25-minute fight with the raging roads of Tarrant County, Texas. My new life has begun, and I vow to honor God and fates and the goodness of the fine managers at

Flagstaff Cablevision for using Staffing Solutions and giving people like me a job.

My boss's name is Connie. She walked me over to a small round table and explained the task: to manage a heaping U.S. Mail bin of statements and checks sent by the city's cable users. She showed me how to use a cutting machine that slices the top edge of the envelopes. I'm to remove the checks and the "Return" portion of the statements, write down any variances between amounts due and amounts paid, then make rubber-banded bundles.

I become a slicing, scribbling, rubber-band bundling machine. For the first time in many years, I am working at a job having a direct and obvious point of accomplishment: an empty bin. In 1976, I worked briefly as a bank teller and appreciated that job for the same reasons. At the end of the day, you either "balanced" or you didn't, but the job was done when you did. In these kinds of jobs, there's no sitting around in meetings, conjuring vague and unachievable "Goals and Objectives," drafting "Blueprints for the Future," Targeting Audiences, Marketing Communications, Strategizing, Positioning, Totally Quality Managing, Briefing, De-Briefing, Debunking De Bullshit.

Of course, a couple of days into Honest Work and I was about to go bonkers. My neck and back were stiff and sore. The appearance of packed mail bins was relentless. Occasionally, the tedium was broken by a written rant on a statement, like "Bring back the Adventure Channel!" and "I'm not paying your fucking late charge!" To the latter, I dutifully wrote down the payment variance amount.

I also discovered a significant number of uncanceled stamps on envelopes that just go straight to the trash. Surreptitiously, I rescued a total of $8 worth of stamps for future road-life correspondence. That's a value of 75 minutes worth of wages! Spotting those stamps also helped relieve the monotony of the slicing, checking, sorting and bundling.

My working life is rigid as a temp at Flagstaff Cablevision. Being an hourly employee, I have to come and go as if punching a clock, with one hour for lunch and two 15-minute breaks, one in the morning, one in the afternoon. There is no schmoozing with others – I don't know them, they don't know me.

There is, however, Brian the cable guy. As I hunch over my table, I hear him making his way along the cubicles, talking to this person and that one. He has a voice like Bing Crosby (*Can he sing?*) and an off-center view of the world and a weird and witty sense of humor. Brian is the only employee who will go out of his way to speak to me. I like him, even though I rarely look up when I hear him coming.

I've identified the office screw-off as Mark. All day every day is a party. I swear, the man never works. One morning, I could hear Mark collecting money to order pizza delivered for lunch.

"Hey, Sarah, you want in? It's just a dollar. Connie 'll match it from petty cash!"

Oh boy, I sure wanted pizza. I listened to Mark invite every person between his cubicle and my table. Surely he could read my loud thoughts: *I have a dollar! I'd like pizza. Please ask me.* One by one, closer and closer… But of course, he didn't ask me. He skipped me and moved around to the other side of the room, asking everybody else to the party, one by one, right in front of me.

What goes around comes around. In my old office life, I too treated many temp employees as if they were invisible. They were always quiet and mousy, just like I must have seemed, and because you're never going to see them again once their assignment is over, it never seemed worth the effort to make them feel like a part of the office. Shame on me.

You may remember that on many days, I require an afternoon nap. This is particularly important with a boring job. Fortunately, the coolness of Flagstaff's higher elevation means that I can snooze in my car. I started spending my lunch hours in the parking lot of the nearby Radisson Hotel. It was restful just to roll down the windows and listen to the wind rushing through the tops of the tall pines. Sometimes I wandered inside to sit in the lobby and read *PC World* or *The Wall Street Journal*. Given my home situation of little real furniture, it was lovely to sit around in over-stuffed opulence.

What an impoverished group we are in our little house on Philomena Street. Many mornings at 8 a.m. or soon thereafter, the phone rings. It is a bill collector, one of the wolves nipping at Heather's heels. If I am at home, I will answer and invite the person to leave a message, which he or she never does. Heather always takes the call when she is at home, showing a forthright responsibility that I feel should count for something.

"I just can't pay you right now," she says.

One day, Heather announced that she had applied for Food Stamps, an experience she described as the most demeaning of her life.

"They were so rude and I felt so low," she said.

"But you're the perfect candidate," I said. "You are whom Food Stamps are for, somebody temporarily struggling, a student and a single mom creating a sound future. It's not forever."

Katie will never know the extent of Heather's financial woes, for everything goes into her care and her mother's studies. After day care and Heather's classes, the two head for the park. After that, when Stella comes home, Katie squeals over another round of attention and the two of them take Misha and Aimee out for a walk. There is no money for movies, other than video rentals, or brand new toys or clothes, but I can't imagine Katie having a happier or richer childhood.

Heather's focus did have its blind spots. One weekend, Bill arrived from Oregon to take his daughter away for his scheduled visitation time. Heather spent the weekend scared, anxious and sleepless. Stella and I did our best to divert her with a night out on the town, complete with Thai dinner in a restaurant, but she could not be distracted.

I was relieved when Bill showed up precisely on time on Monday to return Katie to the house. Heather scooped her up and fled for their afternoon in the park, some grocery shopping, and no doubt to assess the damage.

Two hours later, they returned and Heather was in a fury.

"Do you know what he did?!" she cried.

I cringed. No, oh please, not some kind of abuse…

"We were in the store and Katie looked up and said to me, 'Mom, don't be a smartass.' She had to have heard that word from him. Can you believe that he used that kind of language around a three-year-old?!"

Being well-familiar with Heather's own "colorful" vocabulary, I had to do a little stalling to come up with some supportive outrage.

"*That fucking asshole*!" she blasted.

Nearby, Katie had launched a busy play session with her toys and appeared not to have tuned in for another new language lesson. Or, maybe she wasn't hearing anything new at all.

I found myself promoted, sort of, at Flagstaff Cablevision. There was no higher pay nor did anyone hand me a brass name plate. But eventually, there were no more brimming mail bins. Sarah showed me the next phase of the job: organizing and totaling stacks of payments. I successfully turned on the calculator. Then came the moment of trying to fake my alleged skill of using a "10-key by touch." That did not go as well, but it didn't seem to matter. I was at least accurate and gradually getting faster, although I'd opened the mail so fast that I was speeding myself right out of the job.

"I don't think I'll be here much longer," I said to Brian the Cable Guy. "This is supposed to be a two-week assignment, but I don't think there's enough work."

"Connie told me that I can use you to stuff new-customer 'welcome bags,'" he said.

And so I helped Brian, who turned out to be something of a vagabond himself. We exchanged our "travel America" stories and he told me about taking a year to get from Wisconsin to Arizona. I should try camping, he said; it's really easy, especially with free access to Arizona's extensive national forests.

It was time to report all these doings and travel trivia on my new Web site. I dedicated Saturday to exercise and work. I went back to Buffalo State Park again, and beautiful as it is, the place is just too high. The elevation is thinner on oxygen than I'm used to, and I find the running a big fat chore, so I think I'm going to hang up the running shoes for this portion of the trip.

Later I hauled my laptop computer to the Flagstaff Library.

Have you ever found yourself in a place that, by nature and tradition, should be pleasurable but isn't? There is something ill about that library. It is a beautiful building in a lovely setting, right at the edge of a park, but inside, everything about it says "Leave!" Hard wooden chairs. Signs that always seem to demand or warn. Not a lot of books or periodicals. Hard-looking patrons. Silent staff intent on being invisible. I asked Heather later about the library, and she said that because it draws the unwashed homeless, there's tension among the librarians and not a chance of maintaining upholstered furniture free of body dirt and odors.

I did not work there very long. I left to wander downtown prior to attending the weekly free concert in the outdoor amphitheater. As I waited for the talented kiddies comprising the Suzuki Strings to assemble, I wandered into a souvenir shop where I considered buying a T-shirt with two skeletons talking. One says to the other, "Yes, but it's a dry heat." I finally decided to skip the over-priced shirt and leave with the free humor.

The shop manager also bent my ear over Flag's great divide of interests between commercial development and keeping the city small. She was vociferously anti-development and, like several others I've heard expound on this issue, viewed Californians as Forces of Evil responsible for new, large Barnes and Noble and Home Depot stores. "Californians" railroaded those developments, she said, moving in with their money and moxie, cutting down trees and town history and drawing trade from her part of town on the north side of the tracks, to the south. A few days later, in the university library, I would hear the opposite side of the issue, from a man bitterly condemning "Flagstaff's small-minded, no-growth ways."

The weekend brought rest and pleasant diversions, but it also brought a crash.

"I am SO homesick," I told Heather and Stella. It was Sunday evening and I lay on the sofa doubled over, as if I had a stomach ache. That's how it felt. A great, empty void filled my head and heart. I missed my cats, my sister and brother-in-law and my neighbors Carolyn and Vernon. I missed my mommy. I missed my job at The Arc, my bed, my refrigerator, my routines – Dallas dinners and the symphony with Chuck, Saturday nights in downtown Fort Worth, Mexican food and Texas diners, my jogging route, my minister's Sunday sermons, my radio station and Channel 33, my weekday coffee gang, the Texas sky, flag, and bravado and all the rhythms and rituals I'd so easily shucked.

"OH THIS HURTS!" I wailed.

Some relief came on the day of my 50th birthday when I drove through the mountains to Payson, Ariz., to meet up with my cousin Kenny, Aunt Lugene's son, and his wife Judy. At last, people with whom I shared a long connecting history, even if they were infrequently-seen relatives. Judy is from my hometown – I'd gone to high school with her sister – and so there was much to talk about as we whiled away the afternoon at a lakeside picnic spot in the mountains above Payson. It was thoroughly pleasant.

At home in Flagstaff that night, I found the blue-enveloped greeting card my dad had given to me in Kansas. "Liz Moore" was neatly typed, along with "Somewhere in the USA – Open May 20." The typing in the enclosed note was less perfect – Daddy refuses to use the self-correcting feature on his electric typewriter – and after reminding me that 50 is "a half a century," he wrote, "We can't imagine where you might bE but hope it is a fun time. We will bE thinking of you. Your coming has helped Mother. Happy birthday, WE love you."

My job at Flagstaff Cablevision ended abruptly. The last of the monthly billings had been opened and calculated and Brian was caught up on welcome packets. I poked my head into my supervisor's office.

"Connie, is there anything else you need me to do?" I asked, hoping for something else to extend the life of my little paycheck.

"Actually," she said, "there isn't, but will you be available next month?"

Her question made me feel good, but I will be hundreds of miles away next month. Lately I've been thinking of traveling to the Northwest for the weeks of late spring/early summer. Ken and Judy urged me to seek work on a boat to Alaska, their favorite vacation destination.

The quick release from Flagstaff Cablevision meant that once again, my days were blank and uncharted. I felt the surge of anything-can-happen adrenaline.

I also remembered my pre-trip pledge to do something for the community that took me in. Some kind of volunteer work.

"The Red Cross office always needs somebody," said Stella, who used to work for the organization. "Want me to call them for you?"

And so at 12:30 p.m. the next day, I found myself in the Red Cross office located in a small shopping center down the street from our house, listening to a dismayingly long list of ideas atop the mind of the director. Apparently, she had never found herself with an extra professional body on her staff - a FREE one - and her Things To Do list sounded like all the parts of a three-year strategic plan. I listened, completely bored by prospects here. It was too early to get back in an office and return to the kind of work I'd left just six weeks earlier. In the spirit of my adventure, I wanted to go hand out blankets to flood victims in a school gymnasium. Or comfort the families whose homes had just been blown away by a tornado. Roll bandages maybe? But today, Flagstaff didn't have a single disaster going on.

I would be dutiful anyway.

"Wow, that's a lot," I said, when Cheryl finally took a breath. "How 'bout I help you promote the teen baby-sitting classes?"

And so for the rest of the afternoon, I studied the summer baby-sitting program, wrote a marketing plan and a press release and 45 mailing labels. I don't think I've ever packed more into four hours behind a desk. Isn't that always the way it is, though; you do some of your best work when there's no career or paycheck at stake.

I didn't get to continue on with Cheryl's list. At home, Staffing Solutions called and I was thrilled to accept my next assignment.

"You'll never guess where I'm going to work," I exclaimed in a phone visit to Texas with my old boss from The Arc, who now commutes from Arlington to Plano in a new job with a national youth soccer association. Al

Abeson asked if I might be near Portland, Ore., in early June. He was organizing a get-together of old friends and colleagues from a chapter of The Arc while in the area on a soccer trip. The idea of dinner with favorite old work buddies sounded heavenly, and so I made a snap decision regarding time and destination: Portland, Ore., June 5. I'd be headed toward the Northwest around that time anyway.

"So what's your new job?" Al asked.

"I'm going to work at the Grand Canyon National Park Airport - 'in Security,' so to speak."

The airport needed temporary workers to help make security badges.

To some people, a downside to the assignment might be the 140-mile round-trip commute from Flagstaff. (What was it I said a few pages back about giving up time-consuming commutes?) I didn't care. My mileage would be reimbursed, I would work at the job only every other day, and most importantly, IT WAS THE GRAND CANYON, for cryin' out loud!!

It was also an AIRPORT, a work place that has always held a mystique for me. Thirty years ago, when I saw the great film soap opera "Airport," I wanted the glamorous job of the beautiful female lead, the blonde lady who rushed around, crisp and coiffed, solving one crisis after another, while not having to be *on* the plane dealing with the suicidal bomber. The dirty work was left to Dean Martin and Jacqueline Bisset.

Now I was going to work at an airport at one of the most beautiful places on earth, or so I've heard and seen on 4" by 6" Kodachrome cardboard. I've never been there.

Again I had that exhilarating, first-day-of-school feeling as I left the house at 7 a.m. and found little Hwy. 180. I had no idea what I would find on the route, although I expected a difficult, winding, up-and-down drive. For sure, I passed through mountains, climbing more feet to an elevation of 8,000, and valleys and then a sudden descent into an eerily beautiful, flat plain of browns and purples, with misty low-rise mounds and mesas.

It was one picture-perfect surprise after another: rich forests, a sparkling stand of white Aspens, a meadow of shimmering gold, and once there was a large patch of black where fire had eaten the trees down to jagged picks. There would be more fires in this drought-stricken place and time, and one day, I drove another part of Hwy. 180 through smoke so thick it eclipsed the sun. Sight-seers and the curious lined the road with binoculars and video cameras trained on a large blaze eating its way through forest just a couple hundred yards away from the parked cars.

The route to the airport from Flagstaff had little traffic (at this pre-summer time of year anyway). There were no stop signs or lights, not for 50 miles until I reached the wide spot in the road called Valle. Here was a collection of souvenir stands, gas stations and one big motel, all plunked down just yards from the highway where huge tour buses roared through town. This was where I finally reached a stop sign and a sharp right turn to join the buses and bus-sized RVs headed for the Grand Canyon. My heart beat faster as the landscape changed again, from semi-desert to forests, and I knew that somewhere very close, Arizona would suddenly open into a gash of pink rock. But I was not a tourist today, and I had to follow the sign at the turnoff for the airport without seeing the tiniest hint of the natural wonder.

As usual, my mental image dissolved when I reached my new office assignment. I had envisioned Dallas-Fort Worth Airport, or O'Hare, and perhaps a hangar-sized building where, after passing through an intense check-in process, a whole team of temps would be clocking in and seated at one long bank of computers to work with printouts and stacks of plastic squares with clips, or perhaps the little beaded chains like government employees wear around their necks. Uniformed security, possibly with semi-automatic weapons, would stand guard over the top-secret operation.

If Mayberry had an airport, this would be it. My tires crunched gravel as I searched in vain for marked parking, then picked a spot under a tree near the entrance to the portable building that was the airport office. It was fronted by a small set of wooden steps and a deck.

The only person there at 9 a.m. was my supervisor, a laid-back woman named Jane Odell. She had that languid, assured air of been-there, seen-that. Jane had not decided how she wanted to approach the badge-making project, so she showed me other duties I need to know while Donna the secretary is out, as she was this week. I can tell I will like this place. It means resetting my internal pace clock that ran so full-tilt at Flagstaff Cablevision.

I soon learned that the airport has no commuter traffic. Rather, the airport is the base for sight-seeing helicopters, small planes and air taxis whose brochures litter the hotel racks and streets of nearby Las Vegas. There's also a lot of attention paid to ground-based matters. Everybody who works here is provided subsidized housing, so the airport office manages all kinds of maintenance issues.

Andy Turanto, the acting manager, arrived, halting his long booted strides toward his corner office to stop and meet me. Andy learned my name quickly and soon made me feel like a welcome part of the little airport family. His own family, whom I enjoyed seeing pop into the office from time to time, includes his wife and two young home-schooled daughters who were unusually charming and graceful in their ability to relate to adults.

Andy introduced me to everybody, employees and visitors alike. One day, the chairman of the airport board arrived.

"Liz, I'd like you to meet Paul Babbitt," Andy said, and then I got to pour coffee for a bona fide Arizona celebrity, relative of a national political figure. Mr. Babbitt's brother is Bruce, the former governor who would later become a U.S. Interior Secretary.

I loved this place and all these nice people!

It is the end of my second day at the airport, and I am headed back to Flag. It is 6 o'clock, and the sun has loosened its grip on the day, mellowing into a golden rest. Turning onto the highway from the airport road, I join a short procession of cars and we all speed up to the pace of highway traffic.

Suddenly, my windshield flares red with brake lights. With both feet, I jam deep on the brake and the clutch. This is no quick slow-down; it's a heart-pounding, seconds-count STOP. Somehow, metal doesn't hit metal. We all just sit there, no doubt wide-eyed, paralyzed, as a large deer bounds safely over the front headlight of the vehicle two cars ahead of me and off to the woods on the other side of the road. The three of us continued at a crawl of 20 mph and then 30 and then semi-normally.

Later, Jane and Andy told me that that particular stretch of highway is especially treacherous for deer that leap out of nowhere. Not only is Bambi's hide at stake, so is the body of one's vehicle and its occupants because the animals can weigh as much as 200 pounds and really make a mess of things. Deer activity at roadways is greatest at sunrise and sunset, so I altered my working hours to avoid those times of day.

By Sunday, I was wiped out by my first three days at work and over 400 miles of wheel-gripping, road-scanning vigilance. I decided to skip church, worshiping banana pancakes with Stella and Heather instead. We are now able to dine together at a real table and chairs – a patio table and four plastic chairs now grace the family room in the corner opposite the sofa. The "dining suite" and bedroom furniture are among a bounty that Stella has been bringing home, thanks to college friends and acquaintances who are graduating and leaving their possessions behind. You would have thought one of us had won on "The Price Is Right," so thrilled were we the day Stella started bringing real grown-up – adult-sized anyway – furniture.

After breakfast, Stella went off to hike up a mountain, a trek I've yet to make, but as my time here draws to a close, I'm realizing I like the *idea* of climbing a mountain more than the reality.

Heather took Katie to the park, and though I said I was headed over to the library to work, I suddenly realized that the house and the sofa could be mine, all *mine*, for a few hours. I fetched the comforter off my air bed and arranged it on the couch like a cocoon where I burrowed in and cracked open a book titled, *Without Reservations*. It's a birthday gift from my sister Martha, and soon I was engrossed in author Alice Steinbach's story of taking a year-long sabbatical from her newspaper career. She "moved" to Europe. The other big difference between us was money. When she arrived in Paris and had to wait a few hours for her room, she went out and bought a load of French cosmetics and a silk dress she saw in a window. Wow. Imagine getting to do that.

Still, so many of her feelings and observations were dead-on familiar, and while I could only envy her resources, I could also absorb a sense of her style and savoir faire and play with that this afternoon. When I was ready to leave the couch and the house, I decided to skip the library and go to "New Zealand." Flagstaff has a lovely restaurant called New Zealand Down Under situated catty-corner from the historic Weatherford Hotel. It's a great corner for relaxing and watching people. At the restaurant, I informed the waiter with the Down Under accent and an arch attitude that I wished to sit on the patio and write and I would like a glass of wine, please. My attitude arm-wrestled his attitude and won, of course.

Another work week has begun, but Jane is off to a meeting in Baltimore, loaded down with two large notebooks full of report papers that I helped her three-hole-punch and organize. We also finished drafts of forms and letters needed to update security badges required of everyone who works at the airport. She seemed pleased with everything I did, and Andy continues to praise my work and say he's glad I'm here. It's SO different from the lock-step procedural and cultural machinery of the cable office.

Here I am, working at the Grand Canyon, and I've yet to see it. I'm not sure how that's going to happen given an 8-hour work day and 2 1/2-hour commute. Sometimes I wander out onto the deck and search the dense green of my surroundings, hoping to see the tiniest sign of pink eroded rock. I listen to the gathering roar of a small sight-seeing plane about to take off, or I watch the vertical rise of spinning helicopter blades. They're going to the Canyon – when oh when will I?

Donna, the secretary whom I've finally met, is planning her wedding. She said that she and her fiancé searched and searched for just the right setting.

"That would seem easy!" I said, thinking of all the exquisite possibilities at the rim or down deep into the Canyon.

Boring, Donna said. She didn't really say "boring," but she did explain that if you live at the Grand Canyon, a wedding here is pretty mundane. No, an Elvis chapel in Las Vegas is just the ticket. She has also reserved hotel rooms for friends and relatives and we discussed ways to bypass expensive hotel catering for a nice but affordable reception. Donna's wedding is scheduled for July, so it will be one of dozens of road stories that I regret having to leave unfinished.

Donna's wedding plants Las Vegas in my mind. Ah, big bad city. Bold bright lights. Gambling, liquor and cheesy lounge acts. I think I need a taste of all that.

At home on the Internet, I book a room just off the Strip for two nights post-Flagstaff. Vegas is on the way to northbound Oregon routes.

Because I'm in the unusual mood to plan ahead, I also write to the Mayor of the City of Corvallis, Ore., dressing up my letter in the written-language-equivalent of the navy blue interview suit:

From: Liz Moore
To: Mayor of Corvallis

Hello!
My name is Liz Moore. I am a Texas-based homeowner who has begun a one-year career sabbatical that is a little more unusual than the typical loaf-and-travel break. I have begun a tour of America that includes actually spending a month to 2 months living, working, learning and "helping out" in small cities and towns in our nation's major regions.

I have just concluded my first month in my first town: Flagstaff, Ariz. While I arrived knowing no one, I leave with many friendships I'll carry forever. I hope and believe my time here left a positive mark on a number of lives and the work place of several offices.

I am now heading up to the Northwest and some friends have mentioned Corvallis. I will want to rent a modest residence - an apartment or room in a house, for example - and work of some kind also is an important part of this experience (pay level is not important; minimum wage or better). Community service is a third ingredient I seek.

How readily can I find these things in your city? If you or city staff can offer any suggestions I will be most appreciative. I will arrive in Oregon and look at a number of places June 1-7. You can learn more about me and my mid-life "project" at my Web site. Thank you for any advice that you might offer.

Best wishes to you and the City of Corvallis.

Why Corvallis? It's near Portland and Salem, where I have several good friends, and it probably has a local AOL access number. I like its location on my Atlas map. Otherwise, I don't know a thing about Corvallis.

The next day I add one more thing to appreciate about Corvallis, Oregon: It has a city official with the moxie to reply with enthusiasm:

From: George C. Grosch
To: Liz Moore

Saw your message to Mayor Berg and as a City Councilor I wanted to respond. When you get to Corvallis give me a call and I'll fill you in on the goings on in Corvallis.

I believe this City will meet your criteria. We are an active, vital, involved community with no lack of opportunity for someone looking for a great place to live.

Housing should be no problem but I do not know your price range. We are a University community (Oregon State University) and students will be leaving for the summer so the apartment market will be more open than usual.

Feel free to call or E-mail me for details. Love your web page.

Thank you, George Grosch! As I ponder the blank page that is June, I feel so much better having a place to start.

In the final days of my eight-day airport job, I finished "the security detail," a filing project, phone answering, typing assignments, and I learned that the airport family was as dysfunctional as every other work-place family. How glad I was to be removed from the emotional office politics of reported jealousies, tirades, and frustrations over pecking order. Oh OK, I'll jump in here and blame the employees I did not get to know as well as Andy, Jane and Donna, whom I found to be swell people.

At long last, it is time to drive out the airport road and turn left instead of right. I had arranged the day to leave early and visit the Grand Canyon. Jane has given me a letter to use to be admitted free at the entrance gate 8 miles up the road. I am SO excited.

It is a long 8 miles. Even after handing over my letter to the park employee at the gate, there's a ways to go, and the Honda seems to tunnel through trees that insist on concealing the western wonder I've waited 50 years to see. At last, signs direct me to Mather Point, and it's only after I turn into a parking lot and walk to the edge does the Canyon reveal itself.

For those who can only see God in the big things on earth, this is the place to get religion. The majesty of massive layered rock cascading one mile deep and 200 miles horizontally in front of you is simply jaw-dropping. The air is still, even with a breeze. The silence is powerful, overcoming the multinational chatting of tourists. Colors change at the commands of sun and haze, the reds, browns, beiges and purples whispering and turning slowly toward a sudden grandeur at sunset. Peer down at the base of this gorge and you can see a tiny sparkling ribbon that is the Colorado River. *What was it like for the earliest explorers to stumble onto this place?*

I intended to park the car, walk over to the edge, look over the side, take some pictures, and head home before the roadside kamikaze deer parties began. But I simply can not tear myself away.

Leaving Mather Point, the Honda and I continue to prowl the rim, stopping here and there for a new scenic vantage point. Eventually, I park the car and follow a tourist-free hiking trail that takes me up and out for miles with nothing but a few feet of ground between me and a 5,000-foot plunge to the Canyon floor. My shoes are too thin and flimsy for such a trek but I'm too mesmerized to care, and I walk, then hobble for as long as there is any daylight at all.

At least I had the presence of mind to use the last bit of light to return to Grand Canyon Village, pick up my car and reluctantly leave the park. By then it was pitch dark, so I bypassed the isolation of the mountain road back to Flagstaff and took a more heavily traveled route.

As I headed toward I-17, I stole quick sideways glances at the day's final natural wonder: the forest fires. High in my view out the car's window, jagged lines of orange etched the black of night as the trees and landscape of Kendrick Peak blazed on.

I was sorry to lose my bond with nature, especially as I drove up the interstate's entrance ramp. Feelings of high stress returned as I joined rushing traffic; the Honda seemed to be the only car among trucks. Semis roared northward, buffeting us rudely in their smelly, dirty, windshield-caking wake. Alas, I might as well get used to it, because it's time to pull up stakes in Flagstaff, rejoin highway life and go north.

7 THE TRIP TO OREGON

We said our good-byes with an evening feast around the patio table in the family room. I gave the household a camp chair because Stella and Heather liked mine so much and they still need furniture. Stella gave me her self-published cookbook, "Food is Love – and other fattening ideas," which included our favorite dessert of pound cake, pie filling and whipped cream.

The next morning, I collapsed the air bed and hauled all my stuff out, piling it in the driveway so that I could pack it piece by piece, systematically and tightly into the car. Once more, my world would be contained in an 8- by 5-foot space on wheels, allowing me to roll on to a new American experience. I did not think too hard about how much I will miss my two housemates and Katie, and the two dogs, who had also captured my cat-loving heart.

There was one more smoking break with Heather – she smoked and I drank orange juice in the back yard – and I was gone by 8:30. I stopped by Staffing Solutions to drop off my final time cards, and then I found I-40. Anticipating a boring few hours, I peeled the cellophane off a Texas going-away gift of audio cassettes titled "New York Stories." I popped one into the player, but the vignettes about East Coast urban life failed to engage me, so incongruous were they with the desert and western openness around me.

The route took me to Kingman and then northwest over spectacular terrain where huge dark red rock formations looked as if they had been heaved and shoved out of the earth. And then there was water! It's been a long time since I've seen it. Torrents of the Colorado River fed the mightiness of Hoover Dam. Beyond it, Lake Mead lay vast and blue and still.

Those were the last signs of God's grace; the sinister spread of Las Vegas soon beckoned me down from the hills and onto the Devil's playground.

I descended upon The Strip, a beguiling stretch of hotel casinos and multi-story signs rivaling the dazzle of Times Square. There is, in fact, a small-scale New York skyline anchored by "New York, New York," one hotel representing a whole trend in increasingly-ambitious concepts fueled by obscene amounts of money amassed by the winning side in gambling. Sometimes the hotels are so large that it's a time-consuming effort to walk outside and over to the one next door, which is likely to have a theme representing an entire civilization or culture. There's Egypt and ancient Rome in the Luxor Hotel and Caesar's Palace, glittering European capitals in Paris Las Vegas and Monte Carlo, Hollywood glamour in the MGM Grand. To beckon you inside to the real party of gaming tables and slot machines, there is an outdoor circus of sights and sounds: an erupting volcano in front of The Mirage, battling pirate actors on sinking ships in front of Treasure Island, a 12-acre lake at the Bellagio, a Coney Island-style roller coaster at New York, New York.

I didn't spend the night at any of these places. My hotel was the Key Largo a few blocks east of The Strip. I had never been there but was soon charmed by the throwback-Vegas feel of my lodging, with its cramped, dark and smoky casino and a lazy coffee shop in one corner. Three stories of rooms were built around quiet courtyards of tropical vegetation, fish ponds and a large swimming pool. One could almost envision Elvis appearing poolside at dusk with a guitar and girls.

Best of all was my room, not that it took much to please me. I slept in a real bed for the first time in a month. Instead of one snowy TV channel, I had 50 clear ones on cable. And in one corner of the room, there was a little bar with a phone jack where, on one 50-cent local call, I could plug in my computer and spend a couple of hours on the Internet.

But, thirty budgeted dollars were burning a hole in my pocket.

On my first night, I went to Bally's and converted $10 into a satisfyingly hefty roll of quarters. I soon lost the heft at the video poker machines, chosen because they usually allow me to lose the quarters more slowly. Not this time.

Time to find a non-gambling amusement and lo, there it was. A monorail! I felt like a futuristic cartoon character as I climbed out of Bally's and joined the other shorts-and-sneaker-wearing tourists on a vast platform wired for sound. Drumming our ears and psyches was one of the many disembodied voices that lull and hypnotize the hordes who are either trying to leave a casino, or deciding whether to enter one. *Welcome to the MGM Grand/Bally's Monorail System...At this time the monorail is on final approach into the station...there is no eating, drinking or smoking while on board...for your safety...you are getting sleepy...Return to Bally's and give up the quarters you pathetic little tightwad...*

The train did not fly and dip and swoop the way I wished, but it was very cool to soon find myself at the MGM Grand. I dropped a few quarters into slots and stared at lounge acts. The shows, heavy with "golden oldie" themes and impersonators, couldn't beat the entertainment of simply watching people. Most amazing were the gray-haired grannies completely mesmerized by slot machines. Over and over, they would drop the coins that had long ago lost any significance as currency, and the players never even reacted when they hit something that released a jackpot. They scooped the change into the wide well of a cardboard cup and mechanically played on.

After my evening of wandering the casinos, I went to bed early and arose early for a 3-mile run. At 7 in the rising sun of the morning, the casino landscape is exposed in all its gross, tawdry starkness. The fantasy confections are mere buildings, monstrous in size, garish in color and shape and sprawl, hollow without people, creepy with that 24-hour outdoor sound system repetitiously droning on. Employees shuffle into work or listlessly sweep, pick up trash and wipe the brass and glass of doorway entrances.

Aside from my groovy lodging and Internet connection, I had fun one time during my two days in Vegas. I returned to the MGM Grand to visit the "lion habitat," a glassed-in jungle housing several of the King of Beasts. The lions lounge mostly, sometimes yawning and stretching and making their way up on their feet for – *oh my god, what??!!! Leaping? Roaring??* – we gawkers crowd each other and step on small children for a closer vantage point at the glass walls. The lions tease us, deciding not to move after all and instead, settle back into a nap. One of the cats is highly annoyed as two handlers try to play ball with him.

Despite their grand and distinctive themes, the casinos are basically alike inside, especially in their relentless pressure on people to gamble. There are no clocks and no windows. Any places to sit are going to be in front of a slot machine, a gaming table or inside a restaurant. Once you're inside a casino, it's hard to locate the exits, so you find yourself wandering in circles on carpet with large dizzying patterns, peering through weird, dim light, but then you can't help but focus on the intense color and brightness of a device or game. The sounds are all ding-dinging bells and the clang of coins amplified by metal when they hit the trays. There are clicking wheels, dice falling on felt-topped tables, shouts and yells of delight and despair. Who can resist the action? Plus, if you don't gamble, you really feel out of it (I even feel like a dork as I write all this about not gambling.)

All that said, there is much to admire about Las Vegas, even beyond the fact that it makes use of the desert for something other than weapons testing and toxic waste dumping. Name America's appreciatively unique cities and there just aren't many. Las Vegas is a place where the idea of it is bigger than the reality – a swaggering, sexy, dangerous, anything-can-happen idea. Enough people have "struck it rich" to put stars in the eyes and hope in the hearts of the rest of us. And, true to American ideals, the city is democratic in the way it makes people suddenly rich and eventually poor. Las Vegas was the "first" of its genre and is therefore entitled to its sins and excesses. In fact, Vegas simply wouldn't be Vegas without sins and excesses.

I am more than ready to leave town and head off to a cheerier spot: Death Valley. The place implanted itself in my brain through 1950s television on "Death Valley Days." I just have to see where 20-mule teams hauled borax. Where the average high temperature in July is 116 and yearly rainfall isn't even 2 inches. Where the lowest point in the Western Hemisphere is near a spot called Badwater.

Driving out of the city toward the northwest, I can't imagine that Death Valley can look worse than what I'm seeing – mile after mile of flat brown desert, just like in the movies except that on film, something zany is usually going on between at least two characters in a convertible. Oh wait! Here's an interesting landmark: a prison. Bet there aren't many escapes there.

At least I don't have far to go up U.S. 95 before it is time to turn left and drive another few miles to my destination. It's also time to have lunch. An attractive business right at the turnoff promises a clean, spacious convenience store and directly behind it, a restaurant in the same long block of a building. I can either buy groceries or splurge on a sit-down meal. I decide to walk through the store to the back, taking one step up into the plain dining room through a doorway.

After ordering as the only customer, I realize I need something to do while I wait for my lunch. I trot back to the car to get my Atlas so that I can study the route to, through and beyond Death Valley National Park.

Conveniently, the restaurant has a side door and therefore a shortcut to go back to the side parking lot. Stepping outside, I spy a part of the building I had not noticed, a section attached to the back that has its own small entrance behind a secure gate. Next to that door, there's a plain, black and white-lettered sign. My jaw drops when I read it: It advises that Nevada state law requires that "latex prophylactics" be used in this establishment. Another small, more-artistically lettered sign told me that I am dining at Madame Butterfly's.

Oh. My. God. Little Honda, I don't think we're in Kansas any more.

I finally shut my mouth and start walking back to the dining room again, incorporating this new thread of sophistication into my innocent little world. Of course I'd read at some point that Nevada has legal prostitution, but I never expected to be a "patron" at a brothel. (Well, sort of. I mean, is it all the same business? Groceries/restaurant/sex, all on the same set of books?) I return to my little table against the wall in the restaurant and try not to stare at a door marked "Employees Only!" Madame Butterfly must be on the other side. Is that her "act"? The tragic heroine of the famous opera? Do customers find her in full costume and white makeup and is that a turn-on? What's going on back there right now…

"How are those chicken fingers?"

I'm startled by the cook, who suddenly appears in the doorway of the kitchen. I pretend to not be thinking what I'm thinking but rather, engrossed in the map I've retrieved from my car.

"Good! Say, can you tell me the best way to see Death Valley? It's just up the road, isn't it?"

And so begins a half hour of conversation. The cook is an interesting fellow, somebody who traveled the U.S. extensively before deciding he likes this barren part of the world and chose to settle here – but on this side of the state line, not California's. Oh how he hates California. His reasons seem to be similar to those of the bashers I met in Arizona; Californians are greedy developers who enter and pillage the sovereignties of their neighboring states.

Meanwhile, nobody else ever comes through the restaurant for either dinner or nooner. I buy some ice cream and jump in the car for the short drive northwestward along Hwy. 190. It is the hottest time of day, and the road seems to descend as rocky hillsides rise to wrap the Honda and me in desolation. In this area, points of interest have names like "Funeral Mountains," "Furnace Creek" and "Stovepipe Wells."

Taking the cook's advice, I find the way to a scenic lookout called Dante's View. Narrow and blind, the little road climbs and turns for 11 slow miles to an elevation of 5,475 feet. What a sight! Befitting Dante, the view swept miles of valley walls graded in browns, tans and buff shades, all ending at a vast floor of white salt. I absorbed the eloquent description of a sign explaining what I was seeing: "This is the chemical desert, and in a few days a living thing out there would be embalmed like salt cod – preserved forever and thoroughly dead."

The sky was blue and the air was cool and sparkling clear. Several foreign tourists milled about, and I approached a stylish young Frenchman. I asked if he spoke English and then requested that he take my picture.

"Sure, no problem," he said, taking my camera. "Do I have to speak English to take a picture?" (*Another smartass, Heather!*) He also shrugged off the view. "It's the same at the Swiss Alps but there is snow there."

I drive back down the road and up the thermometer. Man it's hot.

Misunderstanding signs for a Visitor's Center, I stop at the Furnace Creek Inn and Ranch Resort, a "4-diamond" retreat built in 1927 by the Pacific Borax Co. The inn is perched on a hillside and below it, there is a rock and concrete tunnel. I follow the passageway, eventually emerging into the cool pastel beauty of a lobby. Classical music wafts about. It's a startling world in which everything denies and defies the damnation outside.

As I returned to my car, I chatted briefly with a groundskeeper with skin like shoe leather. He was the brownest white guy I've ever seen, illustrative of the few among our human species who thrive in the most extreme reaches of our land. A man like that couldn't live in, say, Scotland.

At the real Visitor's Center a mile away, I paid the National Park's entrance fee of $10 and watched a truly educational video. Why, Death Valley isn't "dead" at all. Wildlife come and go, mostly at night, and there are more than 900 kinds of plants.

"What's the hottest temperature you've endured here?" I asked a park ranger.

"I've seen one twenty-nine," he said.

I made one more stop at a place so often photographed that it represents Death Valley to most people: the Sand Dunes near Stovepipe Wells. I stopped my car on the side of the road, where a lady from Miami, Fla., stood and waited on her husband and son who were "playing" out in the dunes. She said they had left Yosemite at 10 a.m. That park and its mountains have kind of emerged as my next overnight destination, so I was heartened by the news of a relatively short distance.

Eventually, I walked out among the dunes with my camera. The hot sand fought the rubber soles of my running shoes, eager to say HELL-o to the skin of my feet. I couldn't catch up with the men from Florida, but I met up with two girls. Our conversation went something like this:

They: "OO. OW. You're smart to have thick shoe soles OUCH."

Me: "They're not thick enough. OW. Would you take my picture?"

They: "Sure! OUCH OUCH. Where are you from? OO. We're from Germany."

And then we hopped and danced on the soft deep sand like marionettes as we fulfilled our touristy obligations and beat a speedy retreat back to the road.

With utter faith in the stamina of the Honda, I drove up and out of the Valley, even turning off the air conditioning in the 107-degree heat. I had already asked my car to take on great fetes of motoring performance and didn't want it to over-heat. Smugly, I noted a highway sign warning that the next gas station was 47 miles away. One of my rules of the road, something I've never bothered about before, is to drive on the top half of the tank, so I'm always good on gas.

It was a relief to rejoin green-grassy land and tree-shaded road, even if I was diving more deeply into the allegedly evil state of California. I wasn't seeing Hell fires yet, certainly not with the rise of the snow-topped Sierra Nevada mountain range and then the charming town of Bishop, pop. 3,800. I decided to stop and spend the night there.

Hwy. 190 became Bishop's main street. I drove slowly through the center of town, captivated by a real Main Street lined with mom-and-pop restaurants, banks, stores for clothing, jewelry, hardware, furniture, baked goods, gifts, pharmaceuticals and sporting goods and in the middle of it all, a two-screen cinema showing first-run movies. It's what my hometown looked like in the 1950s and '60s, before hard times and the big-box discount stores cheapened, homogenized and corralled the shopping experience to the specifications and benefit of a few corporations. Today, I couldn't wait to relive the old-fashioned experience of strolling down Main Street, wandering in and out of stores that weren't warehouses.

Later I learned that an aged Kmart lurks at the north end of town and is about to be super-sized into a Big K. If they don't watch out, Bishop will lose the charms of its Main Street and find it converted into a dismal string of T-shirt and souvenir shops, fast-food stands, "antique" malls and vacant store buildings plastered with front-window For Lease signs.

On the way into town, a billboard led me to the Thunderbird motel, advertised as being a half block off the main drag, so it was convenient but quiet. I cruised by first. The lodge was small and old, but there was no litter nor junky cars. Roses grew in a patch of ground beside the office. Spaced around the two stories of guest room walkways were terra cotta pots with little evergreens. In short, the Thunderbird looked proud.

I checked in and found I'd summed up the place correctly. I got a lot for my money; the room was well-furnished and while I always hope for a microwave OR a refrigerator, I got both.

An evening walk and dinner on Main Street and an early-morning run from edge to edge of town on flat streets, all below a backdrop of stunning mountains, made Bishop a winner. I'd like to have stayed, but Oregon has become a firm goal.

Onward to Yosemite and what a beautiful drive that was! I had been thrilled to see slivers of snow on the mountains around Flagstaff; today I saw SNOW. It blanketed the peaks like the views in a Christmas card.

Just outside the park, at chilly Tioga Pass – I was more than 9,900 feet higher than this same time yesterday – there was a tiny lodge complex with hand-hewn log cabins and a shop offering souvenirs and food. I considered buying picnic food, but a café with room only for a few little tables and a horseshoe bar was too tempting. I sat at the bar on a stool made out of a stout short length of upturned log and had one of the best meals of the trip so far. It included a California version of a BLT, with avocado added to the thick bacon, lettuce and tomato and everything draped over a fresh puff of croissant roll.

"Pie for dessert?" the waitress asked.

Definitely. Cherry.

"Would you like that with Haagen Dasz?"

"Oh…well, OK…sure..yes. Definitely."

A couple sitting around the curve of the horseshoe laughed with me in recognition of that slippery slope from nutritional sensibility to lusty indulgence in one of the great little joys of life: vanilla ice cream on warm, freshly-baked pie.

I hated having to pay $20 to enter Yosemite. The fee includes a seven-day pass, but I wanted to merely cross, driving and looking along the 39-mile length of Tioga Road. I looked at forests, meadows, lakes and the steep faces of rock domes, stopping once to meditate on a broad slab of granite beside glass-clear rapids. Perhaps the greatest blessing of the day was a general absence of traffic, because later I read of hellish jam-ups of creeping cars, SUVs and RVs that clog the park in the middle of summer. It's nice to be ahead of the onslaught.

I'm starting to feel squeezed by time, which is dwindling; distance, almost daunting; and these dang park fees, exorbitant for someone merely passing through.

No more stopping. Press on, press on, out the other side of the park, around steep, switch-back roads down into the San Joaquin Valley and some of the nation's most important agriculture. In fact, simple open-air stands close to the road offer immediate access to items I've known only from grocery store produce sections and Del Monte-labeled cans. Hand-lettered signs promise STRAWBERRIES! APRICOTS! SWEET CORN! RED ONION! ALMONDS!

And so I brake once more today, stopping to pick up baskets of cherries and boysenberries and a few oranges. It seems the Tioga Pass lunch merely whetted my appetite.

After that, I really do "step on it," glad to finally reach the broad runway of Interstate 5. I fly past Manteca, Stockton, Sacramento, Orland and Red Bluff. There isn't any scenery, or maybe I don't look for it, keeping my eyes on the dotted-line ribbon of the road.

Bone tired at the end of a 400-mile day, I now sit on the edge of my motel bed and hook up my laptop to quickly check e-mail. The room is dark except for the low wattage of a lamp. The screen glows as I Read, Write, Send, Reply and Save.

In the silence and the dark, bits of musical notes trill. The frame for Instant Messaging pops open.

"Hi. It's Linda."

"LKBowen" was my first best friend 40 years ago. In 1950, I had no best friend until she emerged from her mother's womb three months after I was born.

"Where are you?"

"Redding, California. Trying to get to Portland, Oregon. What are you doing up so late? It has to be after midnight in Bismarck."

"Can't sleep. Menopause. Hot flashes."

"I totally understand."

Our chat is warm and comforting and strange. Working alone in a silent and unfamiliar place, an old friend's words are a sudden and welcome link, like a flame that first catches hold in the fireplace. You write and they write back, all in real time, and you are talking to this person that you love without making a sound.

"Are you coming this way?" Linda writes.

Maybe. Maybe so.

As I continued up north through the rest of California, my eyes locked on the growing image of a stout, snow-heavy mountain called Mount Shasta. So when an exit sign materialized for Mount Shasta City, I couldn't resist. I veered off and drove into the central business district, parking close to the center of town, but instead of wandering along the business district, I was more curious about the residential neighborhoods. I walked the old, uneven sidewalks, peering into yards and being nosy about others' ways of life.

At one driveway, I noticed wood piles. The logs were wide and I stopped to learn its age, counting rings. One log had so many that I quit at 80. Besides, the occupant of the house stepped out, an older man in a flannel shirt.

"Are you a wood cutter?" I asked.

"Yes," he said, and we continued to talk, although not about wood because suddenly my thoughts turned controversial as I wondered about the loss of an 80-year-old tree. Why and where? Was it a beautiful tree? Was its demise really necessary?

Instead, we talked about my trip. The wood cutter didn't hesitate to voice *his* controversial thoughts.

"Did you go to Disneyland?"

"No, I'm -"

"Why not?" he snapped. "Disneyland is wonderful! Nobody should miss it. There's a lot to see and do there."

I started to explain that I couldn't get around to every place but then he interrupted again and told me to be sure to find a good fishing spot. I didn't dare tell him I don't like to fish because by then, his face was locked in a disapproving scowl. I was glad when he said he had to go back inside and take a pizza out of his oven. If I wasn't driving about on his trip, then there wasn't much use talking anymore.

As I cross the state line into Oregon, I think, and feel, *I'm home.* There's the potential Corvallis hospitality ahead to provide my second American "life." More importantly right now, I'll soon see no fewer than six old friends, all drawn from my old life at The Arc.

One of them, Judy Kearney, has invited me to dock at her townhouse in Portland so that I can make the June 5 dinner organized by my old boss. Judy is in New York City on a week's vacation, but she's told me where to pick up a key. Stay and enjoy Portland and don't leave before I get home, she said.

This is why Oregon felt like home. Besides, it is so beautiful. I-5 followed the curves of low, gentle mountain slopes thickly forested by Douglas firs and Ponderosa pines. The trees soar, and we outsiders are thrilled by their size and mass when we see just one picked to grace places like Rockefeller Center at Christmas time. Today I saw millions of them, with little towns sprinkled here and there beneath their branches on ridges, river banks and valleys.

My first stop in the state was for gas. To my surprise, a sign on the pump advised, "State law prohibits self service." And sure enough, an attendant bounded out of the station and over to my car.

"Sit back and relax," he said.

When I paid the bill inside the station, I asked the clerk where I might wash the fruit I bought in California.

"I'll do that for you!" she said. "Don't use the bathroom sink for that – who-knows-what gets in that sink! I think whole families take baths in there sometimes."

My next "friendly Oregon" experience occurred later in the afternoon in a roadside park. This was another 400-plus mile day of driving and I needed a nap. It was too warm to sleep in the car, so I opened the trunk and rummaged around till I found my flannel-backed vinyl tablecloth and a pillow. I spread the covering plastic-side-down on the grass and stretched out, lying flat on my back below the towering pine trees.

Nearby, a man and his wife shared a picnic table. I encountered the man later as he was walking around and I prepared to resume the drive, folding up the tablecloth and walking back to the car.

"How was your nap?" he said.

"Great! I feel better."

"My wife and I were admiring your ability to do that. You looked so relaxed."

We chatted some more and within five minutes, he was sharing the proudest achievement of his life: Getting sober. I've known people who don't divulge that sort of information in five or 10 years of friendship.

"I tried AA and church and everything else," he said, "and then one day I just dropped to my knees and said 'Lord, help me.'"

"You seem like a happy man," I said. Indeed, he smiled constantly. I left ahead of the couple, and a ways up I-5, I heard a merry beep-beep and they passed me, both waving.

The really beautiful scenery eventually gave out, flattening into a long string of dull miles. I noted with some disappointment an exit for Corvallis, apparently situated in this nondescript patch of the state. I thought about detouring to at least see the lay of the town, see if it "spoke" to me before I bother George Grosch, but by then, I only wanted to gulp the miles that stretched between the Honda and Portland. Finally the land prettied up again. I reached the southern fringe of this exciting, liberal, funky, smart, cosmopolitan port city, and I started watching for the signs for exits and turns that would lead me to Judy's town house.

Using the key she'd left with the neighbors, I let myself into her home which is narrow in shape but stacked on three floors, with a garage and her pottery studio at the bottom. Having decided on two suitcases, a tote bag jumble of shoes, my computer and a sack of lunch leftovers, I schlepped up the steps like a bag lady and entered Judy's living room. *Ah! This is pretty much my idea of urban living perfection.* Hardwood floors, cozy furniture grouped before a bay window, original contemporary art on the walls....oh, and hundreds of books and compact disks. They were tasteful too.

I drop everything and stare. This is mine, *all mine*, for a week.

A three-page typed note welcomed me. Here are the best parts:

"To begin with, bedrooms and bath are upstairs, the guest room to the right as you get to the top of the stairs. There are a few hangers in the closet, and the top two drawers of the dresser are empty if you want to unpack a bit. Washer and dryer are in the pantry area off the kitchen, detergent and fabric softener on top. There's not a lot of food around, but there might be an open bottle with a little wine in it – and some beers – help yourself. *The Oregonian* is delivered in the morning and on Sunday, also the (New York) *Times* on Sunday...You're here during the Rose Festival, so there will be stuff going on downtown, and the annual arrival of ships..."

So many little luxuries I haven't had in a while.

I didn't seek out the Portland Rose Festival or anything else beyond the front gate. Instead, I drank Judy's wine and settled in to all the other creature comforts and never left until the next day when I met another old pal from The Arc, Bill Lynch.

For 17 years, I aspired to be as smart and vigorous an advocate for people with disabilities as Bill. He and I had worked and played, laughed, argued, compromised and debated anew through about three dozen meetings and events of our employers. The flip side of meeting "wonderful new people" on this trip is that I'm always having to introduce myself and tell relevant bits of my life history. I certainly don't have to do that with Bill.

Sunday was unseasonably warm and sunny, so the air was heavy with humidity from the more common condition of rainfall. After brunch at the Daydream Café, Bill took me on a walking tour of an old tree-lined neighborhood near Belmont Street. It didn't matter that I'd chosen to skip the festival – the signature flower of "The Rose City" was everywhere. At one point, I waved the insects away to smell one, something I've generally given up since growers seem to have quit "making" roses with a scent. This blossom did have one, and as smells do better than any of the other senses, it transported me back in time, to the roses of my Kansas girlhood. I was *in* my hometown of the 1960s. I was *that* age and of that mix of experience, wonder and hope. I saw the face of my boyfriend Mike, who was in love with me, who brought me roses from the yard of his big red brick house, although by then, my ardor for him was fading and falling away like the petals always did.

All that in the single whiff of a Portland rose!

Back at "home," it was time to update my Web site. That laborious activity took up the rest of the day and nearly all of Monday until the long-anticipated dinner with my friends Al Abeson and Bill and three more work colleagues from Oregon and Texas. We all agreed to meet at an Italian restaurant in Beaverton.

Having spent so much time immersed in Internet technology, I decided to be high-tech cool and simply pull the directions to La Prima off a Web site map. (I could have just called the restaurant to ask the way, but that would be too easy.) I got in the Honda and followed every street and turn like a laboratory mouse, a dumb one at that, in a particularly tight and complex maze, negotiating one confusing neighborhood after another and even the streets of Portland's town center. Later I determined that the freeways would have delivered me in 10 minutes, not 40, and I would have been on time. But again, I was meeting dear old friends to whom I didn't have to explain myself. They just seemed glad to see me and we had an exhilarating evening of pasta and wine and gossip and free-wheeling old war stories of association life.

The week is well under way, and it's time to roll this whale off the beach. I can't have Judy return from her vacation and not have a plan. *Well, Judy, I guess I've drunk ALL your wine and beer — how 'bout running out and getting us some more? And you might want to take care of those dirty dishes in the sink, and then would it be all right with you if I stay here a while, maybe till the fourth of July, Labor Day at the latest?*

Today is Tuesday. Judy will be back on Thursday.

My day of searching for a home begins with lunch in Salem where Rick Berkobien – part of the Arc group – now works for the state legislature. The novelty of seeing Salem was my visit to the Oregon Capitol Building, a long white block of a building topped with a "dome" that was actually a cylindrically shaped structure topped by a gold statue of a man. It is said to be the only state capitol in the nation that looks exactly like bowling trophy.

After lunch, I drive farther south to Corvallis although I haven't called George Grosch to announce my visit. Unfortunately, it is an overcast day and Corvallis has an overcast business district. Realizing a little sunshine might change everything, I decide to stay a couple of hours and give it all a chance to somehow metamorphose into something out of a Broadway musical. Like River City, Iowa, in "The Music Man" when Professor Harold Hill arrives with his suitcase and soon has unruly teen-agers dancing around the library and quarreling school board members singing harmony on street corners.

I found Oregon State University and toured the campus, stopping by the student center to look at roommate notices on the bulletin board. But now it feels like Flagstaff all over again. Back in the center of town, I park the car to experience the city as a pedestrian, cashing a check at the bank, wandering through a book store, peering into restaurant windows, all the while circling one block and then another and feeling increasingly dispirited. At a corner, I stand next to a lady who is also waiting for the light to change.

"Excuse me," I said. "Do you live here?"

"No," she said. "I live in Newport, straight west from here on the coast."

Trying not to scare her, I told her the abbreviated version of my story and explained that I was looking for a home for a few weeks in Oregon, maybe in Corvallis. Did she know anything about Corvallis?

"Why, you should go to the coast!" she exclaimed. "I'd say you could stay with us but we're leaving for Minnesota!"

House sitting. It's called house sitting, lady. Ever thought of that?!!

The coast. That's where I want to go. I just couldn't admit it to myself. But what are my chances of finding an affordable "home" at such a beautiful and popular summertime destination?

I have to try.

The next day at Judy's, I couldn't bear the idea of jumping back in the car, heading to some random dot on the map and doing the street wandering again. In the town house, I parked myself at the dining table, made up some of Judy's gourmet coffee, and opened the Internet on my laptop. I typed the Search words "North Oregon coast" and then "lodging" and "rentals." Soon, the screen filled with beckoning prose and colorful frames of oceanside condos, houses and inns. And, my worst fears were confirmed. Selections began at $70 a night, a thousand a month.

I picked five properties and wrote my short introduction and polite inquiry.

I took a break to let things cook. And to cook, literally. After walking around the corner to a luscious little food market called Zupan's, I bought groceries and otherwise worked feverishly to dramatically transform myself into the model guest. I replaced the booze, cooked, cleaned the house, and tried to rewrite and organize hastily-taken phone messages. Judy's friends would call and I suppose I loved Judy's life a little too much because I talked to them all at length, as if they were my friends.

"You stole my friends, too??!!!" Judy exclaimed after arriving home and learning that I'd taken rather generous advantage of her hospitality.

"Well, it's not exactly like that," I protested. "Although I'm worried about Kate's situation with her new boyfriend…"

"What??!"

"Oh, I've said too much already; I can't violate my friends' confidences. If Kate wants you to know, I'm sure she'll tell you."

"YOU STOLE MY FRIENDS!!"

And then we laughed uproariously and ran with this joke the rest of my time there and on my Web site and probably into the ground, but that's the great thing about friends who share a similar sense of humor. It takes mere seconds to get on the same wave length.

Besides, I was in a happy mood by the time I heard the downstairs door open late in the evening and Judy climbing the stairs with her suitcases. I had a new home on the horizon. Today, a couple of hours after writing to the vacation properties, I received a reply from Peg Miller inviting me to meet and talk at the bed and breakfast she owns in Wheeler, Oregon.

8 MAGGIE'S PLACE

I'm a modern pioneer this Friday afternoon, steering my covered Honda wagon to a town and a set of people that, sight unseen, I intend to love no matter what. They will be my life throughout this month of June. I'm driving 84 miles to the very edge of America, the Pacific Ocean. You can't drive farther west than that, partner.

As the shopping centers of Portland fall away, forests enfold me. I feel alone in this verdant world made greener and denser by steady rain dropped by enormous, sagging gray clouds. There's not much traffic except for long trucks bearing freshly cut logs. They roar past, making me feel like a little girl in a toy car in this out-sized world.

At a scenic overlook I pull into the crescent-shaped parking area to take a picture of the way the clouds drape the treetops. As usual, there is an imperfection: power lines slicing the view. I take a picture anyway and return to the car.

Depress the clutch, turn the key. Engine goes rahr-rahr-rahr. But no vah-room. It's my car's Honda "thing" again. A friend with the exact same make, model and year finally had hers fixed, but I never did. I've preferred to live with the mystery. Sometimes, the car simply doesn't start after being driven and then parked a short while. But it will start again after a minute or two, and as long as I'm not needing it to escape from quick, in-and-out bank robberies, it seems like a problem I can live with.

HONNNGK. A log truck says hello to me. I know I'm the object of the greeting because I'm the only person, the only WOMAN there. The egg salad sandwich I've unwrapped and started eating turns dry and tasteless. The Zen moment ends. *Keep moving, truck.* He does.

I turn the key again. Rahr-rahr-rahr, vah-room. Thank you, God. Blood returns to my face. I depress the accelerator with confidence and the car moves. I won't stop now.

Wheeler, Ore., "Pop. 390," is one mile long and climbs five blocks up a steep hillside from U.S. Hwy. 101. The town is tucked into Nehalem Bay and is halfway between Tillamook and Seaside. A few blocks of stores and restaurants face the peaceful water, and in their midst, I find the large Cape Cod building that contains Maggie's Guestrooms. The front door is between the building's other tenants, a ground-level apartment and an art gallery. I ring the doorbell and peer inside up a narrow flight of carpeted stairs.

Peg Miller, a.k.a. Maggie, hurried down the stairs. She is a short, compact woman of indeterminate age, with thick wavy dark hair and brown eyes like saucers that take in everyone and everything.

"I'm checking somebody in, but come on up," she said.

The stairs led to a short hallway and Maggie's sitting room where the other guest, a thin, pale, spooky woman lounges in a chair. I sat on a couch facing a window of cold gray light and the three of us settled into conversation. Melinda, the guest, was about my age, with a wan face and ethereal presence. She seemed haunted really, so while she spoke quietly of her work as a sculptor, you just knew her real life must be tenuous. She has lived many places, including two years in Korea, worked many vague jobs, and all was recounted without explanation, nor much inflection, raising more questions than revelations.

Normally, I would be fascinated. Now I was annoyed, antsy. Melinda was in no hurry to adjourn to her room and Maggie was being the gracious innkeeper, or perhaps she was too curious to shoo away the guest, so this scenario of getting acquainted went on for what seemed like hours. I began to wonder if Maggie was merely curious about me, too, and we would never be alone to talk business. Perhaps she just wanted to meet me, the traveler behind the interesting e-mail, and sell a guestroom at a lucrative summer rate. What was I doing here?

Finally, Melinda floated away and Maggie and I were left alone. I got right to the point.

"I would love to stay here. Can we do a deal? Can I pay less, but work for you?"

"I do have projects," Maggie said. "But it's the busiest and best time of year for income. The Wheeler Crabfest is coming up and the Fourth of July and summer crowds."

"I can be out before the Fourth," I offered.

A few math calculations later, we agreed on a rate that Maggie thought she could live with, and I felt lucky to get. I will make it worth it to her.

Maggie's Guestrooms is a gutsy endeavor. Two years ago, the proprietor was living a much different life in her hometown of Chicago, Ill. She was hard-charging through the world of business until one day, she met an Oregon businessman from Nehalem named Garry, and love slowed her down. Maggie jumped off the corporate treadmill, said good-bye to her mother and sisters, and followed Garry back to the great Northwest.

Today, Maggie says, "I am a recovering Irish Catholic Workaholic Democrat."

She bought a building that was bypassed by others who found it daunting. It housed the Wheeler Post Office in the 1930s and little had been done to modernize its three stories of intriguing spaces. Maggie had no trouble envisioning its new life: an art studio and gallery for Garry, the guest rooms, each having its own bath, and her own apartment on the second level, and an attic for artistic pursuits: poetry readings, workshops and writing seminars.

There are three guest rooms and each has a decor and books to match a theme: Art, Travel and Music. I have the Music Room. Somewhere in passing during conversation, I must have mentioned my love for George Gershwin, because when I moved in and unpacked, I found a cassette player and a tape of "Rhapsody In Blue."

The room also has twin beds and antique furniture, including a six-drawer bureau, a graceful little cabinet and a small settee. It's wonderful to have a furnished room and not have to make do with an air bed and cardboard boxes. I added my camp chair, an instant spoiler to the decor, but I can curl up there and read and write in my journal and listen to Gershwin concertos. There is no TV; it is in the sitting room, and I will not mar the setting by bringing mine in. It can't pick up a channel way out here anyway.

My move-in day was a particularly dreary Sunday. Huge thick clouds full of rain covered and concealed the mountains that allegedly ring the bay -- if they are there, I do hope to see them before I leave. When the rain fell, it was blown about by the wind, chilling me and making my spirits sag. It was hard anyway to leave Portland and the merriment and comfort of Judy's townhouse and now I had second thoughts about moving to this tiny, probably weird, little hamlet.

Fighting off my mood, I set out to find the Pacific Ocean. (The bay did not count.) I drove eight miles to Rockaway Beach, parked the Honda at a beachfront motel -- and still couldn't see the ocean. But I heard it as I trudged through wet sand that found its way into my shoes. Finally, I reached the edge of pounding surf -- here was the Pacific Ocean!

I appreciated that milestone mere minutes, then scrambled back to the car. Back in Wheeler, I seized on an improved mood and optimistic new view of my life by ordering steamed clams at Nina's Italian Restaurant, which is right up in the next block from Maggie's.

"You didn't have to do this!" I exclaimed, meeting Maggie the next morning at 8 in the sitting room. There are no other guests, but she has laid out muffins, juice, coffee and tea on the antique sideboard.

"Oh it's just for this morning!" she said festively.

As I urged her to do, Maggie has a project idea for me: a decorating touch for my own room to complement its theme. There is a small corner closet and the idea is to "wallpaper" its interior with old sheet music.

As the rain continued, it was not hard to stay in and throw myself into the work with all the care and precision of someone who has absolutely nothing else to do. The large, aged pages carried dates circa 1915 and titles like "A Holiday Excusion," "Down the Trail to Mother Dear," "Pic-Nic Dance," "My Hula Hula Love." There were far more pieces than I needed, so I layered and angled my choices, gluing and nailing them to permanence with brass tacks. I picked "Minuet of the Graces," with the added romanticism of "The Moonlight The Rose And You," and the whimsy of "A Pleasant Story and the Pranks Afterwards."

Late in the afternoon, with the closet finished and the rain over, I went back to Rockaway for some extended walking and picture taking of the broad flat beach and startling outcroppings of black rock. Unlike California and many other states, all of the Oregon coastline is open to the public. Summer crowds have not yet arrived, so it is easy to find a place to park and walk to the shoreline. I came upon a man walking two dogs. He noticed my Texas license plates, so he told me about his son who lives in Keller, another suburb of Fort Worth, and works for American Airlines.

I am not a water person, but I find the ocean captivating. I am both drawn to it and afraid of it, pulled by its rhythmic roaring and splashing of waves, a force bigger than any civilization, not to be captured or tamed. It is the one natural wonder that human beings cannot alter. We can't put malls or condos on it. There are no shorn ski runs. No traffic jams. And today without tourists, I can walk for miles without seeing a soul.

Back in Wheeler, I indulged in another restaurant meal. I had to try the Sea Shack, a sprawling, weathered building across the street from Maggie's at the dock of the bay. Over a beer and clam chowder, I took stock of my situation, counting the uncertainties first. Can I find a paying job? Satisfying community activities? Interesting friends?

For the most part, I've felt great, sure of what I'm doing. Especially at Judy's in Portland last week, I felt a swell of happiness and well being. This trip, these days without structure and a plan, are working for me. All my life, I've been able to hide behind others – people and things. Family, a short marriage, good jobs – throughout my life I've leaned on the institutional aspects of providers and let them define me. Away from such day-in, day-out shelters, it's just me and the world now. I'm having to put myself "out there," accepting fate, trusting strangers and asking them to trust me.

But I'm also no more than three days from home and the familiar institutions of my old life if things turn sour. I'm not *that* far "out there."

It's Day Three in Wheeler and time to mingle. The weather has improved a lot, even beyond the "sun glimpses" that Maggie jokingly promises.

On the corner of our block and facing Hwy. 101 is Common Grounds, where coffee is a dollar. I paid two to cover the refills I would need while reading the *Oregonian* and gazing out the large front window at lumber trucks rumbling through town, a sight and sound that contrasted with the little tugboat that bobs on the water on the other side of the highway. I was not rushed. A Santana album played. Business was slow, but it seemed to be the time for the proprietors to bake things and make sandwiches for the lunchtime crowd. In the evenings, I learned, Common Grounds is a site for meetings, poetry readings and musical entertainment.

After four cups of coffee, I went back to Maggie's. She greeted me with an invitation.

"There are several women who meet on Tuesdays. They're an interesting group; would you like to join us?"

"Sure! Where do you meet?"

"A place on the corner, Common Grounds."

Oh no! More caffeine? So I bought herbal tea this time for Maggie and me and we settled into a table for six. I sat at a corner and listened and watched the other women. The discussion was mostly about business. After all, two of the women owned nearby buildings and I quickly learned that no one has an 8-to-5 work life. They run businesses, work for others' businesses, lease out property, teach, consult and pursue freelance arts, AND they help the town at-large through civic committees and event planning. It appears to be the accepted price of living in a lovely but tiny gem of a community with a short tourist season and no large employers.

The conversation was also about Dick and Barbara Matson and their impending move to California. Dick is retired from corporate life in Portland, and his movie star-beautiful wife, who reminded me of the actress Gena Rowlands, paints at their Wheeler gallery. When they have events at the gallery, such as artists' openings, Dick plays jazz piano for the guests.

Barbara joined us this morning and was the only one to prod me out of my passive observation. She had a warmth and generous personality that matched her looks. Such a nice woman; no wonder the talk about their departure was sad.

After spending the entire morning at Common Grounds, it was time for me to go off and take care of some practicalities. The closest place to do that was Tillamook, 23 miles south of Wheeler on 101. I had another tire leaking air, so Maggie and Garry told me how to find Les Schwab Tires. There is no Walmart in this part of the world, but I would find Fred Meyer's, a Walmart-style super center, to get some provisions for my room.

The coastal road to Tillamook curves back and forth in a game of hide and seek with ocean views. I drove straight to the businesses I needed without being lured off by a giant center and symbol of Tillamook County's dairy industry, the Tillamook Cheese Factory. A "Visitors' Center" beckoned, but there's time to return and play tourist.

While a grease-streaked young woman fixed my tire, I ate Les Schwab's free popcorn and read *People* magazine, so naturally all that pleasant diversion made the repair seem fast. Then it was off to Fred Meyer where I bought $35 worth of groceries for my room. (Must Stay Out of Restaurants.) I now have a loaf of bread, cereal bars, a variety pack of cereal, two kinds of sardines in a sauce, a bag of potatoes, which can be baked in the crock pot, a can of almonds, a small can of spinach, a bag of baby carrots, a jar of Tang, assorted teas and a hot water immersion coil, a roll of foil, and a four pack of individual bottles of red wine.

Back in Wheeler, Maggie allowed me to use her Internet service where I found 17 e-mails, none of it junk. Friends and relatives were checking in with me, and not-so-subtly demanding an updated Web site.

After catching up on all the e-mail (but not the Web site), I finally had a sense of accomplishment this day, so I got back in the car and drove north across a bridge to tiny Nehalem and then to Manzanita seven miles from Wheeler. Maggie explained to me that our bay "community" consists of the three villages. Beautiful Manzanita is the largest. It sets off the highway and is squared off from its beach front, unlike Rockaway's stretched-string layout. There is also the dramatic Nehalem Mountain that lifts Hwy. 101 and points it northward on to Cannon Beach, Seaside and Astoria. The mountain's face drops sharply to the sea.

Manzanita's beach is broad and flat, with a tumble of massive driftwood scattered about. The sun had more permanence today, so there was a sunset to stay for. Even past 9 p.m., the light was golden and brilliant, deepening and briefly making the ocean shimmer like fire before yielding to the night. There's nothing like sunset and a beach and unstructured time to bring out a little loneliness. It would be nice to be walking with somebody. But that is not my life.

The next morning, I wrapped a potato in foil to start its day-long process of baking in the slow cooker. Then Maggie invited me to help myself to milk and a banana to go with my cereal box du jour, Fruit Loops, and Tang.

Over coffee in her sitting room, we sat down and pored over papers — books and articles and brochures — and ideas, people to meet and talk to, places to go, and all of it was about some sort of creative process. I think Maggie sees me as a real writer. Yes, I call myself that as I move around the country and try to explain what I'm doing. But I use the title more to justify and legitimize my trek as needed and not scare people off. (Nobody ever asks "A writer for WHAT, exactly?") So here's Maggie embracing me as a ***Writer.*** And now I've become a part of her vision for Maggie's Guestrooms, as a haven for artists creating beautiful things.

"But Maggie," I said, "I just want to paint your hallway!" This was, in fact, one of the numerous little "real work" projects I'd coaxed her into identifying. Clearly, however, such things are not expected of an *artiste*, so we were at rather amusing odds over how to spend my life in Wheeler.

Eventually, I did agree to let her show me around Nehalem Bay, so we got in her car and went for a drive. First stop was a community center that has brought new life to an old public school in Nehalem. Staffed mostly by volunteers, the center is a civic gathering place with classes and a fitness center with a swimming pool where Maggie works out several times a week.

Next we wandered into some Manzanita shops, but I find such places irrelevant to my life. I can't afford to buy stuff I don't absolutely need, nor do I want it. Where would I put it? Any day now I'll be tooling down the highway and the trunk of the Honda is going to pop open, spilling my possessions for miles along the road. I hope I won't feel compelled to go back to pick them up.

"OK, now I want to show you 'CART'M.' It's a recycling center," Maggie said.

Swell. (*Yawn.*) Being in Oregon a couple of weeks now, I've become well aware of Oregon's mastery of recycling as law and cultural rigor. What's not to admire in recycling? Really, I do. At the same time, coming from a state that is relatively backward in that regard – Texas has lots of space for piling up garbage – in Oregon I've been feeling guilty about creating any trash at all. You have to stop and think before throwing away so much as a gum wrapper. So the idea of visiting a recycling center has all the appeal of a duty. And so my tug of war with Maggie goes on.

"I'd love to see this, this, 'kartem,' did you say?"

"I think it's an acronym but I'm not sure what the letters stand for," Maggie said, steering the car along a maze of back roads that evoke an odd sense of both beach and forest.

Finally, "Here we are – the city dump!" she announced.

We had reached a gate incongruously decorated by an abstract artist with block lettering for CART 'M and a whimsical design. Up the road was a complex of buildings and busy hives of people. One swarm was mastering a small hill of used building materials, and near the base of the hill was a field of toilet bowls and picture frames. Other workers were directing traffic as cars and pickups full of every kind of junk imaginable drove up, stopped and waited for direction: old tires here, refrigerators there, newspapers and cans over there.

And then Maggie led me to the centerpiece of the whole place: the resale store, a magnificent and orderly complex of glassware and dishes, pots and pans, tools, furniture, doors, toys, Christmas decorations, mattresses – all rescued from the discards and displayed for purchase. I bought a silverplated fork for a dime.

I learned that in the first year after opening in December 1998, all of this sort of junk sold for $33,000 and found new lives.

"Liz, I want you to meet Ron Hintz," Maggie said, introducing me to a man who seemed to be the general foreman of everything.

"And this is 'Iron Man,'" Ron said, bringing me into the artistic realm of CART 'M. Ron built Iron Man out of scraps, including a railroad spike to make Mr. Man anatomically correct. A jaunty purple scarf and a beret completed the look.

Ron also showed me his turtle built from a metal plate, four bedsprings and a shower head.

I love this place!

The vibrant industry of CART 'M and the industrious townspeople of Wheeler, combined with the prospect of a lot of lonely beach combing, made me long for work again. The next day, Maggie fretted over her lengthy list of Things To Do Today. One thing was to prepare Andy's room for other weekend guests. Andy is a young Englishman, whom I hardly ever see, who is in this part of the world to help lay telecommunications cable across the ocean floor. He comes and goes and if he's gone for a few days, he considerately packs everything up and stows it in Maggie's apartment so that she can book his room.

"I'll clean Andy's room," I offered.

"Don't do that!" Maggie protested. "Why don't you..."

"No," I said. I don't want to write or go meet interesting people.

Andy is in the Art Room, which is now available for this coming weekend of the Wheeler Crabfest. My work of making up the bed and cleaning the bathroom went fast, although I lingered in that different corner of Maggie's Guestrooms. The Art Room looks much different from the pale green serenity of my Music Room. The Art Room has yellow walls, a colorful bedspread and a bright area rug. An old desk is angled in the corner and there are books on art.

Finally, I could put it off no longer: Get out. Hit the bricks. Peddle my wares. Get a job.

Maggie and Garry, her beau, had advice about that.

"Go see Dave Dillon at The North Coast Citizen," Garry said.

"Yes! He always needs writers," Maggie said.

Why was I not surprised.

So naturally, I drove someplace else. First stop: the Bunkhouse, a rustic little restaurant I'd noticed on the highway going into Nehalem. It looked friendly, busy but not so busy that the wait staff looked stressed.

"Can I help you?"

The young woman stopped and smiled at me in mid-stride, holding a water pitcher.

I attempted to match her breeziness in attitude and pace -- in my old professional life, I would have called it Sizing up the Company Culture and being in tune.

"Do you need waitresses?" I said. "I'm here for a while and would love to help out."

"Sometimes we do!" she said brightly. "Do you have experience?"

"Oh yes, I've done it all!" I said with my quick wave of a hand. Sure, that fib (and gesture) didn't work in Flagstaff, but this is a new country, different café, unique set of needs. I'm even more sincere, having tried repeatedly and in vain to be a waitress. The goal that eludes me has become a calling.

"Leave me your name and number," she said.

Wow! I don't even have to mess with an application! There are no questions about who I am, where I live, nor how long "a while" is. I know she'll call me, I just know it.

"Call any time!" I said. "I'm very flexible. Morning, night, whatever...If somebody is sick or doesn't make it in, I can be here in five minutes."

Emboldened with new confidence, I left the Bunkhouse and drove into Manzanita, parking on the main street to start door-to-door appeals. At a pink and purple shop with the fun name of "Bad Woman," a not-so-bad woman lounged on a front step and allowed me to go into my spiel.

She warmed up to the idea, but couldn't offer me anything herself.

"Try Manzanita Fresh Foods," she said. "For such a short time, they could even pay you under the table! Talk to Jim and tell him Yvonne sent you."

That's the spirit, Yvonne.

On my way to the grocery store, I stopped at Three Peas in a Pod, another cute shop where the head Pea said sweetly that her grandchildren are here for the summer to help out. At a deli, a fast-moving Korean man barked, "Out of applications. Come back tomorrow." I also struck out at a garden center, a T-shirt shop and, probably, Manzanita Fresh Foods. Jim was not in. I sat on a bench outside and waited but he never turned up.

By late afternoon, my spunky little tail was dragging.

Heading back toward Wheeler, I drove through Nehalem and looked reluctantly at the parking lot where Garry told me I would see Dave Dillon's gray Mercedes. It was there.

The *North Coast Citizen* sits atop the Dockside restaurant beside the Nehalem River. I parked near the Mercedes and climbed the tall flight of wooden stairs to the second floor newspaper office. Do I knock? Walk right in? The office wasn't marked, and while the door opened, no one seemed to be there.

"HELLO," I call out.

Dave appears, a big man with a gray beard and intelligent eyes behind glasses, and he tells me to come on in. I am instantly comfortable in the chaos of desks and files and computers and the flurry of paper that characterizes a small newspaper office. I spent four years working in such an environment in 1970s and I loved it. But do I want to retrace those steps, however briefly?

I tell Dave my story, again framing my wanderings in the respectability of a "career sabbatical," and emphasizing my need today "to find something to do."

"Maggie and Garry said you sometimes need a writer."

He regarded me quietly and then he said, "Think you could write something about the Wheeler Crabfest this weekend? Talk to people and see where they've come from and why."

And how, Mister! I suddenly wonder why I've been so reluctant to revisit my journalistic training.

The invitation must be an act of pure faith. The Crabfest will be THE social event of the season and Dave is entrusting it to me, a stranger with an odd, if not dubious, story about roaming the country, living here and there. *Shouldn't he at least give me a writing test or ask to see samples?*

It isn't a "regular" job, but it's something. It's work!

Buoyed by this turn of events, tonight I explored Wheeler on foot. This entailed climbing its steep grid of narrow streets (the town is too small for sidewalks). The houses are modest and weathered, with eclectic yards. Higher I went, and gradually, my picture of the bay expanded, from the highway-level view of the steadfast presence of the tugboat in a circle of water, to a wide horizon of ocean and sky and imagination.

At the top of the hill, a man was playing with his little girl and their Chinese Pug dogs. His name was Jim and he was a contractor from San Antonio. Nearby, his wife, a prosecuting attorney, tackled weeds at a furious pace, frankly admitting, without stopping, to dealing with her stress through this activity.

So I talked to Jim, and he reminded me of the recovering alcoholic I had met at the I-5 roadside park in southern Oregon. Like him, Jim quickly went from small talk to his own story of survival and new-found love of life. A fork lift accident had put him in a coma for three months. He showed me his scars of the cuts that nearly severed his body, and he talked about his changed priorities toward caring for a wife and child.

Reluctantly, I came back down a hill bathed in the golden light of sunset. As I approached Gregory Street, I saw Maggie and Garry and others among Wheeler's business set congregating outside Common Grounds, which was hosting a musician and a poetry reading tonight. Some people lounged in the town's unique willow chairs, found along the main street, outside the Treasure Cafe, and inside the little passenger shelter of the bay's excursion railroad.

The chairs are the creation of "Willow Bill," a man with a waist-length ponytail and many jobs, some paid, mostly volunteer. Again it struck me how a town like Wheeler survives and thrives because of the contributions of individuals and very little commerce. Any person can make a big difference.

I loved Wheeler tonight.

It is Saturday, and there's much to do. In addition to the Crabfest and my reporting gig, I'm getting ready for Judy Kearney's visit. She is driving over from Portland to attend the festival and spend the night.

I tidy up my room and then head over to the party, paper and pen in hand. It's a sparkling day and by 11, parked cars are lining the highway. Business at an arts and crafts fair set up in the parking lot is picking up. It's easy to find visitors there and in line at the red and white-striped food tent.

"Hi, I'm writing about this event for the *North Coast Citizen*. Mind if I ask you a few questions?" And with that opener, I met the Milners from Nehalem, the Ridens family from Hillsboro; the Recks from Portland; Rob and Tashia from Longview, Wash.; and Helen Knoche, the former mayor of Grand Mound, Iowa. I sat at one of the tables outside the tent with Doug Hudson from Jackson, Mich., his daughter Lacey and brother Jim from Boise, Idaho.

I worked hard and fast gathering quotes, facts and "color," because mainly, I just wanted to EAT. I could hardly wait to get my own paper plate heaped and heavy with the large pink and white shell hiding tender crab meat, with drawn butter and an ear of corn and cold creamy potato salad on the side. The temptation threatened to derail my professionalism as a roving reporter.

At last, Judy arrived and with one more day to interview and then get the story written, I put aside the pen and paper.

We began our day with the long-anticipated lunch. The sun was bright, the breeze cool, the mountains clear, the bay serene, the tugboat bobbing. There was even a quirky music scene, with a folk guitarist and a belly dancer. Later we drove to Rockaway Beach, gluttons for their festival, too, which had the appealing name, "Wine & Cheese and All That Jazz." But the beautiful weather that favored the Wheeler Crabfest didn't extend the eight miles south to Rockaway, which remained enveloped in a mysterious, cold fog. We parked the car, walked a block, walked back to the car and left.

We mostly wandered the rest of the day, continuing on from Rockaway to Garibaldi, not that it mattered. I was starved for conversation with an old friend, somebody who knew me, with whom I shared some history. That is a difficulty with this odyssey I'm on. I'm always meeting and spending time with brand new people. The first weeks of a friendship are merely a developing stage, and thin, and then, just as a little of that "shared history" has a chance to take hold, I have to move on. I miss the deep bonds of long-time friendship, and the occasional cell phone conversation with my neighbor Carolyn or my sister Martha back home just isn't the same.

And so Judy and I talked and talked, eventually making our way back to Wheeler close to bedtime.

Sleep, did I suggest? Silly me. I'd heard rumors that one of the Wheeler residents was bringing in a live band for an outdoor party. I didn't consider the implications, although looking back, I can now see that Maggie was a little anxious about the reported plans.

Sure enough, the band was rockin' and a rollin' and a BLASTING away about 30 yards from Maggie's Guestrooms. Sleep seemed impossible, and though it was midnight and we were tired, Judy and I wandered the streets of Wheeler, hoping to hear the band stop or the amplifiers explode and die. The noise could be heard from every corner of the town, but I guess everybody else was invited to the party, or no one had the nerve to ask the hosts to tone it down, or other townspeople had simply fled.

Finally, we went back, the irony of being in the "Music Room" lost on us. Judy's bed was closer to the window, but she had brought a CD player and earphones and so she plugged into her own choice of music. I somehow willed the uninvited guitars to become white noise and drifted off to sleep.

A few days later, I returned to my room from being out and found an envelope slid under the door. Inside was a check and a note from Dave Dillon. The story, he said, was "Perfect! You write good stuff."

I am capable, yes I am! Still, I didn't want work so dangerously close to my old professional life. Nothing else was materializing, so I went back to CART 'M and presented myself for an afternoon of "whatever you need."

The many needs of the recycling center are constant and recurring, maintenance-types of jobs, such as cleaning, sorting, stocking and organizing shelves in the resale store. I took up a broom and swept a floor littered with bits of trash too small and inconsequential to be sales-worthy. I also attacked the driveway in front of the building with a long-handled bar with a wheel at each end of the bar so that it rolls.

"What is that?" a drive-up patron inquired.

"It's a magnet," I explained. "It picks up nails from this pavement so that your tires won't."

"Hey, that's nice! I appreciate it."

And so I'd also slipped in a little PR for CART 'M.

I spent two hours volunteering followed by a trip to the Manzanita library and then tonight, I went to a bar.

I entered Gale's Bar with a little trepidation and adjusted my eyes in the dark, low-ceilinged space. I wanted to drink a beer, talk to somebody, and absorb a limited amount of nightlife in my bucolic Oregon existence. Men do this sort of thing all the time, but a woman alone is a different story. Her presence is not nearly as casual and off-hand.

Still, I tried to be cool as I took my place at the bar. I seated myself between a young woman trying to talk about her problems to the busy bartender, and a man and woman having a quiet conversation. The place had a fair crowd, all appearing to be locals. At a table with a row of bottles with candles stuck in the necks, four young people played instruments. The musicians weren't the official entertainment, but they seemed to be rehearsing or just playing for fun. I relaxed.

I thought about speaking to the woman next to me but decided I'd be sorry, sucked into tales of woe. I sipped my beer and let the bartender deal with her. On the other side, the woman departed, leaving her friend alone.

"You're so quiet," the man directed my way.

You're so predictable. But I let the conversation begin. His name was Bob, a 60-ish engineer retired from a career in aeronautics and sales. Soon I found myself trying to keep up with the topics of computers and ways of doing business. Reaching my limit, I moved into the more comfortable confines of my trip. Suddenly, I felt totally ridiculous talking about American geography and small-town life. Bob was trying to look interested in my story, but his little half-smile came off as a leer.

I took note of his departure to use the restroom. When he came back, he sat closer to me, right on the next barstool.

Our next phase of conversation was the beginning of the end. I told him about volunteering at CART 'M.

"I just love that place," I said. "I think it would be fun to have a totally empty apartment and then furnish and equip it with things from thrift stores and garage sales."

From leer to a-ha! I could almost hear the click of the light bulb. Bob made his move.

"I've done that!" he exclaimed. "I've been going through a divorce and I have a house now with everything second-hand. Would you like to go over there with me and see it?"

"No, I can't do that."

"Why not?"

Because I don't go home with men I meet in bars. Geez! Don't make me lose my unfailing ability to be polite, Bob.

He pestered. He wheedled. He cajoled.

"Nothing else is expected," he said.

I wrapped things up quickly and left for the seven-mile drive back to Wheeler. The evening had turned annoying and dispiriting. Even so, I was glad I'd branched out and done something just the slightest bit daring.

Maggie's Guestrooms glowed with lights burning in every window and I was glad to be home safely from my walk on the wild side.

Distances seem so much greater on the coast. Nehalem feels "out of town" to me and yet it's just two miles and a bridge away. It's the same distance as my neighborhood grocery store is from my home in Texas.

So on the morning I woke up and thought impulsively, "I think I'll drive to Astoria," the 45-mile drive seemed like a major journey. My reasons for the trip were mundane: banking, shopping for a digital camera, maybe seeing a movie.

Indeed, Astoria was a relatively exotic destination. Situated where the mighty Columbia River meets the Pacific Ocean, it is the oldest American settlement west of the Rocky Mountains. I crossed a drawbridge to get there, then contemplated continuing over the four and a half-mile Astoria Bridge, which was obviously created from an Erector set with many, many parts, to

Washington. I could then add my eighth state, but I decided to let Washington remain unseen beyond that scary bridge. I was interested enough in this city of 10,000 with its gritty, working class, seafaring complexion.

I found a parking place in the City Center and a Wells Fargo bank where I deposited several little job checks totaling $319. I withdrew $200. Easy come easy go.

Outside the courthouse I asked two lawyer types about a good lunch place and they sent me to the Urban Café. Its theme was Ladies Who Lunch. I preferred Yo Ho Ho and A Bottle of Rum, but decided to give it a shot and I'm glad I did. Starved for both greens and protein, I ordered an interesting steak salad and, since my days are numbered in berry country, a piece of lodenberry pie.

The movie choices were standard summertime fare, meaning brainless kiddie attractions, so I went shopping at Fred Meyer's and found neither camera nor a gift for my mother's upcoming birthday. I drove around Astoria's steep streets and headed south.

I made a spur-of-the-moment stop at Seaside, another coastal town with its own personality. This one: Old-timey tourist's playground. Cheap souvenirs, candy shops, arcades, and there's a 1920s era "Promenade" that turns the tawdry into cool, this place by the sea, by-the-sea, by the beautiful sea... I ate stale popcorn and walked the long paved path that lines the wide beach.

On my meandering drive back to Wheeler, I make one more stop. Cannon Beach is another village, quiet and upscale, with a concert scheduled tonight at the Presbyterian Church. I've seen posters for the event featuring a community chorus performing show tunes. Being very late, with no ticket in hand, I merely cruise the church to verify that the concert is probably over so that I can go on home.

Instead, I find the church windows open and voices singing "All the Things You Are." Words and jazzy accompaniment drift out into the summer night. I sit on the church steps to listen. Soon, a chorus member standing at the back door between songs spies me and motions me in.

Slipping into a back pew, I settle in for the remaining performance by the three dozen chorus members who span many ages, but everybody is either young or young at heart.

Some of Richard Rogers' songs exceed vocal range here and there, but who cares. The sheer pleasure is the fact that these singers were having fun. Fun with the audience, fun with each other. Expression, warmth, personality and a love of singing. Seventy-five-year-old women wearing black sequins were cute and coquettish as they sang "I Enjoy Being a Girl." A big man with gray beard and long hair sang "Some Enchanted Evening" with great tenderness. And then came "Oklahoma" and "Surrey With the Fringe on Top," from my least favorite musical, but I thought I would cry from a sudden wave of homesickness.

After the show, the church parking lot was clearing out quickly. As I walked to my car, one of the singers in her lovely black ensemble walked ahead of me and I called out to her.

"I loved your show."

She turned and smiled and asked where I'm from.

"Texas."

"That's where I'm going soon, for 10 months!"

Jeanne teaches Spanish and English as a second language and of all places, she is moving away to work in Weatherford, Texas, which is near Fort Worth.

Then came Janet, another singer who was not in a hurry to go home. We all stood in the deepening twilight and talked about our lives and situations, each of us barely able to keep from interrupting with the next question, answer, fact, observation, one-liner, or a laugh. Everything was fodder -- children, husbands, no-good ex-husbands, good jobs, bad jobs, food, diets, movies...

"Hey! Anybody want to go to a movie?" somebody asked. We all looked at each other, considered it, but with bad night vision, I had 16 miles on a perilous highway ahead of me. Jeanne and Janet also looked at their watches and decided it was too late for them, too.

"So," Janet said. "We're like ships that pass in the night." Again I was reminded of how I'm always saying 'bye to people I'd like to spend more time with.

Back at Maggie's, a friendly young couple from New Orleans had checked in and were watching TV in the sitting room. They invited me to join them, but it really was late, and my friend Bill Lynch from Portland was coming over the next day to roam the coast with me and shop in the antique stores.

Suddenly, it's my last week in Wheeler. And, it's time to make good on my promise to paint the short hallway that connects the guest rooms with the sitting room and the stairway. I can see why the project is near the top of

Maggie's list. The walls are dingy and scuffed, "off-white" when they were last painted, way-off-off white now.

Maggie has purchased four kinds of paint and hauled it home from Tillamook. She has also assembled everything I need, including a paint roller and pan, masking tape and drop cloth for the floor. The worst part of a painting project is all the prep work, and as I covered the floor, taped woodwork and assembled the tools, I decided it was a whole lot easier to clean rooms and serve breakfast and anyway, I'm just about ready to get out of the bed and breakfast business.

Even on a ladder I'm afraid of heights. Teetering and trembling, I somehow managed to connect the roller dipped in white paint with the flat surface of the ceiling, dragging the handle back and forth until that part of the job was done. The walls will be easy.

With that thought and therefore, a quick leap to the notion that the painting project would fly from now on, I rewarded myself with a pizza at Nina's Italian Restaurant. Then I drove to Manhattan Beach for a walk, but suddenly felt so intensely tired that I didn't even get out of the car.

A 9 p.m. bedtime helped a lot. The next morning, I got myself up and out for a run for the first time during my stay on the coast. I ran to "the next town" – Nehalem – staying far to the outer edge of the shoulder of 101. At 7 a.m., the log trucks, Tillamook companies and tradesmen were barreling down the highway. It's not the best place for a run.

On day two of the painting project, I got to dip into the yellow paint for walls.

"Do you think it's too yellow? I'm not sure about it," Maggie said.

I truly think the color is pretty and right for the space, but understand her uncertainty. You either manage to pick out the PERFECT shade, or you live with an imperfect one and it bugs you every day that you look at it. And then maybe you paint again.

"This yellow is wonderful," I said. "It will make the hallway look sunny in the daytime and golden at night."

Maggie was away all afternoon as I made great progress. I was more accustomed to the job and no longer afraid of the ladder. I drifted into the groove of a contented painter, deftly moving between roller and brushes, ivory and yellow. Soon the aged and scuffed walls looked bright and clean. The yellow paint indeed looked sunny this afternoon, clinging to the long-ignored, taken-for-granted wood paneling and making it gleam like satin. It was becoming the Cinderella of walls.

I had reached the end of the hallway and it was time to adjust the drop cloth. Perhaps I had become a little too mellow, the practical and attentive side of my brain turned off. I picked up a corner edge of the drop cloth and dragged it into the next frontier of my work area. The open gallon of yellow paint was perched on the folds of the cloth. I guess I thought it could go along for the ride and somehow stay in place.

But of course, it didn't.

I froze and watched helplessly, my blood running cold like, well, like sunny, golden, satiny yellow paint on carpet. The can was on its side, giving up its contents in a gushing river of ooze that pushed into every dark green fiber of exposed carpet. My second of shock turned into minutes of clawing and scooping with my hands as I tried to at least stop the flood from getting worse. I ran to my bathroom and grabbed Maggie's fluffy white towels, throwing them over a puddle that had become long and wide.

And then I heard the key in the lock downstairs, the tinkle of the little bell, usually a welcoming sound of an arrival – and the dreaded sound of footfalls, one by one, louder as they made the ascent. *No! No! Go back! Go back! I can fix this!* I continued scooping and sopping up and praying the damage would somehow just, disappear. Could I throw my body over it and somehow make the scene look natural?

Maggie took one look and gasped. Her hands flew up to hold the sides of her head, and her eyes popped round and horrified.

"I can fix this…"

"Well, it IS water-based paint," she said, calming down far faster than I had managed. "Use lots of water…"

It was the first bit of good news, a ray of hope.

For two hours I attacked the puddle, sopping up paint, pouring fresh water over it and pressing hundreds of squares of paper towels over the wound. Eventually, there was a manageable stain to clean up. Long after Maggie said it looked "fine," I continued to clean. Finally, the spot was as diminished as it was going to get.

The next night, Maggie faced another near-disaster and this time it was Garry's fault.

The two of them were gone for the day, off to an art exhibit out of town. I used the quiet time alone to *carefully* finish the painting project.

As I headed out to my evening walk on the beach, I heard a high-pitched sound around Maggie's, but couldn't identify it. Deciding it was an innocuous power line noise, I left for my drive to Rockaway.

I returned an hour or two later to the noise times 10 – smoke detectors throughout the complex were screaming, from Garry's Ekahnie gallery at street level, to the hallway of the guest rooms, to the downstairs apartment of poor Joel, who had just returned from a trip to California. Joel and I scrambled to find the source that set off the alarms, and I managed to disable the upstairs alarm, but we could not do anything about the ear-splitting wail in his apartment.

Minutes after frantic phone calls to summon Maggie, she came flying through the front door, scaling the steps two at a time – with a cop in hot pursuit.

"Ma'am – Ma'am !!"

The officer was trying to stop her for driving 49 mph in a 25 mph zone.

"I thought you were following me to the fire!" Maggie said, still frightened, but gradually realizing there was no fire.

There was, however, a burning candle in the gallery. Stuck on a high shelf, the candle had been forgotten after being lit 48 hours earlier for an open house event.

Today is Thursday. Having missed her exercise class this week, Maggie spoke of wishing she could go, so I said I'd be glad to serve the breakfast to guests this morning and I waved her out the door. The couple in the Art Room have stopped here on their coastal bicycle trip to Oakland, Calif. They prove easy to please, passing on the muffins in favor of Wheeler's legendary Treasure Café which is open only a few days a week to serve things like hazelnut pancakes.

Once again, I made it out for my run to Nehalem, shutting my eyes tightly as the log trucks threw bits of wood in their wake. Then I cleaned up and went to Common Grounds for coffee and the *Oregonian* newspaper. Since beginning this trip, I've felt out of touch with national and world events. Usually an avid newspaper reader and TV news junkie, this makes me wonder for the first time what it is that's IN the news that I think I need to know.

Suddenly there's so much to do, because I'm leaving on Saturday.

I drove to Tillamook to get the Honda an oil change and to pick up a few things at Fred Meyer's, including fluffy WHITE towels for Maggie to replace the pale yellow ones I created.

And then I wanted to work one more time at CART 'M. Most of the work day was over by then, but I tackled a wheelbarrow full of dead potted plants. Most were in plastic pots, but I saved one piece of chipped pottery for sale in the store. Nearby, an employee and volunteers were working diligently with a large piece of iron on wheels.

"It's going to be a bug in the Fourth of July parade," Belinda explained.

After the plant toss, there was a little time left to tidy up the toy department, which is also an opportunity to be a kid again and imagine the dolls and stuffed animals coming to life when nobody's around a la "Toy Story." I restored dignity to the dolls, setting them in elegant repose on a shelf. I picked out the action figures and left them to choose up sides in their bin. All the jewelry and other little girl things also got sorted, even though the entire toy world will come apart again and get strewn all over the place at the hands of the next little customer.

Tonight there was a wonderful party, and I got to dress up and wear makeup. Maggie insisted that I join the Nehalem Bay citizenry in saying good-bye to Dick and Barbara Matson. The party was held in an upstairs party room at the Sea Shack, which had been decorated 1960s-prom-style with crepe paper and balloons. Maggie's creative eye also had caught the possibilities in a CART 'M find – a miniature "grand piano," about two feet long, to represent Dick's love of music.

Carrying it into the restaurant, Maggie noted that it might make a swell addition to the Music Room.

"With a tiny Liberace-style candelabra," I suggested.

At the party, I met and talked to new people and watched thanks and affection lavished on the Matsons through gentle roasts and emotional toasts. Suddenly, I felt that my good times in Oregon were really just beginning, but I am leaving. Have to leave. I regretted being too solitary around here.

Take Alice and Frants Poulsen, for example. They offered a burst of friendship at the very end. I was aware of Alice because she had also answered my exploratory e-mail before moving out to the Oregon coast. She hadn't been able to offer me a home, but she worked for a property company that sometimes needed summer help with housekeeping tasks. Somehow, though, we just hadn't connected.

Alice was accompanied by her Danish husband, whom she met in England when both were in Naval careers. They were worldly and fascinating, and conversation was easy and fun.

"What are you doing tomorrow," Frants suddenly asked.

What am I doing? I had not begun to pack, and typically it takes an entire day to round up everything from closet, drawers, shelves and tabletops and then shoehorn it all back into the car.

"Nothing!" I said.

And so at 10:30 the next day, I walked across the road to the dock and met the Poulsens, who had already arrived in their great little motor boat. Frants told the story of how he bought it from a man for $650, then fixed it up. But then what else would one expect of a naval officer?

I am such a non-sailor! Everything about this excursion was strange and adventurous, from having to wear a life preserver, to where to sit in the boat. I didn't even know how long the ride would last, whether it was for minutes or hours. It was three hours, in fact, just the right amount of time for a thrilling taste of the sea-faring life.

Alice took the wheel and guided the boat under Frants's gentle direction. I watched and learned, such as finding out that the red and green buoys weren't placed at random, but served much like painted lines on a highway. We traveled south and it was fun to see the backs of familiar landmarks I'd passed many times on Hwy. 101.

The bay also has traffic cops. You don't have to break a rule to get stopped, and we were. The officer asked to board "for visual inspection" and he checked everything – written records, lifesaving equipment, the working order of all sorts of devices, and then he pronounced everything in working order. But of course!

The highlight of the trip was the seals. Big, sluggish, dog-faced and adorable, they huddled on a remote beach, watching us peer at them through binoculars.

Lots of crabbing was under way. Nets loaded with fish as bait hid deep in the water, attached to orange floats. Alice was careful to steer well away from the nets. The crab have to be a certain size to keep, and at one of the docks, we watched a family inspect their catch, holding up the writhing creatures to gauge whether they were large enough.

Alice had packed a delicious lunch for us, and then we pulled into Brighton Marina for coffee.

By 1:30 I was back at the dock in Wheeler. In wisely saying yes to going out on the boat, I acknowledged to myself that packing takes up whatever amount of time is available to me. So I accomplished that chore in an afternoon rather than a day.

The next morning, I cleaned my room and loaded the very last of my possessions, then peeked through the French doors of the sitting room to see if Maggie was at her computer. She was, so one more time I relaxed in the upholstered chair of her office space and ate "guest food" – muffin, juice and coffee.

Then she handed me a brown envelope and she said, "I'd like to have bought you some grand thing but I wrote you this letter instead. I hope it's helpful."

I might have disappointed Maggie as a resident artist, but once again she caught me with her astonishing care. Like my fondness for Gershwin, and subsequent appearance of a tape player and "Rhapsody In Blue" in my room, my desire for road work in the months ahead had not escaped her quiet attention. And so, voila! The brown envelope contained a "letter of reference."

Told to drop by early to say good-bye, Garry showed up, and we all took turns taking pictures in front of Maggie's Guestrooms. It was something to do instead of saying good-bye.

Our eyes were red when we finally did get around to good-bye.

"You'll be back," she told me. "I'll make you a great deal."

9 LEAVING THE WEST

Portland is behind me, and the Honda and I are on Hwy. 84 deep in the lush darkness of the Columbia River Gorge. I'm driving east with an achy heart. I miss Wheeler and all its good people and quirky individuality. It's not easy leaving such a cocoon-like existence; now the Honda provides the only familiar environment. I face hundreds of miles of brand new territory, and few decisions are set in my mind.

I do know that I'd like to spend autumn in New England. But it's early July so I have time for another stop and another little lifetime somewhere in between.

I want the Midwest. I've had mountains and seacoast and now I want to go "home." I want flat fields, blue sky, thunderstorms, cows and horses, pickup trucks, town squares, county fairs, and the secure grid of roads and streets that run north and south, east and west. I want the wood frame houses of my hometown, with front yards and sidewalks where kids roller-skate and mothers push strollers. I want a movie theater, Walmart and roast beef on Sundays. Baseball, swimming pools and shopping malls. A place so ordinary that people simply live their lives and there are no tourists or vacationers.

In between here and there are some "shoulds." I should see Glacier National Park and/or Yellowstone, some of the most beautiful parts of America. That is why I chose this route, and I drink in the river views of dark abundance, how the water rushes swift and deep.

Rather suddenly, the river begins to meander elsewhere and the landscape has flattened and dried out. Near Pendleton, it is downright desert-like. How can this still be Oregon?

The interstate veered into Washington and I somehow managed not to stop at fruit stands.

Soon I was crossing the panhandle of Idaho. Ah! The allure of Coeur d'Alene. An exquisite lake and picturesque towns nearly slowed me down, but I was headed toward Glacier National Park and felt compelled to keep moving northward. At every stop for necessities (gas, food, rest room) I checked my big Road Atlas. I was making progress.

Reluctantly. The truth was, I didn't want to deal with another national park, another big park fee, another day of in-transience. I decided to skip Glacier.

Liberated and single-minded, I picked Bismarck, N.D., as my destination. I am invited to visit my childhood best friend, Linda Bowen and her husband Mike. They're actually visiting their daughter in Wyoming right now, but Linda has told me how to get into the house. They will return to Bismarck on Saturday. Today is Monday. If I can get there in a couple of days, I can have the house to myself for a while. A HOUSE! With a kitchen, and a washing machine, and furniture for lounging, a yard and suburban streets for running, tabletops and electrical outlets for writing and Web site work, and then my friends will return for lots of conversation and reminiscing about our shared hometown.

I drove far and fast over some of the best scenery of the trip. Out of Idaho, over rounded folds of mountains in western Montana, under vast blue skies of puffy clouds. The snowy peaks of Yellowstone far to the south beckoned, but I responded only with a camera. Aim and click. There. Cross that off the list.

It was three days of beautiful but lonely miles, 1,268 to be exact. Only the days' gas stops offered human contact, but the stations were places to get in and out of fast. Employees and customers alike looked hard. Not to stereotype the locals, but I couldn't help but think about dangerous militias and belligerent rednecks. The Technicolor appeal of Montana was further marred by the blight of video poker, Keno and other gambling. Wherever the pit stop games were accommodated, the space was dark, dirty, stale, depressing.

I spent one night in Missoula and the next in Billings where I was nearly shut out of motel space by a Gold Wing Motorcycle convention. Leaving Billings early in the morning, I drove all the way to Forsyth 101 miles east for a late breakfast. I liked that little town. It had a busy grocery store, several restaurants, stores, offices and -- Ta DA! -- the Roxy, a gen-u-wine theater showing first-run movies. All the business facades stood side by side sentry-like, and everything faced a set of railroad tracks.

I chose a corner cafe to satisfy my craving for a protein-rich plate of steak and eggs. The homey decor had so much kitsch that a fully decorated Christmas tree on this July day looked perfectly normal.

After breakfast I wandered a bit on foot, staving off the drive. The numbing aspect of simply putting miles behind me is wearing off. I'm tired and antsy in the awareness of how far I have to go. So I found a general store of narrow aisles and shelves packed with goods, including cheap cassette tapes of music and stories. I picked out a romance tale to spin out diversion from the Honda's tape deck. I can't enjoy anything too demanding in an audio-taped book. If my mind wanders or something happens on the road, I can't back-track on the story very easily. The novel was simple and predictable.

At home in Texas, a real drama may be developing. Things aren't working out very well for my wonderful tenant Lisa. I learn this in a check-in, catch-up call to my neighbor Carolyn, although I already had some suspicions. Lisa's job in Dallas has not worked out and she has signed up as a temp worker, a drastic change of course for her. We're only three months into the rental contract, and I'm counting on her ongoing diligent care of the home front and my cats. But being so young, and giving up other career and educational opportunities, can she survive the failure of this significant risk taking? I'll bet she wishes she were back in Chicago.

"Oh don't worry," Carolyn says. "She'll be OK. She really seems to be trying to adjust and deal with things."

So I'm not going to worry.

At long last I reached the end of Montana, the last of the gigantic states and the last of the West. I felt regret about the bypassed opportunities, but that dissipated quickly as I flew across North Dakota, the miles to Bismarck dropping lower with every green sign. At 6:30 p.m. I pulled into the driveway of the Bowens' house on Mustang Drive on the hilly, developing frontier of northwest Bismarck. I found the back deck, the key inside the barbecue grill, and I let myself in.

Behold! My palace. It is an immaculate space with a living room, family room, bedrooms, bathrooms, two fireplaces, an office, a kitchen, and Linda's vast collection of milk glass displayed throughout many built-in shelves. It is a roomy, sunny, clean, comfortable, quiet, private, well-furnished, well-stocked world of order, convenience and affluence. I am sprung from the cramped life of a car and motel rooms. Tomorrow I will wash clothes and cook in the kitchen and write in my journal, catch up the Web site, learn my new digital camera and go for a run, catch up on e-mail, call Texas, explore the city, wash the car and get a haircut.

The next day, I rolled out of bed, didn't get dressed, didn't brush my teeth, didn't put on makeup and the whole day followed accordingly. I had fallen hard into the lap of luxury and I couldn't get up. I watched TV, starting with the "Today" show and rolling right on through the afternoon's movies on Lifetime cable. My greatest sense of accomplishment came from watching somebody actually win a million dollars on "Who Wants to be a Millionaire?"

I also contemplated my friendship with Linda. We were best friends all through grade school and high school and then our differences sent each of us off in opposite directions. She was a math whiz, majoring in it in college and becoming a teacher. I ran as far from math as I could, choosing English and journalism at a different school. We did marry in the same summer -- I got to wear her selection of a bridesmaid dress of beautiful pink organza; she got stuck with lime sherbet-colored dotted Swiss.

I married "well"; I thought she made a big mistake. Mike Bowen was a year younger than us, an uncommunicative boy from our hometown, just another kid in the church youth group – Linda could do SO much better. Four years later I was divorced. Twenty-seven years later the Bowens are going strong and Mike is a winner – a nice, successful, affable man whom I like to be around. They have two great kids. I, Miss Know-It-All, am wrong again.

For their 25th anniversary they bought a grandfather clock that stands tall against a wall of the living room. The thing bongs every 15 minutes. I hate that constant reminder of the passage of time, but on a worthless day like today, I suppose it serves me right.

"You didn't have to do this -- Mike will take us out to eat!"

They have arrived home and I've cooked a meal straight out of 1950s Kansas from recipes picked out of Linda's cookbooks: a ground beef casserole, green salad, fruit salad, cornbread and chocolate cake.

"I can't imagine driving 600 miles and then wanting to jump in the car again and go to some restaurant," I said, glad to see that a big smile belied the words. "But you know, cooking here feels like your mother's kitchen, and we're still baking cakes and playing house!"

Soon we were off on a merry-go-round of family updates and hometown gossip, moving from the dining table to the family room downstairs.

"Where are you going next?" Mike asks.

"I've been thinking about Iowa," I said. "Know anything about great small towns there?"

The three of us pored over an atlas, browsed the Internet and shared hearsay about places like Pella, Winterset and Mason City.

In Wheeler, Maggie had given me a copy of *Modern Maturity* magazine because of a feature on America's best small towns and cities.

"Iowa City was one of the favorites," I said. "I actually know somebody there, and whether I choose it or not I'd at least like to visit him."

His name is Tom Walz and he is one of my favorite people encountered through my work at The Arc. I met Tom in a group of people who were given a brief period of fame through an early-'80s television movie called "Bill." The movie starred Mickey Rooney in the title role, although the actor's sad-eyed portrayal didn't much reflect the real man behind the central character. William "Bill for Short" Sackter was a happy, optimistic bon vivant who had put his past behind him – as a 44-year resident of a Minnesota institution, taken there at age 7 because his mother couldn't deal with his mental retardation. Bill was in the first wave of the de-institutionalization movement of the early 1970s.

Lucky for Bill, he was discovered washing dishes at a Minneapolis country club by the young man who would eventually write "Bill" and win an Emmy for it (as well as the feature film "Rain Man" later on, earning an Academy Award for that). In those early years of the decade, Barry Morrow was very much pre-Hollywood, a struggling young writer and film maker whose curiosity and compassion caused him to reach out to Bill and help shore up community support and access.

Back to Tom Walz. Tom was one of Barry's professors in the social work department at the University of Iowa. He was enlisted for the help-Bill effort as well, and Tom cunningly set Bill up in business at the university to run a "coffee shop" at North Hall. By then, however, the facts of who was helping whom were not at all clear. Both men and a growing circle of friends were totally charmed by Bill. His charisma and story of survival and community success also attracted journalists, speaking engagements, awards and there was even a trip to President Jimmy Carter's White House where Bill blurted out to a surprised-and-blushing First Lady, "Gosh you're pretty!!"

Bill was a charmer, and when he suddenly died peacefully in his room in an Iowa City boarding house at age 70, Tom and Barry and all of us who got to know Bill grieved for a long time.

I've seen Tom a few times in the past 18 years, mostly at Arc functions. He always said I should visit Iowa City and see all the "Bill" points of interest – the coffee shop, the boarding house, the synagogue where he had a bar mitzvah as a middle-aged man.

But I haven't talked to Tom in a couple of years; he doesn't even know I've left The Arc.

"Use the computer to send an e-mail," Linda offered.

"I'll bet he isn't even in town," I said, recalling Tom's missions to places like Mexico and Egypt and India. His social work interests and studies stretch worldwide.

But it's time to go SOMEwhere. I've now been beached at the Bowens' for six days. Linda and I have spent our days driving around and talking, just like we did at 17. The topics are essentially the same, just the later-in-life versions: Work (School), Men (Boys), Gossip (Gossip).

It's time to make my next move to Iowa or Michigan or Wisconsin. I'm not really sure where I'm going but I need to leave tomorrow.

So I wrote to Tom, explaining the end of my job, the career "sabbatical," and directing him to my Web site.

The next morning I am up early to do all the packing I failed to do last night. Since last Wednesday, I've managed to bring just about everything into the Bowens' house – the ridiculous stacks, bundles and hangers full of clothes, the tote bag with all seven pairs of shoes, papers, books and the journal and computer I still managed to neglect this week. It's all in a jumble on the floor of daughter Mindy's bedroom where I've camped. As I struggle to pack it up and pack it in, Linda is baking brownies for me. We speculate about what the weather has in store for me; the vast sky over these great plains is dark and heavy with clouds.

But my mood is sunny. I did hear from Tom, within an hour of sending him my e-mail inviting myself for a quick visit. I'm to go straight to his house on Davenport Street and if he's not there, let myself in and take my stuff up the stairs to the guestroom. I don't think he even bothered to look at my Web site nor does he understand what I'm doing. That's just like Tom -- he simply says "Welcome!" No questions asked.

To help me cope mentally, a long day's drive is divided into "legs" and I've decided to call Fargo a leg, even though it's 200 miles. Nearly all the way, rain varied from heavy to torrential. In Fargo I stopped for gas and lurked in the convenience store hoping to hear "Fargo speak" made famous by the quirky, 1996 movie that used the city's name as its title. I wanted to hear just one "Yah" or "You betcha" but I left disappointed. The clerk was MinneSO'n.

The other leg was reached at Minneapolis. I did an odd and moody thing there. My last trip to Minneapolis had been in 1992 for the year's national convention of The Arc. Today I decided to find the hotel and simply walk through the memory of being there. It was an act of pure nostalgia. It was also a bit of a brainteaser – I couldn't remember the hotel's name, just that it was downtown and attached to a mall. I wandered in and out of hotels until I finally recognized the Marriott because of an escalator that descended diagonally toward a restaurant, and the floor of strangely low-ceilinged, cramped meeting rooms. I remembered the week's swirl of people and activity and inspiration – I LOVED that part of my job, and today I mourned its loss briefly. It had all come back like a dream, and then in an instant felt empty and irrelevant. My detour down memory lane was abruptly over.

The drive was fairly speedy today after I tried out a customer service I'd heard about at Cracker Barrel restaurants. For a small fee, they basically lend you an audiotape book. All I had to do was pick out a tape from the rack and put its $27 cost on my credit card. If I return the tape within a week to any Cracker Barrel, they credit back the cost less $3. So a Danielle Steele yarn kept me entertained over the many dull miles of Minnesota.

At sunset I checked into a hotel with the words "Conference Center" in its name. If you're traveling alone on a budget, don't stay in a place that is more facility than you need. This one also had one of those dank swimming pool/atriums and other kiddy amenities. The rings and pings of video games bounced off the walls as I padded out in search of ice and Doritos. The breakfast bar the next morning offered coffee, juice, doughnuts and four kinds of sugared cereal.

Soon I was crossing into my 14th state. Iowa is cornfields with roads, at least the northern rural part. It seemed natural and desirable to leave the interstate and try out Hwy. 218, which took me from one small town to the next. In Charles City I stopped for lunch, gleeful at seeing lunch specials of things like ham and scalloped potatoes and a side of Jell-O. This is the life I want for a while.

I stopped for gas on the southern edge of Cedar Rapids at mid-afternoon and pressed Tom's number on my cell phone.

"Where are you?" he asked. "Hurry if you want to go to an auction with me. I've got my eye on a piece of furniture so we'll need to leave as soon as you can get here."

Social Worker and Wood Worker -- I'd forgotten that Tom even carries both those titles on his business cards. And, he may be retired and entering the very group he represents as a gerontologist, but he still moves at a pace that's three times as fast as anybody I know.

So I picked up my pace and sped the Honda south on 380 to I-80 and Iowa City and the Dubuque Street exit. The Honda's tires rolled noisily over bricks below huge leafy trees arced from each side to form a big green canopy. I reached a pink frame house and there was Tom sitting on the front porch. He leaped to his feet.

"C'mon!" he said, directing me to the alleyway behind the house. We jumped into his little red pickup and flew eastward out of the city limits to an auction complex called Sharpless. The parking lot was jammed, with cars and trucks parked any which way they landed, everyone apparently intent on the same objective we had: Don't Miss That Buy!

The low dusty buildings stretched deep and wide to contain everything a person might possibly need for life and home -- furniture, dishes, food, tools, farm implements. Three auctions were under way and three rat-a-tat callers were in command of business. They stood above their crowds, lording it over a dinette table suite or an ancient chest of drawers and skillfully moved the bidding higher. In a blaze of words and arithmetic, the callers fired up the competition between coveters of the items at hand until one bidder prevailed and "SOLD" was declared.

Lending an air of an earlier century were the Amish Mennonites, some jostling elbow-to-elbow with the farmers, wives, lawyers, Methodists, students and all the other more usual species of bidder. "Amish" and "exotic" may not belong in the same sentence but I was excited by this new marker of time and place in my journey.

Gosh, the Amish are just so *different*. With their beards and un-made-up faces, black hats and bonnets, suspenders and long sleeves, to me they are a sort of national treasure, so quiet and devoted to a private life of religion and community without modern conveniences – century after century. Or did I just write something that's *anti* the American way?! Whatever, Tom's just asked me to go buy a loaf of honey nut bread from the table of an Amish bakery. I also pick up a plump rhubarb pie.

Gradually over the evening, the considerable array of items that had filled the auction barns was disappearing. Now the line at the cashier's window was long. Tom won the bidding skirmishes on the furniture he wanted. We prepared to leave.

"That stuff in the middle is free," Tom told me, and I made a beeline for a central pile of cast-offs that nobody wanted. Imagine that! I picked up four glasses, a plate and two wastebaskets.

"I have an idea," I explained to Tom in the truck as we drove back to the house. "I'll get an apartment and furnish it with auction finds that I can recycle at the end of my stay."

He didn't say much.

10 CRISIS IN KANSAS

Tom's house is my new home. "Stay as long as you like," he'd announced. I also feel a little needed. Separated from his wife of many years, Tom just moved into the place a few months ago. He is very independent, but I think he could be a little lonely, and he can certainly use the housekeeping/cooking support. In one way he's just like my dad – appreciative of the miracle of a meal on the table.

The house has the feel of the 19th century rural Midwest. It is old and old-fashioned. The kitchen is a distinct room, large enough to accommodate both cooking and eating. The kitchen's north door opens onto a sweet little front porch where squirrels drop from the trees and skitter along the white porch railing.

Next to the kitchen and adjacent to the living room is a small dining room which Tom has turned into an office. A large desk seems to get little use. Far more important is an easy chair and lamp, with an ottoman and an old metal freestanding ashtray, which holds Tom's pipe and tobacco. Every night, Tom settles in here to read a fine book and puff on his pipe to the sounds of classical music. On Friday nights, he sips brandy.

Rounding out the first floor are Tom's bedroom, the house's only bathroom, a back utility porch, and a flight of stairs down to the basement.

I love my room. It is up a steep stairway next to the kitchen. A finished room of the attic, it is tucked under the slant of the roof, with two small windows, one facing the attic window of the house next door, the other overlooking the lower back roof and the yard. There is no air conditioning up here, just a box fan, but Iowa is not Texas and I think I can get along without AC in a gentler summertime.

The house is perfectly, adequately, comfortably furnished entirely from "a few dollars worth" of auction finds.

"Hurry!"

Full-summer sun is pouring into the house at 7 a.m. on my first morning and Tom has zoomed into the day in usual fashion. I have agreed to fall in with his routine. This means racing off to Bruegger's downtown for a couple of sacks of bagels to sell at Wild Bill's Coffee Shop. Then it's off to North Hall on the University of Iowa campus. Tom continues a busy professional life here of and writing and teaching, including a course on Ghandi.

"Wild Bill's" is much as I had imagined. Its substantial furnishings include a magnificent wood and glass counter acquired from the demise of an old-fashioned drug store. The room has square tables and chairs and there are things besides snacks and coffee for sale, including student arts and crafts and many of the auction finds that Tom has stripped and sanded and varnished to new glory.

Bill Sackter's spirit of opportunity lives on in the young men and women who work in the coffee shop. They too have minds that are wired a little differently – labeled retarded or autistic or mentally ill by the medical community, slow or "special" or maddening by the rest of the world. Mental retardation was the subject matter of my professional life, and I found it regrettable that society generally can't appreciate the disability because the world is too much about "keeping up."

I could even make a case that we so-called "normal" people suffer a brain dysfunction when we over-think and over-intellectualize and construct elaborate mental gymnasiums as we deal with each other. Our power to sort, analyze, filter, weigh and finally present our thoughts and "reveal" ourselves doesn't seem to have much to do with a capacity to experience the richness of life. The man who smiled and said good morning and served my coffee this morning has a job, home, friends and boundless optimism. In that vein, I can think of plenty of smart worldly people who are miserable failures. Who's disabled here?

I spent much of the rest of the day in Tom's office, which has two, maybe three desks – I'm not sure how many there are because of all the scholarly clutter. At his desk he races through e-mail between students' and colleagues' visits and trying to solve others' problems that seem to mostly involve various lifetime issues.

I too am happy to be Tom's shadow. At 68, Tom has a ring of white hair with a few flyaway strands on top. He's not thin but he also hasn't settled into too much of a paunch, thanks to weekly games of basketball that he'd no more skip than the Wednesday auctions at Sharpless. His large eyes are magnified slightly by his eyeglasses, which is vaguely unsettling when you ask a question or assert some point and he fixes his intelligent, appraising gaze on you. Tom is a world traveler, and not just to the easy parts of the world.

"Tell me about meeting Mother Teresa in India," I said one evening as we lounged on the front porch watching squirrels and fireflies.

Tom had been part of a visiting group of Americans in Calcutta. They were walking through the city's teeming streets, making their way to Mother Teresa's order of nuns for an arranged appointment.

Suddenly, they saw a woman lying in the street. She was naked, dirty, sick, perhaps dying.

"We didn't know what to do," Tom said. "Everyone was simply stepping over and around her and going on their way. So we did too."

Tom's group reached their destination, and after the exciting introductions to a woman who was, after all, a world celebrity, Tom told her about the woman in the street.

"What should we have done?" he asked.

"And she simply turned to the nuns and said, 'Bring her here.'"

So here is someone that I know, witnessing an example of Mother Teresa's well-known response to the question, "Why bother?" Why bother to feed and care for dying people. Her reply was that God did not call her to be successful, just faithful. It is one of my favorite citations on faith.

Next question.

"Where do you think I might get a job?" I asked. "I really want to be a waitress."

Here comes The Gaze.

"Well, there's Hamburg Inn," he said, his voice devoid of inflection. "I know the owner."

His lack of enthusiasm was infectious. Somehow, a university town's hamburger haven didn't hit me right. It sounded too busy, too young, too...*hamburgery*.

"You can help me," Tom said.

He described a project he's been contracted to do that involves interviews and a survey of all manner of homes for older adults in southeastern Iowa. From assisted-living apartments to nursing homes, all have to be contacted, mostly in person, and asked Twenty Questions about what they provide. The outcome will be part of an Internet online directory.

"OK!" University *research* associate. How important!

Our household is really humming along. Tom won't take any rent money, so I've busied myself as housekeeper and cook. Being simply furnished and because he's not there very much, the house is a cinch to dust and sweep. On the cooking front, Tom's sole dinner repertoire is "Rosemary Chicken," so there is nothing in the cupboards but the one spice. We went to the grocery store and I stocked up on rice, canned soups, fresh fruit and vegetables and just a few more spices, and beer. I love being in charge of the kitchen.

"What time is dinner," Tom will say at 5 o'clock.

"Oh, 6:30 or 7."

"Plenty of time to get this Sharpless desk refinished," and off he goes to the small garage that sits on the alley behind the house to – sure enough – refinish an entire piece of furniture before dinner. The few times I've tried to refinish something it's taken me weeks. However, I know how to cook lots of things beyond Rosemary Chicken.

On Saturday Tom went out of town for one of his speaking engagements so I was on my own. I went downtown to while away some hours, to try a restaurant, work in the library, and wrestle the tight parking situation. (I've already picked up a parking ticket after tarrying too long one morning over coffee and the *New York Times* at Bruegger's Bagels. I intend to ignore it along with the other two tickets picked up in Arizona and Oregon. I don't think these municipalities treat their guests very hospitably.)

I spent many hours in the library trying to make my new digital camera talk to the laptop computer. Am I *really* free on this trip, saddled to technology the way I am? No! These things are anvils on my time and concerns.

As evening arrived and the library closed, I wandered out to find the "Ped Mall," a street closed to vehicles and open to pedestrians. I sat on steps and watched people and listened to live jazz music.

"Liz, where are you?"

I have answered my cell phone. My brother in Ottawa, Kansas, has called me.

"It's Mother..."

She is in the Ottawa hospital, he said, and nobody knows yet exactly what's wrong. Ed and my sister-in-law Sharron had welcomed our parents for the usual Sunday dinner routine: Mother and Daddy attend the Lyndon Presbyterian Church's 9:30 service, then drive the 30 miles eastward to Ottawa for a meal. This is always followed by a nap for Mother, and Ed and my dad go out for a drive and "senior Cokes" at McDonald's. Not quite weekly, the get-together is nonetheless frequent and regular, but today, Mother is not her usual quiet self. She tries to explain what is wrong and can only say that she is sick and "uncomfortable."

My questions and Ed's answers are heavy with the punctuation of silence. In the past six years, our mother has needed a number of trips to hospitals, and the growing fear among family members OTHER than our dad is that their situation is becoming too difficult to manage on their own. There have been falls at the farmhouse, and for the first time, my dad has not been strong enough to get Mother upright and has had to call 911. These incidents are then conveniently forgotten in later conversation with Ed and Martha and me, but because "outside help" is now required, word leaks out in Osage and Franklin counties.

The words "nursing home for Mother" have begun to creep furtively into quiet conversations and e-mails.

"I've got trips to Kansas built into my plan this year," I told Ed. "Sounds like this is a good time for one."

The drive to northeastern Kansas is an easy one, not even a full day's journey. It's a straight shot west to Des Moines, then a quick drop down I-35 and an angled route across northwestern Missouri. Lunch was in Eagleville. I ventured into the tiny town instead of picking up fast food off the fast highway and was rewarded with the oddity of communal dining – strange to a city girl anyway. The only table available was an over-sized one, so as I was finishing my meal, two farmers and three teen-agers sat down with me to make the restaurant completely occupied. I didn't feel like initiating conversation and they didn't either.

As I neared Kansas City, exit signs indicated I was right at Liberty. My Sun City Aunt Lugene and Uncle Fred lived in Liberty in the 1950s and '60s. It was my favorite kind of weekend when my parents would load us kids and the suitcases into our '57 Chevy and head north out of Southeast Kansas on a

Friday night. Three hours later, including 30 minutes or so of being lost in Kansas City, we'd pull up to the house on Orchard Street and my aunt would be ready for us with a wonderful dessert. My dad and my uncle then engaged in an interminable conversation about how the Smiths had managed to get lost and where the crucial wrong turn might have occurred – and I recall that this conversation was necessary *every single time*. Meanwhile, my teen-age brother sat there like a Sphinx. A borderline juvenile delinquent, he was alleged to skip school and drive to KC with his friends, so he knew the town like the back of his hand, yet had to keep his mouth shut when my dad would take that inevitable wrong turn.

The memories were strong, and I found myself taking the Liberty exit and setting out to find the house on Orchard Street. A little driving around and inquiries at a grocery store led me to the house that I last saw in 1971. My, how it had changed! It had shrunk for one thing, reduced in scale and choked by the development of apartment units, tract housing and the roads to serve them. Thirty years ago, the backyard view stretched over pastures. There had been a lavish strawberry patch and a patio nice enough to accommodate my cousin Carolyn's wedding guests. Now the backyard is neglected by everyone and everything but weeds.

Is it obvious that I'm not in a big hurry to get to Ottawa? I am full of foreboding and dread.

"The judge says you may come in."

My brother, "the Honorable Edwin R. Smith," has seen me peek into the doors of his courtroom in Ottawa's Franklin County Courthouse. I have withdrawn because a full cast of players is presenting a case. He has sent the bailiff out to say I can come in if I want to. So I do, settling in for an hour or so of a juicy she-said he-said case that's either about rape or revenge.

Later in Ed's office I resist saying a word about the case as he hangs up the black gown and settles in behind his desk. Besides, weighty family matters are at hand.

"Assuming nothing is seriously wrong, and Mother can be released soon, I'm going to talk to Daddy about placing her somewhere," I announce.

"You are," he said, not as a question, or reiterated fact, but in sheer incredulity. "I'd better tell you what he's said to me. He is adamant about taking her home from the hospital."

"I am not here to agree with Daddy. I did not drive seven hours to do that and not have my say. It is time. She is not safe in that house and he can no longer handle her care. He could hurt himself and then they'll both be in a mess."

Gone was the judge's impassive poker face. In its place was a brother's constellation of emotions flickering in rapid succession: surprise, uncertainty, understanding, amusement, fear, folly, agreement, skepticism, and finally, the look that said, *It's your funeral, kid.*

"I don't think you understand," he said.

"Oh I understand," I said, trying not to feel like such a naive kid sister. "Right now, let's just go see Mother."

The Honda and I followed Ed in his car straight south on Ottawa's wide Main Street to Ransom Memorial Hospital. I was glad that my dad had already left the hospital for the day, returning to the farm before dark. There was no one in Mother's room, but she was awake and she peered at me, her head poking out above the sheet and blanket. She looked tiny and restless.

Her greeting revealed a mental state that was a boxing ring of dreams, physical pain and the effects of medication, random memory, unresolved tasks and issues, frustration and depression and just plain dementia. Her greeting was, "Are you... here... for... the... the...." The sentence was not finished and I seemed to be a stranger to her.

"I'm here to see you, Mother! It's me – Liz – the GOOD kid."

The joking would be lost on her, but it helped me to swallow the lump in my throat.

She managed a smile that was as brief as a candle's flame in a breeze and soon she was asleep.

I slipped out of the room and found the hospital's social worker at the nurse's station. Yay! An ally in this battle! She can help us stabilize our parents' situation, use her training and expertise to counsel and help them understand – even embrace – the necessity of change. She can even make the arrangements to transfer Mother from the hospital bed to a fine long-term care facility close to the farm when this latest medical crisis is over.

"Your brother is right," the social worker said flatly. "Mr. Smith is adamant about taking your mother home."

She listened patiently and sympathetically as I erupted again, repeating the thundering spiel I'd spun out in Ed's office. But my rhetoric is fired at the wrong audience. Even to my own ears, my words feel like a rehearsal that may or may not lead to a live performance.

We left the hospital and I took Ed and Sharron out for dinner at the Chinese restaurant near the hospital. We managed to set the difficult parental issues aside and talk about lighter things.

And so it was nearly 9 p.m. before I headed the Honda west across Franklin County and into Osage, the dark night lit only by occasional oncoming headlights and the dim street lights of the tiny towns of Pomona and Vassar..."*I was quite impressed with your father when we first started dating,*" Mother said, her smile mischievous. "*We were in college in Emporia and I didn't know a lot about his part of the state. So when some other kids told me he'd dated a 'Vassar girl' – Well! I just didn't know what he would see in me!*"

The classic family story makes me smile, but the loneliness of the night and my dread of the deed ahead soon returns. Maybe Daddy will be in bed asleep; I'll have time to plot the conversation out for daylight and breakfast time tomorrow. I'll even practice – both what I want to say and how to react when he fires back.

Road surface rumble strips warn me that Hwy. 75 is mere yards ahead – it's a dangerous intersection where Hwy. 68 suddenly intersects with the busier north-south artery – so I slow completely to stop, look and turn south into Lyndon. Then it's west 4 miles to the farm, then south again – if there's a street or a road in Kansas that runs diagonally, I've never been on it and its engineering must be a mistake.

The house is well lit and, of course, Daddy is still up, stretched out in the gray-blue recliner, his old long-haired cat Tertia perched on his lap as he awaits the 10 o'clock news. I plop down on the sofa beside the chair and offer up a breezy report on my new "home" in Iowa, the quick trip down, seeing Ed's courtroom, and then a report on Mother.

"She seemed tired but I think she was glad to see me," I said.

Daddy responds jovially – in fact, he is a little too animated for the hour. The news and a bowl of cereal are always his last acts of the day, accomplished with little conversation. But there he is, oddly talkative, strangely nervous. I feel off balance. Something's coming.

"One of the 'professionals' at the hospital told me they think Mother should be transferred to a nursing home," he said.

There it is.

"I don't think they realize what a good situation we have here at home," he exclaimed, "how well it works!"

He turned his head toward me. The floor lamp between us spreads light across his face – his eyes are wide with brows arched high.

Right, Liz? Right??

There comes a point where words are less important than timing. I don't have the words, but it's time.

"Daddy, I'm not sure I can agree with that any more."

I said it gently but plainly.

"It seems to me she has deteriorated," I said. "She's needing an environment where there are more people, more medical, safety and emergency features to help make her situation more secure."

My dad's face fell – the eyebrows, the smile, the hope of surely having an ally. He looked down and he looked 86 years old again and I'll have to live with the memory of that suddenly-sad countenance forever. But he didn't get angry. He just looked away and didn't say anything at all and I didn't rush to fill the silence.

Finally, he said, "She really has deteriorated." And then, "Let's go to Emporia tomorrow and look at Presbyterian Manor."

Just like that. Obviously, despite the claps of thunderous protests, Daddy *had* been thinking things over. And as in most other difficult moves in his life, his Kansas-bred stoicism kicked in for some brisk decision making.

The next day, Ed and Sharron and I clamored and stumbled all over one another like Keystone Cops, anxious to help Daddy, amazed by his change of heart, scared he would change his mind. We ALL crowded into Whitey the Buick, trying to secure our group in a sort of mental Velcro to stay headed in the same direction. I drove, putting the pedal to the metal for Emporia and wher*ever* Daddy was willing to look. We hovered and soothed and continually reassured my dad that his decision was so right.

I stayed in Kansas for a week. Mother's medical emergency turned out to be the most worrisome episode yet. She had pneumonia and while that was being tackled, a large "mass" was discovered and tests scheduled. My sister and brother-in-law rushed up from Texas, and we all spent heavy hours shuffling between the hospital and houses and restaurants in tight pathways of worry and waiting.

The mass was benign. Mother was OK. It seemed likely that Daddy would change his mind about the nursing home transfer, but he didn't. He settled on a facility in Osage City, a mere 10-minute drive for him from the farm. Not only can he have meals with her there, he can take her out for short trips and visits home.

My whole being heaved a sigh of relief – for both family and self – as I returned to Iowa to resume my escapist adventure.

11 CLEANING APARTMENTS

It's a few days later, and the irony is not lost on me that I am visiting nursing homes for Tom's Internet project. We actually started my training to do the surveys shortly before my trip to Kansas. I went with him to facilities in Iowa City and small towns nearby, sitting next to him in the administrators' offices while he rattled off the survey questions about numbers of beds and kinds of services. Pretty dry stuff really.

Today, on my own in Cedar Rapids, I am much more interested in the subject matter. It is also difficult for me to make these calls, but more as a practical matter than the idea of depressing subject matter. I've made appointments at four places, and they are at unknown, far-flung points of Cedar Rapids which is a lot bigger than I expected. I wrestle a large fold-up map draped over the dash and gear shift and passenger seat of my car, then try to reconcile what's on the paper with the streets I'm seeing. AND arrive at the appointments on time.

First place: Tree-shaded one-story apartment buildings built in 1969. The manager answered my Twenty Questions patiently, having paused from lunch preparations for an employee's good-bye party. A handyman breezed in and out. Clearly, this place was at the light end of the assisted living-nursing home spectrum and I liked it.

Second place: Modern complex of apartments and wings of rooms. The administrator arrived late, having had to take an 85-year-old resident with cancer and no family to her medical appointment. I shuddered. Things could be worse for Mother.

Third place: A nursing home in the style of what I know, with an institutional space for congregating and dining in front of the nurse's station. People are older and medicated and sleepy, so a woman in a wheelchair sewing on an afghan offered a welcome splash of color and life.

Fourth place: My personal favorite. It is a historic, red-brick mansion filled with antiques and is for "ladies only," established in the late 19th century because the plight of one indigent woman touched the right people's hearts and the home was built.

So now I know. When I get old, I'll be sure to shop around with a 401(k) that will surely take care of the bills of "the best." That's my plan anyway.

But I'm not old yet.

In fact, tomorrow I start another job that will require energy and spunk: Apartment Cleaner. This is a time of year when University of Iowa students pack up and move out, having finished their summer school session or even graduated. The southwest-side apartment complex is offering top dollar for workers to deal with the aftermath. The job sounds gruesome and foreboding but it is also quick – just a few days' commitment – and it pays TEN DOLLARS AN HOUR, a fortune in my economy.

"I'm Elizabeth Moore," I announce to the manager, having found the office again where I'd carefully completed an application a few days earlier. Sharon is 40-something, with an unsmiling face constantly etched in worry.

"I want you to go with Amy," she said, motioning toward another employee. "Here's your clipboard – go with her and she'll show you how to do check-outs."

A *clipboard*. I've been doing these wage-earning jobs only a few months now, but I recognize a wage earner's status symbol. The person who carries a clipboard has authority.

"We're training you to be a crew leader," Sharon said.

Crew leader! Boss! Slave driver! AND, I'll make $12.50 an hour!! I'm promoted even before I start the job. Why? Was it my intelligence? My maturity? My work as assistant-to-the-owner of Maggie's Guestrooms? And, maybe this means I won't have to actually CLEAN apartments – I'll tell other people to clean apartments and then mark them up on the clipboard: Good Job (checkmark) or Bad Job ("Dock paycheck"). I am heady with power.

Amy is a cheerless, stalwart soul, all business and with no discernible personality although I cling to the possibility. Otherwise, I am destined to spend the afternoon trudging after her from one apartment to the next learning a distasteful job that's about cleaning up after people. Sure, these departing residents want to please us and get their deposits back – some of them anyway. Others just want to turn in their keys and hit the road, leaving their greasy ovens and dirty carpet in somebody else's hands.

Amy and I do a lot of walking over the 30-year-old complex of two- and three-story buildings. It is a sprawling property, built around grassy spaces and a swimming pool. We walk, run and climb stairs, going in and out of hallways that emit many different odors, mostly unpleasant ones of other people's lives and habits. She shows me how to inspect the units and write down any trouble spots on the clipboard – missing ice cube trays, curling iron burns, broken, dented or stained whatever – then we must get forwarding addresses from the tenants (usually, several roommates are involved) and collect their keys.

We arrive at Apt. 107 and are greeted by Joseph, a student who has finished graduate studies and is heading back to Africa. Joseph is lanky and handsome, full of charm and impish good humor, and his apartment is a mess.

"WHAT IS THIS?!!" Amy cries out.

She is pointing down at the linoleum floor in the tiny kitchen. Dozens of small cuts have left permanent marks that no amount of Top Job can ever eliminate.

Joseph seems to realize that his interpersonal skills also cannot cover up the marks.

"One night, we haf a knife fight in here."

Silence. I decide a little joke might be good to break the tension: "Well, at least you got the blood cleaned up pretty good."

Nobody laughs. Joseph's face has gone slack. His roommate, more of a serious, studious type, stands by silently. Amy is rigid.

"Yes, well...we, uh, well..." Joseph stammered, and then, "What do I haf to pay?"

"Just leave," Amy says.

We hurry back to the office to tell Sharon about Apt. 107 – the floor, the grease-coated kitchen walls and countertops, and the large spot of living room carpet where a deep freeze had set. The manager calls in reinforcements – two temps whose sole assignment for the afternoon is to clean that one apartment. I'm so glad I'm the person with the clipboard.

The greatest hardship of this day is the running back and forth across the complex. Finally I get to clock out for lunch and I head home to change from thin flats to thick-soled running shoes. Amy gets reinforcements of her own: two teen-age daughters and a car. She also tries to snare a golf cart to help us get around, but to no avail. I learn that golf carts are a sore subject. Only the maintenance guys get to use golf carts.

In the afternoon, we were spared more real hellholes, but we also ran out of people checking out – there may be more tomorrow, and definitely a slew on Monday. This meant that I had to put down the clipboard, pick up the cleaning supplies and start scrubbing.

Actually, cleaning was not so bad. I got to stay in one place and work with Amy's daughters, who were a lot more fun than their mother. The three of us agreeably settled on our cleaning specialties. They picked kitchens and I chose bathrooms, the latter being a much smaller space and not requiring the use of oven cleaner.

At the end of the afternoon back in the office, Worried Sharon was fretting about needing more people to work.

"I'm not supposed to work tomorrow but I can be on call," I offered. "I'll have my cell phone with me and will be available after 11."

That will give me time to attend an early service at the First Presbyterian Church. The pastor there is Tom Brown, a long-time minister at my home church in Hurst. I've been looking forward to seeing him and surprising him with a Texas presence in his congregation some Sunday.

Actually, I'll be floating around outside the house all day tomorrow. My host Tom is having company: his girlfriend from Des Moines. I need to clear out completely, because she does not know about my presence. She calls every morning at 7 a.m. On my first day at the house, the phone rang at 7 a.m. and I absent-mindedly reached for the receiver.

"Don't answer that!!" Tom exclaimed, racing in from the back porch. "Don't ever answer that."

"It's just easier not to have to tell her you're here," he explained.

'Nuff said. I understood completely and after that, I never answered the phone and in particular, made myself scarce in that part of the house at 7 a.m. I also added Advice About Women to my repertoire of household support when it seemed warranted, and sometimes when it wasn't but I just couldn't stop myself.

"Tom! You'll be dead if you don't let me help you. I know the kinds of things that will catch her eye," I declared on this Saturday evening.

Not only had I removed nearly all personal possessions from sight, with some things going into the trunk of the Honda and others stashed in the basement, I was telling him that we had to restore the look of the kitchen to that of a man living alone. I threw out the flowers on the table. The toaster, sugar and the salt and pepper shakers had been positioned halfway between us; I bunched them all back on his side of the table again.

"I've been a jealous and suspicious girlfriend myself," I told him, relishing the conspiracy. "I know what's going to make her ask questions."

The next morning I left the house with plenty of things to do to keep myself occupied for the day. First stop: Bruegger's, for a bagel and coffee and *The New York Times*. What a great start!

In the middle of breakfast, who should come in but Tom with the girlfriend. I hunkered down, adopting the pose of a nonchalant, total stranger, never looking anywhere near a direction that might result in eye contact. Even then I stole glances over the top of the newspaper at an attractive, vivacious woman in her mid-50s. She looked happy to be with Tom.

"Why didn't you say something?!" Tom said to me later. "I didn't see you but if I had, I would have introduced you!"

After Bruegger's I found the First Presbyterian Church and a bit of 1980s Hurst, Texas, in the Rev. Tom Finley Brown, perpetually jovial and youthful even at 60. He's been here several years but it was good to hear that he's lost none of his Texas twang, even coming off a six-week visit to Scotland with his petite wife Carolyn. I successfully cornered both of them in the after-church coffee hour and we made plans to meet for lunch this week.

After church I drove straight to North Hall to settle into Professor Tom's office and do some serious work: Catching up my survey paperwork, answering my e-mail, working on my Web site and updating my journal. I had forgotten my offer to be "on call" to the apartments when my phone rang.

"Elizabeth?"

It's Worried Sharon. Fun's over.

This afternoon was no clipboard job; I joined a regiment that included other over-qualified scrubbers, including a harpist and a Ph.D. who speaks fluent German. We descended into a basement utility room and picked up identical buckets of cleaning products: Scrubbing Bubbles, Comet, Easy Off, Windex and assorted sponges and paper towels. Again, the status symbols of this type of work belonged to the swift and the sure. NEW – not partial – cans of Scrubbing Bubbles and Comet, BIG sponges, not the little frayed ones, were snapped up by the keen-eyed, quick-handed, fleet-footed among us. The harpist got left in the dust.

Today's shocking fact learned about student apartment life: The Perfectly Good Things People Throw Away. The dumpsters are heaped with furniture and household goods – chairs, desks, pots and pans, sofas, lamps, bookshelves, dishes, bicycles, plants, sports equipment, rugs, clothing, computers, books, videos and CDs, toys, TVs, vacuum cleaners, mattresses...Why would anyone in Iowa City bother to BUY this stuff? All they have to do is cruise the apartments' parking lots and help themselves to the bounty offered up by dumpsters.

After three hours of cleaning, I went back to the university. Tom called shortly after I arrived to say that the coast was clear.

"I'd like to take you out to dinner," he said. It sounded like atonement for the "inconvenience" of booting me out. Heck, it's his house and I enjoyed (most of) the day away.

"After dinner we have to go dumpster diving," I said.

And so we did just that after eating at the Hamburg Inn near a table where Ronald Reagan once dined as president.

I showed Tom the way to the apartment complex and the spot where I'd spied wooden chairs and a table perfect for refinishing. Apparently, other people had the same idea and the treasures had been captured. Even so, we were able to get a child's pink bicycle and bureau drawers from which Tom will remove the ornate pulls for use on other furniture.

The next morning was July 31, the most important of the job's four-day run. This was the last day of most of the leases, the final day for departing students to clear out and make way for Aug. 1 move-ins. Fifteen of us cleaners and two additional teams of painters and carpet layers had mere hours to literally sweep in to the units and make them shine.

At 7:59 a.m., I punched my time card into the clock in the manager's office. Again, Sharon's greeting to me as "Elizabeth" grated. But I didn't bother to explain that I'd rather not be called by my formal name, which hasn't hung in the air since 1959 when it was last invoked by an angry mother and prim schoolteachers.

I picked up my clipboard and surveyed the tasks of the big day ahead. Good grief. My crew – five helpers I'd never met - weren't due in until 9:15. And then I had checkouts scheduled about 10 minutes apart beginning at 9:30. I hoped there wouldn't be too many apartments like Joseph's.

Today, Sharon had an assistant named Nina. They were buzzing with nervous energy and uncertainty about how to meet the demands of the day. They had at least managed to commandeer a golf cart.

"Go work on Apt. 152," Nina said to me.

I kind of wondered how I was supposed to go scrub bathrooms AND command a crew, but as a great respecter of Authority, I didn't ask questions, assuming that Authority knew what she was doing. I raced over to Apt. 152 and soon found myself scraping black stuff in the bathtub with a pumice stone. A girl named Pat kept me company. She scrubbed the sink and we talked about why we were there. Generally the reasons were similar, relating not so much to personal fulfillment as to paying bills.

At 9:30, I wished Pat a good day, put my game face on and picked up my clipboard. It's SHOWtime.

At Apt. 315 I rapped on the door. Three 21-year-olds let me in and stepped back as I took charge with a businesslike "hello" and no smile. I positioned my pen over an extensive checklist. Kitchen: Not bad. Bathrooms: OK. Walls: No holes. Carpet: "What's this?" I said, pointing to a spot about 10 inches wide.

"Uh, I think somebody threw up there," a member of the trio finally offered. I believe I wouldn't "think"; I'd KNOW if somebody threw up on my carpet but I didn't say anything. I simply checked all the blanks, wrote down the roommates' forwarding addresses, collected the keys, and, already running five minutes late, raced off to the next apartment.

For the next two hours, I was at a dead run, meeting 13 appointments among 40 apartments in five buildings. I had to abandon the fine points of the checklist but developed a handy acronym that I wrote a lot: "PGC" - poor general cleaning.

It is lunch time, and my clipboard is heavy with little brown envelopes full of keys and a pile of checklists with scrawled notations: "OK" or "PGC." But all appointments have been met, and I proudly stride toward a tent that has been put up on the grass near the manager's office where lunch is available to all of us.

Suddenly, a wild-eyed crew member approaches.

"Where have you been?!! Sharon and Nina and Amy have been looking for you!! You aren't with your crew!"

"How can I be? I had to do check-outs…Am I being too logical? About not being in many places at the same time??"

I keep walking, arriving at the lunch tent. The golf cart is parked nearby. Sharon stands there, glaring with fury.

"ELIZABETH!!" She roars.

Nina scowls. Amy smirks. Fifteen other pairs of eyes peer at me.

Oh god.

"WHERE IS YOUR CREW AND WHAT ARE THEY DOING?!"

"My crew? I – I don't know. I never saw them this morning. I've been checking people out. Nobody introduced us and I didn't have time to chase down people I don't even know..." Faster and faster, deeper and deeper I dig.

Snickers ripple through the crowd. I've stumbled onto a blue collar version of a "Dilbert" cartoon world. Logic is not about to work with Sharon, our equivalent of the comic strip's pointy-haired boss. I shut up.

"Where is your crew?!" Sharon demanded yet again, and then, unthinkable happens. SHE GRABS MY CLIPBOARD. She begins calling out names of MY PEOPLE and barking directions. Am I fired??

You can't fire a warm body when that's basically all that's needed for the job – somebody who shows up. Nothing more was said. The fury subsided. When Sharon wasn't looking, I picked up my clipboard and mustered other remnants of my dignity, including oven cleaner and a toilet brush. I went back to work, finished the job and clocked out, head held high.

Some day, I'll show her. I'll show everybody. I'll return to this place in glory – I'll drive right up to the office and shout taunts – from my really fancy golf cart.

"It's time to do a story on you," my long-time friend Kitty Frieden said to me in a catch-up phone call. She and I worked together as reporters many years ago in Abilene, Texas. She stayed in journalism and now works for the *Houston Chronicle* on the editing side of the profession.

And so a few days later, a reporter named Richard Stewart called me and interviewed me for almost two hours. Oh boy. That will be interesting. Or not. I don't know when the story will appear but knew better than to ask. Those things aren't up to the writer.

The interview was spirited and glib, and I did not tell Mr. Stewart that all is not well. I now have an e-mail from my tenant Lisa, who had just returned to Hurst after a weekend with family and friends in Chicago. The message began breezily, full of admiration and congratulations on my adventures. We haven't talked a lot, but she watches my Web site.

"Here's the tough part," the second paragraph began. "While home, I had a chance to talk with several people about the whole situation down here in Texas. They all, without exception, felt I should leave the area. I explained that I had signed a contract and did not feel right changing until April. But they encouraged me to weigh the painfulness and unhappiness and lack of things falling into place job-wise against the commitment to this incredible living space and Minnie and Bigelow."

The letter went on for two pages.

"Oh Liz! I'm so sorry to disturb your sojourn like this," Lisa concluded. "I'm so sorry not to be strong enough to handle this situation the way I planned to."

The letter was painful to read, but not wholly because of the obvious problem for me. I remembered what it's like to be 25 and to be surprised by situations that I couldn't handle "the way I planned to."

However, I need somebody in the condo and I need the bills to be paid and the little bit of rent money fed into my checking account. I decided to cling to the hope of the sense of responsibility Lisa was showing. She was obviously looking for another tenant, or would probably buy me out if that fails.

Knowing she would be on pins and needles for a response, I wrote back that I was not upset, would think about the dilemma and would appreciate her continued efforts to find a replacement.

I have begun planning and preparing my departure from Iowa. It is August and time for my "vacation." Even in this unusual year, I cannot give up my annual week in New York City with my sister. We always get a suite at the Olcott, one of the city's older hotels on the Upper West Side. From that base we tackle the whole city – shopping on the West Side, theater in Midtown, dining Downtown. An artist, Martha branches off to the museums while I like the sociology of Manhattan and wander the streets looking at the art of humanity.

We usually include a friend, and so I am always reminded of those great old movies about flight attendants and Doris Day or other single "girls" living it up in the city. And New York is one place that lives up to its fabled reputation for delivering fun and glamour. Martha's long-time friend Eilleen, recently retired from school teaching, will join us.

This year, the city offers an extra special attraction. My friend Karen, who moved from Texas to London to New York because of her job, has achieved the Impossible Dream. She landed a beautiful apartment and will show it off with a party. Martha and Eilleen and I have put our invitation at the top of our expectations for a wonderful time.

I have to be in New York in 10 days but have given little thought to the logistics of traveling there from Iowa. I certainly don't want my car there, nor do I want to buy a plane ticket. I decide on Amtrak and identify Pittsburgh, Pa., as a convenient place to leave the Honda. I love a long leisurely train ride, and when I return to Pittsburgh in late August, I can go straight from there to New England for my next bit of settled-down life.

I am excited about New York and on one of Iowa's "tax-free" days, when shoppers don't have to pay the sales tax on some things, I went to the mall downtown to find things to spruce myself up. I bought a purse, shoes and a glittery sleeveless sweater, all in black, the color of Manhattan sophistication.

"It's my last week," I said to Tom at home. "How about a little dinner party? I'd love for you to meet Tom and Carolyn Brown."

I de-emphasized the *Rev.* Brown. Tom Walz levels criticism at organized religion, and Presbyterians are about as organized as you can get.

The Browns treated me to Chinese food last week and I had such a good time, I wanted to see them one more time. Plus, as I've said, I'm really getting into this New York state of mind and I'm feeling the need to scrub the apartment cleaning experience out of my life. It's time for a nice evening of a special meal with good people and intelligent conversation.

I was not disappointed all the way around. From the modest supplies of the cupboards and refrigerator, I fixed pork chops and rice, farm-grown squash and tomatoes, green salad, wine and for dessert, brownies with ice cream. We dined in the kitchen – not at all an unusual setting for company in 1960s Kansas – now it felt old-fashioned but cozy. In the living room later, Tom and Tom talked excitedly about auctions while Carolyn and I ran an easy gamut of subjects as diverse as church history and old boyfriends. Once again, the prospect of leaving a comfortable home for the uncertainty of the road and a minimal plan makes me uneasy. Sometimes I am shaken by a recurring feeling, that I am crazy to break ties and float untethered, as if in outer space, subject to obliteration by flaming asteroids of catastrophic fate.

12 NEW YORK, NEW YORK

It's another departure day. Tom is leaving early for a business trip so I get myself up at 6 to drink coffee with him one more time at the kitchen table, then tackle the onerous chore of packing. (There's *got* to be a way to do that in less than four hours!)

Adrenaline has kicked in to make me excited about hitting the road and driving into brand new territory, and yet another attachment I've formed with my host sticks like a Band-Aid. Again, I choose to simply rip it off all at once, and then think and wonder about my next home, my next "family," friends and employers. What will be written on the blank slate of late summer and fall?

The packing and loading of the Honda is still ridiculously drawn out and tedious, so I attempt once again to weed out things I don't need. I guess I'm not so different from those students in a hurry, but at least I leave the cast-offs with Tom instead of the curb.

Also, there have been a few interruptions, including a call from my sister-in-law with an update on things in Osage County. Sharron gives me the phone number of Mother's new address, the nursing home, but she also says that Mother is not putting up a fuss about being there. That's a relief. If she does, it's a certainty that Daddy will find a way to bring her right back home to the farm.

On the Texas front, Lisa is suddenly optimistic about a new opportunity for working in Dallas. She called to give me an update on her situation and there was a new lift in her voice. The prospect of her immediate bail-out of Hurst appears to be averted. I'm happy for her. And for me too.

My two home fronts seem stable. And with the car loaded and a gas fill-up on the way out of town, I'm feeling free and speedy again. An hour later than planned, I finally leave town, swinging onto I-80 to head east.

Before crossing Iowa's eastern border into Illinois, I detoured into Davenport to make one last stop at a Wells Fargo Bank. I've learned there are no branches of my bank in the East, so I probably need to learn how to use my ATM card. I've got one. Even tried it out with a teller's help in Hurst before embarking on my trip. So I deposited my few hundred dollars in Iowa earnings with a live teller and then stepped up to the automated teller. This is a machine which, I understand, is supposed to poke cash out from a slot when you insert a card and type in a code known only to oneself. Unfortunately, my self couldn't remember my pin number. Various arrangements of my birth date failed to prompt the ATM to disgorge cash.

Back to a live teller, and then a customer service representative, I explained my problem. They tried calling various phone numbers, but apparently the Texas Wells Fargo might as well have been on Mars. The Iowa bankers couldn't communicate with the Texas branch that issued the card. Finally they suggested, in that friendly, smiling customer-service kinda way, to go away and solve the problem myself. I'm supposed to go back to Texas for a replacement card. So much for me and technology and the 21st century way of life.

From Davenport I continued east, stopping for nothing but gas. Illinois and Indiana were notable chiefly for their unending miles of highway construction. With every blink of the eye there was an orange and white traffic barrel, and speed-reducing "work zones" warned of bigger fines to pay if I exceeded the speed limit, an impossible fete with the weekday truck traffic.

Calling Dr. Laura. The very best way to make the miles melt away is to join the closest AM radio broadcast of Dr. Laura Schlessinger and her daily dole of advice to assorted callers: pregnant girlfriends, clueless boyfriends, sluts, tomcats and deadbeat dads, cheating wives, philandering husbands and other hapless souls who will burn in hell if they don't bow to her tough-love pronouncements (invariably, sex and babies seem to be at the root of most of the problems). One minute I'm agreeing with the doctor, feeling a satisfying *oomph* with every measured pronouncement – "Hit 'er again, Dr. Laura!" I'll think – and then sometimes the berating just goes on and on and I'll think, "Of all the lofty, judgmental, self-preening load of crap she's dumping on that poor girl..." although, of course I realize that *that* poor girl called Dr. Laura and should know what she's getting herself into.

Anyway, the Dr. Laura show gets me all worked up and involved in something beyond drab countryside and the orange traffic barrels. But too soon, even the powerful Dr. Laura is overcome by a rising tide of static and I give it up, switching the function of my old car radio to the cassette tape deck and an Agatha Christie novel.

On the edge of evening I arrive in Indianapolis and decide to walk around downtown for a while and find a bite to eat. It's a jumpin' place. There seem to be at least two major events under way, something at the convention center and an athletic extravaganza at an arena. I admire a city like this with its ability to draw pedestrian life after 5 o'clock. It's a wonderful break for me just to walk among the jostling crowds, but my other objective, to have dinner, turns confusing and I settle on a mere food court and a slice of pizza.

It is getting dark but I feel like putting away some more miles. I am now on I-70 driving fast. The construction is behind me, so I'm hoping the road will be open and easy and if my mind can work up some kind of absorbing topic of thought, many more miles will simply fall away.

Instead, my mind admonishes me in a Dr. Laura-type scold: *Liz, you promised not to drive after dark. It is a smart promise and you are being stupid.*

Where did all this truck traffic come from? All around me – ahead, behind and passing – are 18-wheelers, all very determined and far more aggressive than I in my wimpy little Honda. We are definitely out of place, but I try to keep up anyway, refusing to be intimidated. It's my highway too.

It is very dark now, and driving has become a battle. I've ignored my problem of poor night vision and now I'm stuck. I can't see anything, just taillights and headlights and my dimly-lit dashboard. I want to watch for billboards that promise a motel – "Next Exit!" – but I can't see signs. I'm out of control on a tiny raft at the mercy of a river current speeding me ever faster toward the falls.

And then it gets worse. The barrels are back. And worse. Four interstate lanes have been squeezed to two, with a concrete divider separating east- and westbound traffic by mere inches. The trucks hurtle along unfazed. A phobia about barriers kicks in. When they run alongside a highway, I am usually able to move to another lane. Otherwise, I think about the smallest turn of my wheel, of striking the wall and flipping over in a horrific accident. Here, that would be the only option in a slight turn of the wheel left. There is no shoulder and so no place to go.

My terror grows with a truck behind me and oncoming traffic of blinding glare. *Breathe. Think of something ordinary. Think of bitchy Dr. Laura's radio program.*

EXIT!

Suddenly the raft ride is over and I am in Richmond, Ind. It's as if the car literally flew off the highway, soaring into an aerial dive and landing gently in this town that even in the dark is especially beautiful to me. Furthermore, God's grace and luck deliver a pleasant Best Western that's only $33. With continental breakfast.

The next day I learn that I'm only 3 miles from Ohio, a pretty state that greets me with a lovely, highway-spanning archway. I have calmed down from the ordeal of last night; plus, yesterday carried the bulk of the miles needed to get me to Pittsburgh.

"Remember me?" I'd written in an email to old Arc colleagues at the Pittsburgh chapter. "I'm wondering if I might leave my car in your parking lot while I'm in New York City for the week."

The neighborhood isn't the best, they responded, but as long as you understand that, we don't mind if you leave your car in our lot.

I crossed Ohio swiftly, clipped a corner of West Virginia at Wheeling, and entered Pennsylvania, 20th state of my journey. I actually have an ancestral connection to Pennsylvania and I thought about my late grandfather when I saw Washington, Pa., which was his hometown. Leon H. Blaney settled in Independence, Kan., but his ancestors were from Ireland and so I always thought of him as an Irishman, tiny and dapperly-dressed, never without a tie. He lived to be 88 but I was only 19 when I lost him. Mother once told me that he had been a theater usher in Pennsylvania as a young man and really wanted to be an actor.

"But that wasn't a respectable occupation at that time and his family wouldn't allow it," she said. *Ah, I wanted to be an actress, and my sister is the well-dressed one...the genetic code...*

Dang it. MORE CONSTRUCTION. It spoils the otherwise-grand entrance into Pittsburgh, whose natural beauty lies in sweeping hills and the snaking presence of three great rivers, the Allegheny, Monongahela and the Ohio. I suppose it will not only look good again one day, but be a dream of navigation.

Now, how to find The Arc of Allegheny County? I've been to the office one time, maybe six years ago. Let's see if I can do it without a map.

Incredibly, I drive right to it. Just make my way through the maze of broken, traffic-choked highways, manage to stay on the right side of the river, and I spy Station Square. I had dinner there on my long-ago first-time visit. The office is mere blocks away at 711 Bingham St.

"Hi, Judy!" Melinda Spriggs says as she greets me at the front door. It's a joke that indicates she's read my Web site. Melinda is young and blonde and big-eyed. I always liked her as a colleague even though our communications were primarily by phone. She was always sharp and appreciative of anything I could do for her out of The Arc's National Headquarters.

"How about the grand tour?!" she offers.

It's strange at this hour, having one foot back in my old life again, hearing about the chapter's programs, seeing the facilities, and trading professional observations about the PR work of association life. Except this time that's all there is to it. It's just a tour, and I don't have to do anything with the information.

With Melinda's work day at an end, we walk out together and she shows me where to park the Honda for its week at rest while I go to New York on the train.

Having not scouted out a place to stay in Pittsburgh, I headed out to find a hotel after first finding the train station and picking up my tickets. I knew the downtown hotels would be pricey, so I chose the suburbs. My only other criteria for lodging besides cheap was that the road TO the suburb and its hotel had to be clear. I actually found such a highway, even at rush hour, and with a "So long, suckers!" at the inbound traffic jam on the other side, I sped out.

Not so fast. Suddenly, there they were again: taillights. Again I was caught in my own predilection for not looking at maps and thinking things through sometimes. I dove straight into the kind of traffic I wanted to avoid. With hundreds of other "suckers," I am creeping mere feet, then stopping, moving six inches, stopping again. Of course, there is no exit.

Eventually, the inches and the feet are strung together to make 13 miles and I find Monroeville and a Days Inn. The Grill Room next door is handy and good and I'm able to unwind over chicken wings and a Rolling Rock.

Tonight I organized my stuff, separating the New York travel gear and organizing the rest to hide in my trunk. The Arc's lousy part of town means that I might as well COUNT on having my car broken into, so for this week's little side trip, I have to lug my most valuable possession, the computer. Before going to bed, I also set two alarm clocks for 5 a.m. If I have to deal with a repeat of today's traffic frustrations, I want to get an early start back to downtown Pittsburgh.

Having finally thought things through, the next day flowed easily with a 6 a.m. checkout and 6:30 arrival in my assigned place in The Arc's parking lot. This gave me an hour to find a nearby convenience store to pick up food to carry me through the 10-hour train ride.

It's a hard, gritty street with both current and historic signs of industry all around me. I join blue-collar workers arriving at the little store as they begin their day. As important as the coffee and doughnut is the banter with the store clerks. The greetings and joking are loud and rough and funny. It was at that point that I was struck and thrilled by the thought, I am in the East! I love its energy and scrappy pace and I'm about to be in the very heart it, New York, New York!

Melinda has given me a ride to the ornate pink colossus that contains Amtrak. Already, the "Three Rivers" Train No. 40 is an hour and 20 minutes late on its journey from Chicago. I flee the dingy waiting room, skip in and out of an oven-hot 24-hour restaurant across the street, and wind up at a bagel bar in a glitzy office building down the street. There I sit and subject every passing office worker to my mental game called "Fashion Arrest." The men generally look alike, of course, but I scrutinize every woman for suits that are ill-fitting, cheap or otherwise unflattering. There are two things wrong with that game, of course. One, I would be the first to go to jail if the game were turned against me. Two, all suits look like strait jackets to me anyway. Plus, it would be cruel to send these drones to jail; they're already imprisoned, marching resolutely in and out with their lattes and little paper sacks.

I'm going to New York and you're not!

I loved the long train ride, even with all its problems. My section had no window. The girl next to me was large, slumped and sprawling, pushing the acceptable limits of seatmate boundaries. A young mother across the aisle struggled with her fussy 2-year-old almost all the way to Philadelphia. I didn't get to see the quaint charms of Lancaster County (but I did observe a young Amish couple who boarded the train, draped themselves with a blanket and giggled a lot).

Just gliding on rails is enough for me. It is soothing and mesmerizing and constant. *"What do you want for your 6th birthday, Liz?" "A train ride to Kansas City, Mommy!" I also get your whole, undivided attention.*

Every once in a great while, one encounters somebody who is perfect for his job. Mark was our train's attendant, trim, nattily dressed and efficient, with the panache of a cruise ship director. The train mostly emptied out at Philadelphia, so Mark perched on the arm rest across the aisle and told me the joys of his work — well, cleaning the toilets ain't so great — but that's OK, he said; it's worth the negatives to meet people and take care of them. Mark also shared a glimpse of his personal life. His story of a paranoid former girlfriend WHO NEVER PARTED WITH A SINGLE BIT OF TRASH was astounding and put me in stitches.

My very first trip to New York was in 1984. Influenced by books, movies and music created out of the romance of the city, a visit was a long-time dream finally realized on a March weekend. I was actually in Washington, D.C., on a business trip, but added 36 hours at the beginning to run up to the Big Apple for a peek.

That trip was also by train. My first disappointment was that there was no "approach." The train rolls through an increasingly dense urban landscape, but no skyline emerges into view. As the train nears Manhattan, it dives underground and travels through blank darkness into the bowels of a nondescript Penn Station.

My next disappointment was not feeling excitement, just bewilderment, at emerging on the street. The city has many entrepreneurs because of wide-eyed tourists like me, and a gypsy cab driver seized the day and $5 by sidling up and talking me into a ride to The Warwick Hotel a few blocks away. He rounded up other unsuspecting passengers as well and each of them paid $5 for a similarly short ride.

So this time — perhaps 70 NYC trips later — I knew to step smartly over to the taxi stand and wait in the short line for an official Yellow Cab. And once I was buckled into the back seat of the car, I immediately plugged in to the buzz of the city and allowed myself to feel everything through the fast breeze of the partially lowered window. It was 10 p.m. and a Friday night in Manhattan was in full swing: crowds flowing in and out of restaurants and theaters, sidewalk cafés brimming with convivial people, pedestrians hurrying across intersection crosswalks. It's a rush; a weekend has arrived.

At Karen's apartment building on 19th Street, I pay the driver and present myself to the doorman.

"You're Miss Moore?" he asks. "You're to meet them at the restaurant at 19th and 3rd Ave – you know where you're going?"

Depositing my suitcase and computer with the doorman, I raced down the block to find Karen with her friend, a former coworker from Dallas, at a sidewalk table.

"Liz, this is Bob," Karen says – although Bob and I, each being close to Karen, feel we've known each other forever. I join them with an order of pasta and a glass of wine. None of us "old Texans" can contain our excitement.

"Can you believe it? We are in NEW YORK CITY – and you LIVE here, Karen!" Our conversation is a pinball machine of stories and quips, plans and ideas. They ask about my trip. Bob and I ask about Karen's new life here. Karen and I grill Bob on his plans for retirement. He too wants to move here. Or maybe Florida. All three of us are 50 and finally living out our dreams from a rich array of choices.

"When will Martha and Eilleen arrive?" Karen asks.

"Tomorrow afternoon. So I'll move up to the hotel then. How can I help you get ready for the party?"

"There's really nothing to do!" Karen insists.

For an apartment unveiling and her 50th birthday, she is having a party tomorrow, splurging on music, wine and catering. Sweet. If we were still in Fort Worth and this were my party, I'd be scrambling to get my place cleaned up, hurrying over to Sam's Club Warehouse to pick out some plastic-encased party foods, and sorting through my CD collection for the background music.

"I just need to go pick up some flowers and get my nails done," she said.

At midnight we walk back to her building, rise 19 stories to her floor, and enter the now-fabled rent-stabilized space, which took six months of diligent perusal of *Times* ads and a lot of traipsing around to find. It is just as I imagined, serene and pastel like a Monet painting. The piano in her entryway is where the Julliard-schooled musician will play. Crates of wine rest in her small bright kitchen and her formal dining table bears crystal and serving dishes. The rooms still smell of fresh paint from the remodeling.

"And here it is," Karen declares, waving Bob and me over to a door on the other side of the living room.

It is the terrace, a space generous enough for a wicker settee, table and chair. But it is the view, of course, that is the awesome, jaw-dropping feature.

It sweeps from the silvery cascade of light atop the Chrysler building in the north to the Con Ed building in the south. Late on a summer night – the wee hours of the morning really – it is the perfect place for three happy friends to revel in the wonderfulness of life.

Karen and I slept in her bedroom and Bob took the sleeper sofa in the living room, so he was the first to get up on the morning of the party and make coffee. He also took up hammer and nails to finish hanging a few pictures and otherwise was being dearly helpful. In an unexpected twinge of homesick recognition, I thought of my Hurst friends Carolyn and Vernon – he is our fix-it person in the same generous way, taking on everything from picture hanging to leaky faucets to cat funerals.

Another friend arrived this morning, nicknamed "the Drama Queen" by Bob, so I was expecting Ru Paul to sweep into the apartment in sequins and taffeta. Instead, an ordinary chap named Richard arrived from Chicago where he has been engaged in a bowling tournament.

It's time to swing into some serious action and the four of us left the apartment and walked briskly the few blocks to the farmers' market in Union Square. Crowds milled around the booths of flowers, fresh produce and jars of sweet, sour and salty things. Except for the ring of tall buildings and nearby subway entrances, the scene was agricultural, and we browsed through both the familiar and the exotic, like purple carrots and a varietal riot of peppers. We finally selected the flowers for several graceful arrangements and Karen ran off to her nail appointment.

Bob and Richard and I went shopping for birthday presents, then settled on a Third Avenue restaurant for lunch.

"I want to dye my hair," I announced, surprising even myself. It's not that I've never done it; it's just rare. The natural auburn continues to hold up against any gray, so there hasn't been much point in going to either the expense of an appointment or the mess of do-it-yourself.

"There's a Rite Aid across the street," Bob said.

"Then you guys need to help me pick out something outrageous."

At the drug store it's a good thing we couldn't find blue because I swear that's what I was in the mood for. Instead, we all voted on the color "Moroccan Spice."

I packed up my things and left Karen's, then toted my two bags onto a Third Avenue bus. Uptown at 72nd Street, I switched to a cross-town bus that rumbled from the east side west through the great leafy Central Park and half a block more to the Olcott. In addition to its proximity to the park, the hotel's location has the distinction of being three doors down from The Dakota, one of the grandest apartment buildings in the city, where "Rosemary's Baby" was filmed and John Lennon was shot.

I love this neighborhood, where everyone from hotel staff to neighborhood bartenders to apartment house residents – and their dogs – are familiar faces, constant and unchanging year after year. However, they may not speak to each other. One night, a couple of August trips ago, a manhole cover exploded, creating such a noise that people gathered on the street to investigate. It turned into something of a block party and I heard more than one person exclaim how nice it was to actually talk to neighbors.

Even The Sentry is around this year. He is a homeless man, another long-time West Side regular, whose occupation is to stand silently and watch the street and passers-by. I don't believe I've ever seen him ask for money. However, there are days when The Sentry becomes completely different, possessed by demons or drugs or both and the sidewalk is his stage for a shouting, incoherent, body-jerking rant.

I was two hours ahead of Martha and Eilleen, so I got to put our suite on my credit card. I nearly choked over the four-digit amount – it's been a long time since I've had to deal with that kind of number – but at the same time, I quietly resolved not to complain about being impoverished.

And unemployed, and road-worn. I suddenly felt the shabby side of my state of affairs when Martha and Eilleen swept in from Texas – it was a jolt to realize that they had arrived from, and would return to, their lovely Fort Worth homes. I have no home and no plans beyond 10:45 p.m. one week from tonight when Amtrak deposits me back in Pittsburgh.

It does not help that my sister, a tiny, svelte clothes horse, looks more chic than ever. Hey, other than that, it's great to see her! Truly. Where's that damn box of Moroccan Spice.

We all hurried to prepare for the party and when I was finished with myself, the dye, face paint, nail polish and black clothes made me feel presentable. The three of us left the hotel and walked the half block to the C train of the 72nd Street subway station, which seems almost attached to The Dakota. There's quite a contrast of worlds in descending down steps into a dark, roaring tunnel, leaving the park views and the grand, filigreed fortress that towers above.

At Karen's building we enter the elevator with a stately-looking couple with good posture also going to the 20th floor. We all barely acknowledge each other, although it occurs to me they, too, are likely from Texas but here we are, donning Manhattan affectations with our finery. You just don't speak or make eye contact in elevators. Sure enough, they join the party.

Looking 35 instead of 50, elegant in chartreuse, Karen answers the door. The room is filling with friends from Texas, New York, London and Washington, D.C., all meeting and talking easily while the pianist plays and a waiter named Kevin moves around with a tray of drinks. After a hundred, mostly work-related functions of cubed cheese and crackers, the buffet is a culinary work of art to me, with prosciutto, asparagus, salmon, strawberries dipped in chocolate, and other delicacies.

I want to sit with Martha and Eilleen and catch up on things, but realizing we have a week to do that, I've told my introverted self to step aside and let the party girl out. Talking to strangers at parties definitely feels like an athletic event to me, involving the flexing of lightly-used social muscles. Some guests are interested in my trek and they warm up to my question, "Where should I go next?" Their suggestions: "Marblehead, Massachusetts..." "Montpelier, Vermont...." "Cooperstown, New York..." But all of the options, which should sound exciting, are making me nervous about the decision looming ahead.

Many of us want to be on that glorious terrace even though it is raining. The terrace of the apartment above Karen's provides some protection and anyway, the rain is soft and fine, muting both the thousands of lights around us and the city's sounds below. Taking a break from the strenuous social action, I stake out a corner of the terrace and laugh with Bob, whose friendship now feels as old and comfortable as Karen's.

Meanwhile, Kevin is making sure no one's glass is empty. Fortunately, I've caught on to that and seem to be doing a fairly good job of keeping the same splash of Chardonnay in my glass.

My sister, on the other hand…

"Where's Kevin?"

Martha, still sitting next to Eilleen on the couch, is holding her empty glass aloft.

What a party! The wine flows. The music rocks. The affectations are long gone. We're all Texans now.

But well-behaved, and at midnight the party is breaking up. A quick conference with Eilleen and Martha confirm they're ready to find a cab and return to the hotel. With thanks to the birthday girl, the three of us go into the bedroom to pick up our purses.

Suddenly, there are only two of us standing there. Martha is on the floor. I didn't see it or hear it – first she was there, and now she's not. Eilleen and I look at each other, stunned into inaction a few moments. Then Eilleen reaches to pull my sister to her feet since she doesn't seem to have much of an idea about how to make herself vertical again.

I'm alarmed, and Eilleen says aloud what we're both thinking: "I've never seen her this way."

Martha is smashed.

It occurs to me that she is emerging from a difficult summer, notwithstanding the purchase of a new Mercedes Benz. I wasn't around to help, or even to sympathize, when she suffered a fracture in her foot and then had to hobble around in a cast for weeks. So it might be argued that it's probably the weak foot that contributed to the fall.

Except that the falling happened at least two more times before we got her back to the hotel, once right there in the gutter, the *gutter*, *Martha*, in front of the Olcott. I will say this for her, she's a graceful drunk.

The next morning, Eilleen and I had to leave the lump in the bed to get started on the day with our usual favorite breakfast routine of the Upper West Side. We walked the long block to Broadway and around the corner to Utopia, a lively, old-fashioned diner. It's a great place to plunge into the New York action, a boisterous convergence of characters and hot-shots, the waiters' shouts of greeting in foreign accents ("Sit anywhere – anywhere OK"), clattering plates, aromas of coffee and bacon and the vaguely theatrical entrances and exits of patrons. In fact, Utopia's cast never seems to change – I've seen the same employees and customers year after year.

Our favorite waiter is Angelo and he is working today: "Hello! Welcome back!" he says to us. "Coffee-two-coffees," he not-so-much asks as confirms, stringing three words into one.

After breakfast, Eilleen and I stop to pick up the Alka-Seltzer Martha has requested, then return to the hotel. As quietly as possible, we let ourselves in, trying not to step too heavily on the hardwood floors as we ease into the bedroom where she is now awake but not *up*.

"How are you, Marth?" Eilleen asks gently. "We brought your Alka Seltzer."

"Are you feeling better?" I ask, determined not to make fun of the situation. It could just as easily have been me whom Kevin took advantage of.

It's hard to look heavy at a hundred pounds, but she did, moving ever so slowly to try to sit up. Meanwhile, the day is feeling half-over to me and I'm starting to wonder what we're going to be able to do with the rest of it. And is my sister "in" or out?

Still speaking softly Eilleen said, "Liz and I think we might try to find Orchard Street."

Eilleen has read about this downtown district, where Jewish immigrants started the New York garment industry and sold goods from pushcarts. Now the stores are closed on Saturdays, the Jewish Sabbath, but on Sundays there is an outdoor market. Today is Sunday.

"SHOPPING??!" Martha has practically bolted upright. "Well YES I'll go!"

She's definitely alive. And fair game.

"And is there anything else we can do for The Princess first?" I sneered.

"'The Princess,'" she repeated. "Yes. I like that."

Martha was back.

We did a lot of shopping that week in New York, or at least, my roomies did. One day they spent three hours at Eileen Fisher's alone, where a sale created a *line* outside the store as women waited for their chance just to get in and pick through the racks of black, purple and orange wrinkled linen. Management even converted floor space into a large curtained dressing room so that more women could try things on. Me? I spent 5 minutes in the store, then heroically gave up my spot to a needy, deserving shopper. I went out on the streets of Soho, buzzing in and out of Rizzoli's and other non-clothing related establishments and eventually excused myself to head back uptown on the C train.

The rest of the week my path continued to diverge from theirs at stores and museums. The three paths converged again at Utopian breakfasts, a Broadway performance of "Chicago," a tour of Lincoln Center, restaurants of every ethnic persuasion, and Café des Artistes where one night we spent a hundred dollars on drinks and appetizers.

We could be frugal as well, not that funds determined everything we did. One day we went to Woodlawn Cemetery to find the grave of one of Eilleen's ancestors. Woodlawn may be in The Bronx, not far from blocks of urban danger and hardship, but its "inhabitants" include famous people who took their wealth with them in the form of ornate stone monuments of pillars and curlicues, angels, crosses, stars and lambs marking their graves. Their names are immortal: F. W. Woolworth, Roland Macy, Herman Melville.... We found Eilleen's family member in the Juniper section with the help of two security guards who were retired NYPD cops. In the quiet, still world of their assignment, the guards seemed happy to have the company.

We ended our week in festive fashion atop the Peninsula Hotel on Friday night. Late summer had the feel of fall as we ventured outside the enclosed part of the rooftop bar. The air was chilly and slightly damp, so we scooted back inside to sit next to a window and gaze down on the gold and platinum of Fifth Avenue facades. We *owned* the city at that point, and so we used our regal positions – we had The Princess with us after all – to sip $16 cocktails and toast the future of trips back to New York.

In mere hours, the metaphor of my coach turning into a pumpkin again would be a rude, hard bump back to reality.

13 NEW ENGLAND

It is 11 p.m. and the August night is blacker than black as I exit the Amtrak train in Pittsburgh. All around me, my fellow passengers are striding purposefully toward the terminal and their parked cars or to a taxi or into the waiting arms of loved ones. Rolling my suitcase behind me, I stare downward, seeing only the hard glints of quartz that flash from the concrete. I am very lonely and a little afraid.

The forces of frugality have won my mind's battle against safety and comfort, and I have decided to spend the night in my car. I want to get an early-morning start on my northward drive toward New England and so there is no way I am going to fork over funds for a hotel.

A taxi takes me across the river to Bingham Street and The Arc's parking lot. To my great relief, the Honda is in its place untouched.

"Can you please wait a moment," I ask the cab driver. "Make sure I can get in and drive away?" He complies and I start up my car just fine and head out of the parking lot.

It seemed like an easy thing to do – find a nice, quiet residential street where I might park at the curb between two houses. The Honda shouldn't draw any special attention; rather, it could be somebody's spare car or that of a neighbor's overnight guest. I want to draw NO attention whatsoever, because stretched across the back seat and through untinted windows, I will be caught in a policeman's flashlight beam or the glance of anybody walking by.

The other challenge is the bedtime routine. I did have the foresight to wear glasses instead of contact lenses today, so there's no messing with a sink and contact lens solution, and I'm wearing no makeup to remove. I also remembered not to drink anything, so I won't need to pee during the night.

All I have to do is brush my teeth and go to the bathroom one more time before retiring.

But try to find a place to do those things at midnight in a strange city. With the search for the right parking spot, the time it's taking to "go to bed" in Pittsburgh is going on two hours.

"Where is the ladies' room," I inquire of the convenience store clerk, paying for a bottle of water.

"Restrooms are closed after 10," he replies. "Sorry."

All around me, creatures of the night, including hard-looking adolescents, drift in and out. I guess the all-night stores are battening down the hatches, but what about decent people who have to be out and about at night? What are we supposed to do?

Eventually, I find another gas station and ask the sullen clerk about a restroom.

"Over there." She points toward a sign in a short hallway.

Inside I nearly gag. The floor is flooded and I smell urine and cigarettes. Gobs of paper toweling and toilet paper are disintegrating in patches of mush on the wet floor. There is no dry TP, nor towels, and certainly not soap. I have soap in my purse at least, and I hurry through essential tasks.

Outdoors again, I inhale the summer air deeply.

Circling close to Pittsburgh's downtown so that I can minimize the potential for getting lost tomorrow morning, I find some pleasant enough neighborhoods, but there is always some kind of problem to discourage a camp-out. Housing is too dense, or there are too many cars on the street, or the area is too upscale and there's little street parking, especially for old Hondas.

Shortly after 1 a.m., I find my spot on a quiet, traffic-free street. I'm parked next to a high wooden fence that walls a backyard, and the two houses across the street are middle-class-nice, with small interior lights on but no humans in sight. I stand next to my car to brush my teeth with the bottled water.

It was an awful night, of course. A street light tortured me, splashing its way into my glass room and prying at my tightly shut eyelids. For warmth, not wanting to dig around in the trunk for my quilt, I used an old sweater, but in the night I had to add a layer consisting of a bath towel and then the flannel-backed tablecloth. Seat belt buckles gouged me in the back – and in the legs, stomach and hip when I tried to get comfortable. Deep sleep was impossible, so I simply lay still and kept my thoughts quiet.

I opened my eyes to a lightening of the sky. Thank you, God; I made it! I disentangled myself from my "bed covers," climbed back into the front seat, and drove to the Amtrak station to wash up and get my bearings.

Now what? And where? Sitting in the station's waiting room, I opened the Atlas, and scoured the maps of Pennsylvania and New York. I settled on Jamestown, N.Y., as a tentative destination.

The wretchedness of the night gave way to a beautiful day and a scenery-rich stretch of driving. I left Interstate 79 and stopped for breakfast in Grove City, then followed the Allegheny River on Hwy. 62 through the picturesque towns of Franklin and Oil City. At 10:30 a.m. I stopped in the town of Tionesta near the Allegheny National Forest.

Still full of gratitude and relief, I was drawn by the sight of an old Presbyterian church with a service scheduled at 11. I've never attended church in running shoes, and I felt scuzzy from the ordeal of last night, but I also felt like saying thanks. A friendly church member named Rachel sat next to me, and I felt reconnected with both my spiritual life and the human race.

Back in the car, I continued the lovely, winding path north. Jamestown was a lot closer than I thought, so I decided to press on to Olean where, for some reason, hotels and motels are scarce. They're not obvious anyway, so I had to settle on a Hampton Inn.

I love that chain, but it's a little pricey for my budget. Just for tonight, that's OK. The comparative luxury is heaven. The hotel feels new and immaculate and there's a laundry room. I am definitely in the mood for clean and I throw myself into an orgy of soap and water, laundering my clothes, lathering my hair, and soaking in a bubble bath. In crisp sheets on a king-size bed, my body rests and stretches out kinks and cramps and forgets the indignities of the night before.

The next morning the breakfast buffet in the lobby is generous. I confess I snagged some extra food for later in the day. I've not been maintaining my financial records as scrupulously as I did at the beginning of this trip, but I'm feeling impoverished from the New York binge and now this costly night's lodging. In addition, my car insurance is due and I'll mail the check to Fort Worth today.

Speaking of my car, the Honda has never performed so well as on these long days' drives. It zips along the freeways and maneuvers the back roads and I've not had a moment's concern about its mechanical soundness. Looking back at its predictable suburban life in Fort Worth, I think the Honda got bored, or vexed at me, and it would present some whiney little problem every few months that I had to get fixed. Now it seems to know I need it to be faithful and responsible, and perhaps this is the trip it has always wanted, like a thoroughbred horse needing to get out of the stable and onto the racetrack.

The day's drive continued my stop-and-go pattern of decision-making. I'd drive a hundred miles, stop, walk around some little town, look at my Atlas, then go again.

At Corning, N.Y., signs for the Corning Glass Museum popped up as the latest excuse not to pick a destination and get myself there. I allowed myself to turn strictly tourist, plunking down $11 to watch a video and tour the large and lavish building that is made mostly of – guess what – glass! It looks like a pleasant airport terminal.

The video, shown in a small, dark theater, was riveting. Images of fire were matched to a soundtrack of opera, and at the end, instead of the usual roll of credits, the movie screen disappeared and the wall seemed to fall away to reveal – why, GLASS, of course – the world of the museum itself with its windows and walkways and all the tourists milling in and out of the exhibits and the gift shop and the glass-making demonstrations.

What a refreshing stop!

I finally ended my day in Troy, N.Y., the very threshold of New England. I settled into a cramped Super 8, opened a beer, and worked on my Web site at a tiny desk squeezed into the corner of my room. I wrote about my New York City "vacation from a vacation," which sounds ridiculous, but this year-long break is feeling like WORK. There's the driving and the writing, finding homes and jobs, working in homes and jobs, keeping an eye on things in Texas and Kansas and managing my finances. I also contend with hot flashes and sleeplessness, and I've GOT to do something about health insurance. I'm developing a list of regrets of sights unseen – I just breezed past New York's Finger Lakes region without seeing a single lake.

Oh well, the trip can't be perfect. Nor is that my objective.

The next morning I picked up a doughnut and a cup of coffee in the lobby and returned to my room to, once again, stare at my Atlas. OK, let's do this through a process of elimination this time.

Massachusetts: Too populous.

Connecticut: Ditto.

Maine: Coastline. Like Oregon. Been there.

New Hampshire: Hmm. Friends raved about their vacation there a few years ago.

Vermont: Hmmmm…

Obviously, there was one last way to decide: Who has the more appealing license plate motto?

New Hampshire's is "Live Free or Die." Vermont is "The Green Mountain State."

WHOA, New Hampshire! Taking yourselves a little seriously aren't you?! I'm not sure I can live up to that declaration if I become a resident. Besides, the Green Mountain State is closer to Troy and if I am somehow deceived, and the mountains aren't really green, I can keep driving on over to New Hampshire and then just do my best to "live free," or else DIE.

As I checked out, I asked the desk clerk if she knew anything about Vermont.

"Oh yes! I lived there," she said.

"Where, and did you like it?"

"I loved Rutland," she said with a big smile and a dreamy look.

Rutland it is.

The first sight that announced "New England!" was a stately old church in Bennington, Vt. I rounded a corner and there it was, its spire soaring high above trees poised to receive the colors of autumn. The centuries-old step back in time is unblemished by billboards, which aren't allowed in this state.

I was tempted to stop in Bennington, but decided to stick to Rutland which was 55 miles farther north on Hwy. 7. Soon I was playing hide-and-seek with "New England," with pretty scenes coming and going – and then obliterated by maddening highway construction complete with flagmen and lead cars to escort one lane of traffic at a time.

I arrived in Rutland around 3 p.m. A dreary, nondescript string of strip shopping centers, fast-food restaurants and automobile shops introduces the city, but I pressed on into the heart of town and New England reappeared. I nit-pick, but no town is perfect. I can't have "peaceful" AND variety, "small" AND an AOL access number.

My first stop is the Rutland Herald. The newspaper's classified ads list a number of apartments, a good sign.

But as I start looking and calling around, the housing possibilities evaporate. No one wants to rent to somebody for a couple of months. Real estate offices douse my hopes as well.

It is a warm day, but not warm enough to make me sweat. Creeping panic does that. OK, think. Somebody somewhere, who maybe doesn't normally "rent out," can be convinced to give me a room. I find a pleasant neighborhood – and a woman mowing her yard.

"HELLO!" I shout, succeeding in getting her to cut off the lawn mower. "Do you know of anyone in this neighborhood who might rent space to me for a couple of months?"

"Try Killington," she said. "It's nice up there!"

I know Killington is a ski resort and I'm surprised to learn that it's so close. Back in my car to head the 8 miles east, I come up with another idea: Maybe one of the small, neat motels I'm seeing on the outskirts of Rutland will give me a good weekly rate.

At the Pine Tree Lodge Motel, fresh blue paint and a profusion of flowers told me the property is loved and cared for. A string of guest rooms facing the highway is anchored by a two-story house having a porch and old-fashioned swing and the motel's lobby for checking in. I step inside and see no one, but there's a buzzer to press.

An Asian man hurries out from his living quarters. As the owner of Pine Tree Lodge, he radiates energy and a beaming smile of welcome, but his response to my inquiry deflates me.

"Oh!" he exclaimed. "You are coming close to 'fall foliage' and a lot of people. I could give you a room now, but I would have to raise the rate or ask you to leave in two week. I am sorry...I wish I could help you..."

I wish he could help me, too.

"This very busy time of year," he continues rapidly. "Very busy. I could give you room now, but that would not be fair to you if I do not tell you that you will have to leave; I cannot do that."

His name is Net Satayavinit and he seems truly sorry. What was I thinking, that I could simply show up in the last week of August, right on the verge of Vermont's peak tourism season, and find lodging on my shoestring budget.

"Fall foliage bring a lot of people. I charge you a rate now, but rate always go up...not fair to you..."

I realize that Net is talking in circles, presumably as apology. But no, I realize, he is trying hard to think of a way to help me. Suddenly, he stops talking, takes a short sharp breath, and touches a finger to his lips.

"Wait," he said. "My wife have a friend... She have a house and a room – sometime we send people over there when we have no room. I talk to her tonight. Come back and we all have tea."

I checked into the Pine Tree Lodge, warmed by the help and hospitality and the glimmer of hope that my next home might be at hand. I celebrated with dinner across the street at the Pizza Hut. Tea later on did not work out because Net's wife, a hospital nurse, came home from work tired I suspect. That was OK with me. I was tired, too, and just wanted to watch cable TV in my room.

The next morning, hope and optimism catapulted me up and out for a run of a few miles on the residential streets of Rutland. As I reached the motel again, Net was getting ready to leave, hoisting a set of golf clubs at the waiting door of an SUV containing three buddies.

"I talk to my wife," he said. "Said you are a nice lady. Her friend Sue a nice lady, too. Lost her husband last year. Thelma talk to her."

Later, after a shower and getting dressed for the day, I walk over to the office to meet Thelma Satayavinit. Like Net, she is friendly and helpful and she speaks with an exotic accent, too – not from Thailand, but Long Island, New York. As we talk, the couple's cat comes charging into the room. Mischief is a black, 30-pound Maine Coon who, after making her assertive entrance, walks back and forth against my legs, then rolls over to have her considerable tummy scratched. It's just one more thing to signal that Rutland might be home.

I like Net. I like Thelma.

And now I like Sue. She arrived at the Pine Tree Lodge on my second morning, stepping out of a white Volvo. She is 49, cute and petite, with short, wavy brown hair and wide, blue, intelligent eyes. Sue is also a registered nurse, working with Thelma in the hospital's rehabilitation unit.

Incredibly, Sue shows none of the effects of personal tragedies that hit her life this very week. Thelma told me that Sue's twin brother in Florida died, but she is not able to travel there for the funeral. In addition, her dog, sick from cancer, had to be euthanized. All of this is layered onto her year-long grief as a widow.

Yet there she sits over tea with Thelma and me, head up, eyes clear, conversation relaxed and cheerful. She seems to be about friends over self.

"My house is actually a little ways outside of town, but it sits on a quiet road next to a farm with sheep," she said. "I have a son who is in high school. We have a fireplace, cable TV, and you're welcome to use the kitchen."

Perhaps I can be of comfort and support to Sue. It's another encounter that's meant to be.

I write her a check for the few hundred in rent and a share of the utilities.

Everything is working out, lining up perfectly.

Except for a phone call. From Texas. My tenant Lisa is the leading candidate for a job in New Jersey. It is clear that she desperately wants to go. I don't feel like standing in her way. I've seen the collapse of her Dallas opportunity and her valiant effort to stay in the condo and make things work, but if we can find a good replacement, why not.

"It's OK," I say to Lisa. "I'll make some calls. We'll work it out."

14 NEW HOME, NEW FRIENDS

I moved into Sue's house on a Friday. It is a brown ranch-style three-bedroom, with a great stone fireplace and hearth and a cord of firewood already stacked outside. As Sue brings me in the front door, her son Jesse is sprawled on the large deep sofa watching TV.

"This is our new housemate Liz," Sue says.

"Cool."

Danny is there, too. He is 40-ish and fixes things – cars, yard, appliances, plumbing, and most world problems. The latter are attacked in loud, non-stop, opinionated yak. Sue and Thelma have not told me so much as "advised" me about Danny and his place in the household. He fights the effects of brain damage caused by a motorcycle accident. The condition doesn't limit his handyman abilities, but it does affect emotions and judgment, so Sue must constantly manage Danny and his many problems and keep him on track with priority projects on a long, unfinished list. Currently, the Volvo needs work and a project to finish out the garage stands idle.

And finally there's Eva, age 55, Sue's best friend who is a psychiatric nurse with a gentle nature and earth mother outlook. She's now my Rutland friend No. 4. Eva has arrived to help with a yard sale that starts tomorrow if we can all finish organizing and pricing and setting up the pile of goods heaped in every available corner of the living room.

"I put friends over housework," Sue has already explained.

My bedroom, first door on the left of a hallway that shoots off the living room, has a double bed, dresser, a small antique rocker, and a wonderful little desk that's perfect for setting up the laptop. Sue's room, the third bedroom, the bathroom and a laundry alcove also line the hallway. Jesse lives in the large, partially finished basement accessed down a flight of stairs off the kitchen.

I unpack and then call a 20-year friend at home in Texas.

"Doris? It's Liz. I'm in Vermont."

"How ARE you?! How's the trip working out?"

"Great, except I'm losing the tenant in my condo. I need somebody... I remember that you were kind of interested in the 'job' and wondered if you might reconsider turning it down."

"I can't believe it," Doris said. "I just signed a lease on an apartment. Otherwise..."

My friend turns rueful.

"Let me see if it's too late to get out of this apartment," she said.

Leaving that situation to work out, or not, I went to bed, begging off the job of price-tagging stuff but vowing to be a good morning worker for the yard sale.

The next day, I plunged into the tasks of the sale – hanging up clothes, organizing tables, selling, collecting money, and doing some buying myself now that I have a closet – Eva sold me her nifty wool blazer for $3. Meanwhile, the chaos of doings in the yard had strange parallels running within our lives in the house. The morning had begun with the sound of Danny's voice in the house, loud and agitated, or was it just more of his standard commentary? Eva was helping Sue write a eulogy to send to Florida for her brother's funeral service. And I face a "Now What?" mode – can I stabilize my condo situation without going back to Texas, and what am I going to DO in Vermont now that I'm here?

Eventually, an early rush of customers subsided, Danny disappeared, Sue finished her difficult composition and things calmed down around our front-yard station. Thelma arrived with doughnuts. Another friend named Patty brought her own consignment of goods. Fortunately, each item was marked with prices of 10 cents, a quarter and a dollar on green "Patty" tags – as the stay-at-home wife of a Rutland businessman, she is the only one of us with the time to be so well-organized.

We all settled into plastic chairs and a growing lethargy on a day that turned sunny and hot.

I asked my standard, first-day-in-town question: "Anybody know where I might get a job as a waitress?"

"I know people at the Norman Rockwell Museum," Thelma said. "They need extra help when the tourists come." (Do people just not SEE me as a waitress?)

I've noticed the museum about the famous illustrator on the edge of town. It is a rustic, homey, tree-shaded complex, but with ominous "bus parking" signs in the driveway. I'm not sure I can bear staring at, selling and handling the merchandise of an American cliché all day long. It's enough to have a bit of Norman in my home – a metal wastebasket decorated with a

1950s *Saturday Evening Post* cover of three little girls. Strictly a utilitarian item, I've had it so long that its origins are long forgotten.

I make sounds of appreciation for the tip but stifle a yawn.

"If you can write, I wonder if you can help me with something," Patty says. "I need to word a petition."

A petition?! Is Patty a rabble rouser?? Cool.

She explained the petition with great frustration. Several times a day, Patty drives past an old boarded-up house on a prominent corner of Woodstock Avenue. The petition would call for demolition of the house, which I've seen, and it does look terrible. Its windows are gone and the boards are completely gray, the paint long ago stripped by weather. The house now exists as nothing more than an eyesore on its weed-choked lot. Supposedly, the owner held off doing something about the property because Home Depot was going to move in on nearby land that would include the house because of access. A big corporation like that would make the problem literally disappear.

Instead, the deal disappeared, and the house still stands.

"I'll be glad to word-smith a petition, Patty, but let me look into the problem itself. What does the City of Rutland have to say?"

And so on Monday, a day that always feels like the start of a work week – even without work – I have lots to do. For starters, there is the condo matter, the civic project, a Web site update and the job hunt. I still have stuff to haul out of the car and I'd like to drive around Rutland to get a little better oriented. E-mail, laundry, check-in phone calls and journal writing are also on the to-do list.

Sue is sleeping late, so I begin my day with a run. We live on a short, dead-end street, but Sue has suggested a route across the highway in a gorgeous residential area – big houses on gigantic lots of their hillsides. Running as a healthy habit is one of the good things in my life that's been ravaged by the trip. By definition, a habit needs habituality and the changing landscape of my year is messing with that.

Back at our house, it was time to dress in business attire for my visit to City Hall. No harm in just *asking* about the boarded-up house – anybody got any plans for it?

My phone rang as I was drawing on my eyeliner at the bathroom mirror.

"Liz, it's Doris."

I gripped the phone tightly and turned my full attention to the voice of my friend in Texas.

"I can't get out of my apartment lease; it's too late," she said.

My heart fell. Lisa has to get out of town and up to her new job in New Jersey. Rutland is a very long way from Hurst, Texas. I do *not* want to drive home.

"But..."

Yes?

"I have a friend," Doris said. "Sara is 59, I've known her about four years and she works for American. She loves cats. I told her about your condo, and she said she's been trying to save to buy a house – this would help her save a little more a little faster."

A cat-loving, older, friend-of-a-friend, long-time office employee for the Fort Worth-based airline, *available*...

"I definitely want to talk to her, Doris."

Later in the day, Sara called me. Wanting to hear nothing but green light indicators, I nonetheless asked why she is in a position to move into somebody else's home for the next six or seven months. What about her own possessions? Furniture? A lease elsewhere?

"I live in an apartment that's pretty much month-to-month," she said. "It won't be a problem for my landlord; he'll let me go."

There was a reassuring maturity and calmness in her voice. No highs or lows really, just an even recitation of her employment for the airline and before that, she had been a police officer in Corpus Christi. She skipped the issue of stuff and I did, too, because Sara sounds perfect. I don't want to hear any complications.

"This is a great opportunity for me to save money," Sara continued. "I talked to my daughter and told her, 'I'm going to start giving you part of my paycheck every month to save for me.' I do like to shop a little too much!"

So she has a little shopping vice – who doesn't in this day and age? At least she's tackling the problem and I get to help her if she holds up through one more step in the process.

"I'd like for some people to meet you and I'm sure you'd like to see the condo," I said.

Next I called Lisa, my neighbor Carolyn and my sister Martha. They all agreed to meet Sara at the condo tomorrow afternoon.

This is a good day and I'm buoyed by this promising solution to a very big problem.

Next stop: City Hall. I have in hand a picture of the house and a list of "talking points" that Patty and I developed. Primarily, the house isn't just an eyesore, it's a hazard, a magnet for vandals, vagrants, animals, and curious children.

It's a pleasure to take my time driving around Rutland's old downtown streets. I'm still in awe of this part of the country, of achieving a lifelong dream of "autumn in New England." Rutland is the vision, all right, with its historic buildings arranged gracefully on sloping, tree-lined streets. My favorite point is along Court Street, where the Grace Congregational United Church of Christ sits majestically next to the Rutland Free Library.

Turning west from Court, Center Street descends steeply to Rutland's old commercial center, and I drive around looking for a municipal building and the office I need. Finding the city's offices, I ask about the existence of a zoning office and am directed to the second floor.

A woman named Carol is at the front desk. From my newspaper years of dealing with city and county clerks and bureaucrats, I'm always a little leery of these people. I suppose their surly attitudes might be blamed on their jobs – on the front lines of public officialdom, they have to deal with absolutely everybody and anybody who pays taxes.

Carol puts me at ease. She's pleasant and attentive.

"There are some people in Rutland who are concerned about this house," I explained, showing the picture. "I offered to find out if there's anything going on behind the scenes, because they're wanting to circulate a petition or take some other action to get rid of the problem."

I paused to wait for the question, "And who are YOU?" *Why, I'm a Texan! Just moved to town – guess you might call me an outside agitator.*

But Carol didn't ask and I didn't elaborate.

"You'll want to talk to Jim Simonds and he's not here today, but let me make a copy of your picture and get the address," Carol offered. "I'll give this to him so that he can be prepared for your call."

Emboldened by the positive reception, I drove home and called the property's real estate agent. The Realtor actually answered the phone.

"So what's the deal with this house?" I asked.

"We're trying to sell it," he said with a heavy sigh. "With Home Depot coming in, the property should sell quickly."

That's not going to happen, Patty says, but I've had enough of outside agitatin' and am ready to quit for the day. I take down some notes from the conversation and say good-bye.

All this work to do and I don't even have a job!

It is 3 p.m. and Sue is at the hospital working one of her 12-hour late-into-the-night shifts. Jesse flies in the door noisily with his girlfriend in tow and as I predicted, shows no interest in the suggestion his mother has left in a note placed next to the kitchen phone. There is chicken marinating in the refrigerator – perhaps he would like to grill it? Instead, there is a fast in-and-out scramble by teen-agers with no time to spare and other places to be.

"We'll get something else," Jesse said, and off they went, having never really stopped when they stopped by. They dropped off books, Jesse changed clothes, and then their car roared away back toward town.

Meanwhile, the refrigerator and cupboard shelves groan with food. It's as if Sue is still caring and providing for five people. Typical teen Jesse is usually elsewhere. A grown son James lives in another town. Daughter Laura lives in Massachusetts. Sue's husband is dead. It's a somber idea that in this way at least, she has not come to terms with the loss of a husband and a nearly-empty nest. Yet she's always cheerful.

I cook the chicken myself in the oven.

One of Sue's talents is gardening. A vast array of flowers, vegetables and herbs is staked out in a backyard shaded by towering pines. There is a compost heap and so in the activities of the kitchen, I can never throw out garbage. In order to keep the compost heap fed, we put food scraps and coffee grounds in a plastic bucket under the kitchen sink. I do this by opening and closing the cabinet door very quickly, throwing remains into the dark slimy morass and trying not to go "ewww." Like Oregon, Vermont is another environmentally-concerned state.

"Thelma and I are going camping," Sue says to me the next morning.

It is her day off and Rutland's warm, late-summer spell continues. "Would you like to go?"

Today there should be a report on Sara. I want to start my job search. And I hate camping.

"Sounds fun," I lie. "But I've got a lot to do and I'd feel too guilty to enjoy myself."

Again, to put my mind in shape for a challenging day, I go for a run in the beautiful neighborhood across the road. Then I shower and dress in job hunter's attire, gather my letters of reference, and head toward town.

First stop: Breakfast. Since arriving at Sue's and making the drive of several miles from her house into Rutland, I've stopped a couple of times at The Seward Family Restaurant, Ice Cream and Gift Shop, a landmark on the city's North Main Street. In Texas, I suppose the equivalent would be a fancy Denny's, if Denny's decided to add souvenirs and 20 flavors of ice cream, with plenty of booth seating and comfort foods like Yankee Pot Roast and macaroni and cheese. This morning the breakfast special was cranberry pancakes. I ordered the pancakes with coffee, then paid the cashier, then asked for an employment application.

The woman obliged, and I carried the piece of paper to a booth off to the side and carefully printed the information requested, as if neatness counts, and doesn't it always?!

Name: Elizabeth Moore

Social Security Number, Address, Telephone number: All easy answers.

Education: Independence High School, Independence, Kan.

Did you graduate? Yes I did!

College? *Be careful here* – Omit the bachelor's degree. But it's OK to put down the one year of junior college. It's true AND believable and doesn't make me over-qualified.

Experience: *This is the tricky part – watch out.* Waitress at Sherwood's Restaurant, Independence, Kan.

Dates of employment: Illegible/ambiguous answer.

The truth? In 1966 I set out to earn money to go to a Barbra Streisand concert in Memphis, Tenn. The plan was to meet my sister-in-law – she and my brother lived in

Oxford, Miss., you see — and I was going to fly from Tulsa to Memphis and she was going to drive to Memphis and we would go to this concert together. So to pay for my trip, I got this HORRIBLE 12-hour-a-week, after-school job in a HELL HOLE and then, well, Barbra was married to Elliot Gould at the time and was pregnant and she suddenly CANCELED the concert! So after six weeks, I quit the miserable waitressing job and used the money to buy some cute shoes on a Kansas City shopping trip. I also decided that a college degree and a professional career were probably the way to go in my life.

I left Seward's and drove into Rutland's center to restaurants called Clem's and Seasons' Circle.

"I'm only here through the fall," I told everybody, against all good advice.

Then I drove out to the Norman Rockwell Museum, home of "over 2,500 covers, ads and illustrations – Open All Year." It looks exactly like a large farm nestled against a hillside, with a house and a big barn beside it. The barn has old-fashioned white lettering identifying it as the museum.

As a reference, Thelma Satayavinit's name went onto the application.

With optimism and a feeling of accomplishment, I stopped at the grocery store called Hannaford's and bought my personal provisions, including beer, which will need to stay tucked away in my closet. I can push a couple of cans at a time deeply back on a lower refrigerator shelf, but not place so many as to tempt young Jesse, although why do I think he's already acquainted with beer?

Tonight, Eva came over with a supply of cat food. Sue and I are providing foster care for Eva's two cats while she moves to a new apartment. The new place doesn't allow pets, so it's not clear to me whether Eva plans to slip them back into the apartment while nobody's looking, or the cats will live at Sue's until Eva's next move. Oh well, it's nice to have cats around again.

I wonder if my two, Minnie and Bigelow, sense the change in their lives, with Lisa about to leave and Sara – I hope – taking over.

Suddenly, good news arrives from Texas.

"Sara is nice," my sister reports in a phone call. She and Carolyn and Lisa met her today at the condo and all agreed that she seems like a good tenant. I like the idea that Sara might be especially deserving of the opportunity – her daughter was a murder victim and Sara is a cancer survivor.

"She was wearing a T-shirt that said 'Cancer Free,'" Carolyn added in another call.

And Lisa, of course, is ecstatic. She is now free to prepare for her move to New Jersey.

It is noon and Sue and Thelma have not returned, so that must mean they decided to stay out a second night. There is a knock on the door and it is another friend of Sue's named Jim, a large shy man about our age. Jim is married, but I think he has a crush on Sue. It's not a wily, philanderer's kind of thing, more of a pet dog-like, gee-she's-nice attraction. Part of it is that Sue would never go for an affair so it's safe for Jim to like her. That's my theory anyway.

"Hi, Jim."

"Sue around? I've been trying to call her."

"Yes, I've heard your messages. She and Thelma went camping. They weren't sure whether they would stay out one night or two, but since she's not back and the weather is so good, I think they must be staying," I said.

"I've got an extra ticket to the Vermont State Fair and the concert tonight. My wife and I already have tickets – Do you want it?"

My mind and hands are well settled into all the things I need to do today. Being a morning person rather than a night owl, I fade out by evening, especially on busy days.

But it's the Vermont State Fair! And the concert is by Starship – a remnant and reconfiguration of the old Jefferson Starship, which used to be Jefferson Airplane. From my day!

"Why not. That's nice of you, Jim."

My promise to myself to get things done today is partially fulfilled. I managed to talk to both Lisa and Sara about the condo tenant change-over. Time is short for Lisa. She needs to fly to California next week for a meeting related to her new job, then get herself moved to New Jersey right after that. To my vast relief, Sara is highly flexible. She offered to move in during Lisa's trip so there can be a little overlap and Lisa can show her where things are and how things work. We'll exchange contract signatures via fax.

The other task needing resolution is a job. No one has called me back from the applications I've dropped around town.

As I weigh the value of working on my Web site versus making some followup calls versus driving out to the fair early, the kitchen phone rings. I start to let the caller hear Sue's voice on the answering machine, but since I'm close, I pick it up.

"I'm calling Elizabeth Moore." It is a man's voice.

"This is she."

"Elizabeth, this is Tom Seward at Seward's Restaurant. I have your application and wonder if you can come in for an interview."

WOO HOOO!!! An interview! To be a waitress. Dreams do come true.

"Tomorrow?" he said.

We're all set for 3 p.m.

I'm glad I accepted the ticket to the State Fair. I'm too hyped to stay home and read or even watch my beloved cable TV.

In the setting sun of this great day, I've found the Vermont State Fairgrounds. I thought Jim told me the cost of parking was included, but when I pulled up to the gate of a close-in lot, an attendant scratched his head.

"I don't think so," he said, looking at my ticket. Then he added, "You're a long way from home."

"Yes, we have fairs in Texas, but I want to see what yours are like in Vermont."

"Oh, go on in," he said. "Don't tell anybody I let you through."

With time to kill before the concert, I crossed a grassy field through a light fog of dust and found the Midway, gaudy with carnival rides, games and food sins of every kind – hot dogs, candy apples, Philly cheese steaks. This is the fair's first day, and everything feels fresh and new. Faces are full of anticipation. Adults wander slowly – children zig-zag among them. All are dwarfed by the rides with their bright lights and growling sounds of speed and swoops and dips.

I look at farm animals and eat a hot dog and find the Vermont Maple Barn. Now THAT'S different from Texas. I try a concoction whose goodness is all in the name: "Sugar in Snow." It's just syrup poured over crushed ice. The syrup becomes gummy and the ice melts. I'll take my syrup on pancakes next time.

A hypnotist has lined up volunteers who sit on chairs across the stage. He tells them to raise their arms, and then he tells them to lower them again and they cannot. He also has them believe their eyes are sewn shut. Those tricks are nothin'! I once saw a hypnotist's show at a mall; those poor people "woke up" thinking they were naked!

There's time for a quick swing through an exhibits building full of products, services and causes. Under the same roof but set up on opposite sides of the hall are a gay rights group and opponents to the state's law allowing same-sex civil union ceremonies. The latter offer black and white bumper stickers that say, "Take Back Vermont."

It is time for the concert to begin and the crowd is embarrassingly small. The vast majority of us are baby boomers. The rest are our grandchildren. I "get" to sit mere yards from the stage – I've brought my camp chair and opened up its aluminum legs and black canvas sling with the mesh drink holders. I'm settled front-and-center on the surface of the track that lies between the performers and the grandstand's bleacher seating.

Was the concert's start 45 minutes late because bands are always too cool to start on time, or because the performers were waiting for some more people to show up?

The musicians drift in and twang a few tune-up notes on guitars. A drummer at his perch raps a few beats. There are random equipment thumps and microphone squeals and suddenly, here's Mickey Thomas and the concert begins.

It's way too loud. I know, I know – I'm a tough audience, but I'm also among the few of my generation to still have full hearing in both ears. I've not been to many concerts.

I find myself admiring the professionalism and showmanship of these guys, who don't seem to care about the tiny crowd. Everybody around me is having a good time, and the sky is clear, darkening into a blue-black brilliance with tiny stars. And nearby the rides glow with spinning lights, and I'm at home in the beautiful state of Vermont, MAYBE with a job, definitely with a home and friends...life is SO good. Sing it, Mickey!

And so he does, and the granny next to me and her grandson and I are soon on our feet to sing along with Starship..."We built this city on ROCK and ROLLLL...."

15 A GOOD WAITRESS

"JESSE!" I cry out. "PLEASE wake up!"

It is 2:45 p.m. and I am pounding on his bedroom door in the basement. I'm due at Seward's Family Restaurant at 3 p.m. for my first day of work.

I've dressed carefully in dark pants, white shirt and a dark green apron that has the Seward's logo right above my heart. Nervous and eager, I'd flown out of the house, raced across the grassy yard to the Honda, jumped in and turned the key. I don't know if the car was doing its "thing" on a warm and humid day, or maybe I flooded it when I tromped on the gas. It won't start now.

"Jesse, my car won't start and I have to get to work at Seward's. Can you PLEASE take me?"

Jesse got home late last night and was getting caught up on his sleep. Sue had left for the hospital at 2, so her son was my only recourse for a ride.

He came stumbling out, mumbled an affirming sound, and we got in his car. At the end of our wordless ride, I promised him, "Thanks – I owe you for this."

Inside the restaurant, the slow hours of the day between meals were also Tom's first hours. He arrives in the early afternoon but works far into the night, which probably isn't unusual for a restaurateur. How do they do it, these owners of seven-day, breakfast-lunch-and-dinner, long-time establishments?

A centerpiece in the simple decor of Seward's Family Restaurant is a large framed portrait of its founder, the late Roland Seward. He gazes from the wall in a formal pose, sincere and watchful, as if his spirit remains in charge and he can observe his son carrying on.

Tom looks like him. He is a slight man, with dark hair combed back. Black-rimmed glasses make his serious eyes even more so, and he doesn't smile much. His movements are purposeful but not rushed, and he is calm but not lenient. He's smart, but in a world-weary way. I don't think I fooled him in my interview when I cheerfully conjured memories of Sherwood's as if the job were yesterday.

"Waitressing..." Tom said as we concluded the interview and I started to leave, "Well, it's a little different."

And so today, I followed my new boss around. He explained the menus and showed me where to clock in at the beginning and end of my shifts, the kitchen and food storage areas, the cook's line, the salad bar, and the deli, a whole different section of Seward's that lies between the dining room and a dairy and gift store. There appear to be dozens of flavors of ice cream here, and a carryout window attracts end-of-summer customers stopping by for a cone.

"Here are the glasses," Tom says as we stop at a stainless steel expanse of shelves. "These are for juice, this is a large size and this is a small," he says, very deliberately and pointedly picking up the correct beverage containers for water, tea, soda pop and milk and the cups for coffee, tea and hot chocolate.

Suddenly, it is occurring to me that I could be in over my head. There are so many details to learn...

I call on Shakespeare for inspiration: "All the world's a stage, and all the men and women merely players." Act, *pretend*. Act calm and you'll be calm, I tell myself.

Tom tells me to "shadow" Sherry, a college student. She points out the way the booths are identified using the letters of the alphabet, and there are five sections: "front," "window," "middle," "side" and "counter." "Window" is the best for tips, so the section assignments are rotated. Least-desired is "counter," which is an L-shaped area that includes the cash register and is mostly occupied by coffee drinkers who linger, perched like birds on a wire.

I also meet Ralph, Tom's indispensable assistant manager. Ralph has been here a few *decades* now, starting out as a young, gawky, timid teen-ager. Today he is in the center of things – the kitchen and the cook's line – pivotal in holding the place together through the chaos of no-show wait staff and disappearing cooks, and he is the bouncer of drunk, belligerent customers. He's the scheduler. I shall be nice to Ralph.

Starting around 5 p.m., the restaurant began to fill with people. I tried to capture and memorize all of Sherry's steps in the process and to try to help in meager ways, like keeping water pitchers filled and silverware wrapped tightly in paper napkins, but I felt woefully lacking.

Because let me tell you about waiting tables. It's harder than you think it is. For every single customer, we have to remember menus – regular green ones, separate breakfast lists, a red and white dessert list, and the day's specials on a single typed page. Is the table clean? Silverware and napkins. Water, with ice, out of the tap, or no water. Other beverages. Cream, straws, iced tea spoons, lemon or god forbid, a milk shake which means having to sprint over to the deli and make it ourselves. Writing the order WITH the carbon under the page of the ticket book. "What kind of potato?" "Oh, sorry. We have no more baked potatoes." "White, wheat or rye for that sandwich?" "A cup or bowl of soup?" "Would you like that brought out to you first?" "How would you like that hamburger cooked?"

And, writing the proper initials or other language the cooks will be able to read. Beverage refills. Order pickup and adding rolls, butter and condiments. Loading the serving tray and then hoisting it up and over to the booth. Delivering, refilling, fetching and correcting. Calculating the ticket. "Dessert?" The dreaded "Make me a maple walnut sundae, peanut butter topping AND a little hot fudge on that, just a little whipped cream but not too much, and no nuts. No *wait*...change that. Mint chocolate chip ice cream..." Adding the price of the dessert or coffee to the check, recalculating the sales tax. Delivering the check. "Thanks for coming in." Ringing up the check if nobody else is at the cash register. Race on to the next table.

Now, multiply that set of details times 30 and you get a sense of one hour at Seward's at the height of the rush.

"Would you like to take a table?"

It's the cheerful, vaguely musical voice of June who trills the invitation lightly. Very unlike the rest of us – certainly the 20-year-olds – June is the happy, gray-haired, rock-solid angel of the Seward's staff. June has been here for 50 years.

"Thanks, but..." Got to stall. I know she thinks I'm eager to start getting tips, but I'd kind of like to feel competent first. Once again I'm embarrassed about my paucity of experience. HOW is all of this going to work out for me? Can't these customers just LEAVE? Dinnertime is OVER. Go home! Put the kiddies to bed! Watch TV! Read a book! Stop hanging out in a restaurant!

At last, they do clear out. Seward's closes at 11, so the last hour of our day is spent tending to stragglers and getting the restaurant ready for the next day. It's called "side work." We wipe the tables, replace the ketchup bottles, clear the salad bar, change the menus and wash the coffee pots. We sweep the floor last, and then a floor washing crew enters as we exit for the night.

"Tom is obsessed with clean tables," June warns me, and sure enough, he makes a random check of the tables post-cleaning, leaning over the tops and dragging the palms of his hands slowly to the edge to feel for dirt.

"This table is not clean," he announces.

"That makes me so mad," June huffs. "He's feeling lint left from the towels; it's NOT dirt."

She shows me how to spray the table with bleach water, wipe it, then go over it again with a dry towel to get rid of the lint.

Sherry gives me a ride home along with two other people. (I guess we all drive old cars – or no cars.) I have $6 in tips. Late in the evening, as the crowd was thinning, I nervously took tables. With the thrill of "instant" cash in hand, my shyness and insecurity are melting away. I look forward to being fully in the action.

Back at the house, Sue is not yet home from work. The phone rings.

The caller identifies herself as a Canadian border official.

"We've stopped a carload of young people. Are you the mother of Jesse Rowe and are you aware that he and some friends are trying to cross into Canada tonight?"

Hmm, what's my role here? It's not hard to figure out what's going on. The Canadian border is just beyond Burlington, which is right up the road. Jesse and his friends are trying to go to Canada for some reason. In my day, in southeast Kansas, "The Border" was Oklahoma, source of Coors beer, dirty movies, under-age marriage licenses and other foreign sins.

Remembering my pledge to Jesse just this afternoon, I respond.

"Jesse's mother is not here. I'm a house guest and I really don't know about the family's plans tonight, but thanks for calling. I'll let her know." And then I decide not to rat on Jesse. See if he gives this up to his mother.

It is the next morning and I am way too tired to run. I ran all day yesterday, from 2 p.m. to 11 p.m., and I'll run again today beginning at 3. But I'm in a great mood, and I talk Sue into calling Eva and meeting for breakfast out.

Sue drives, taking winding, leafy roads to a history-rich restaurant on Route 4 called Sugar & Spice. It sits on part of an old estate of a Civil War brigadier general, whose horse "Old John" is buried there – in fact, you pass Old John's grave stone as you make your way from the parking lot to the restaurant's steps.

Sugar & Spice offers Breakfast, Lunch, and Gifts. And everything nice. (Oops, the more I try to ignore the name, the less successful I am at trying to overlook it.) The place is all rambling dark wood and rustic charm – quintessential Vermont – with big crowds, but the wait is worth it. I get blueberry pancakes with Vermont maple syrup, which is made at the restaurant.

"How's Jesse?" Eva asks Sue over breakfast.

"Oh, he's fine, but he got in really late last night because he and his friends went to Burlington for a game but got stuck trying to find a place to stay. They got lost as they drove around looking for a motel..."

The explanation went on from there and I couldn't follow it, but apparently, Jesse did call his mother pronto and came up with some sort of reasoning for a Canadian border official's call, should she happen to know about it.

Then we talked about the handyman Danny and Sue's great frustrations over his unfinished projects.

"The Subaru just sits there, broken, and now there's something wrong with the Volvo," she said. "He keeps saying he'll work on the cars but he never does. I don't know where he goes, where he spends his time, he doesn't say. He comes and goes and somehow doesn't get much done."

"It could be worth it to just end the aggravation and take your car into a shop," I suggested.

I would have given up on Danny a long time ago, but I've learned that he is another hold-over from the past. He worked for Sue's husband, who apparently was able to get him to finish projects. Constantly on the verge of homelessness and a dalliance with drugs, Danny also needed lots of practical help and support, and the Rowes provided it, from income to advice to intervention to keep him out of jail.

I struggle to imagine myself in Sue's place as a still-grieving widow. Danny has become a needy member of the family. Anyway, how DO you manage those many home-front repairs and maintenance when you've spent your entire adulthood with a mate taking care of *all* those things?

Somebody changed the subject to the idea of side trips we should take. Manchester, Middlebury...even Saratoga which, while in New York, isn't far away. The legendary fall colors of New England are beginning to tint the trees. It's a beautiful time of year to be out and about in a beautiful part of the country. We all agreed to go somewhere on my next day off.

But this is not that day. It is my second day at Seward's and at 3 p.m., having clocked in and reported to the cook's line, I can see there are already too many customers and too few wait staff.

"Uh, who am I supposed to shadow today?" I ask warily.

"Shadow?! Nobody! We need you to take a section yourself. Kristi didn't show up," says Carla, a stocky little dynamo with a voice like tires on gravel. I'm running around helplessly behind her because she's too busy to stop and explain things. "You've got Middle."

Already, booths R and S have people sitting and waiting for, for...*now think*. I grab six sets of wrapped silverware and six green menus.

"Hello!" I smile. "Do you know what you'd like to drink?" *Why are you in our restaurant at this hour of the day? It's not lunchtime. It's not dinner. You shouldn't eat between meals.*

It's water, tea, coffee, decaf coffee at one table, water and a chocolate frappe at the other. I start two tabs in my ticket book, carefully writing an R and an S in their respective corners. Damn. Forgot to position the carbon page under the orders. Damn. Got to go make the frappe. And what's a frappe?

Ten minutes later I have six beverages on a large tray which is teetering on my arm.

And then the real fun begins: I have to take the actual food orders.

"I hope you'll be patient with me today! I'm new!" I say, smile bared, eyes scared... *Please order something easy.*

They don't.

The table of four wants an apple pie, soup and sandwich, a Garden Burger and a hot fudge sundae. I don't know if we have apple pie today because pies aren't listed on the menu and I forgot to look at the list, a thing I should do right after clocking in. I forget to ask what *kind* of sandwich and sheepishly return to the table to ask. I slop the beef-vegetable as I try to ladle it into the cup and create a mess which I have to clean up. I race into the ice cream room and find the vanilla rock hard and nearly impossible to scoop.

Meanwhile, mid-stride in passing me, Carla warns, "Lou is being a bastard today. Watch out for him."

Ah, Lou. The cook. At least three people have warned me about this tall, expressionless, stoic figure in chef's uniform and half-glasses. He'll snap your head off if you try to so much as speak to him, I'm told. He and the assistant manager Ralph are toiling on the line today, grilling, pouring, scooping, spreading, assembling, banging pans, calling orders and shouting questions in the escalating pace of a late afternoon.

"Last year, Carla said, "it was Christmas time and I started singing – because I *love* Christmas – and you know what Lou did? He YELLED at me. He said, 'STOP IT. I HATE Christmas.' Just like that. He apologized later but I haven't spoken to him since."

I manage to get a BLT sandwich delivered and a check calculated and it's time to pick up a customer's meatloaf order from the cook's line.

"Ah, Lou? There's no potato here."

He peers at me over his half-glasses. "What kind do they want?"

I hadn't asked. I will now. If you don't write baked, mashed or fries, Lou delivers nothing, leaving a large bare spot on the plate to teach you.

Back at the table of four, faces are disgruntled.

"I still don't have my pie." "Aren't I supposed to get crackers with this soup?" "Do you have any *fresh* decaf?"

"You've got customers in 'L' and 'M,'" June says to me gently on her way to the line to pick up an order. I glance at the tables and their expectant faces as one of the arrivals says, "Can we get some menus please?"

I am losing control. I am scared and sweating. My heavy trays shake and tilt precariously. I am drowning, thrashing in the waves that rush and rise around me, and there is an undertow pulling me down...down...

"Do you need some help?" June asks kindly.

"No."

For I keep thrashing. L and M get menus and silverware. The pie person gets pie. I tear open the coffee packet for a new pot of decaf. *Extra* crackers for the beef-vegetable soup (can't let Tom see me; *cups* get *one,* bowls two).

I scoop up a $5 tip from a table where the couple had ordered only ice cream and coffee. They had taken pity on me. My heart aches with gratitude.

"Liz, table O needs you," Sherry says.

What now. It's that table of 4 again.

"THIS IS NOT *APPLE* PIE."

I freeze in a realization that I have not, can not, and probably will not ever get her simple request met. In a moment that feels endless and still, our eyes lock, hers angry, mine horrified.

"Just...bring us our check."

"Liz, you need to watch the cash register," Tom reminds me.

What?!! Sure enough, no one is there and a line is forming. Tom is having to handle some sort of a crisis in the kitchen and can't do it. The counter person is off making desserts.

"June? Can you take beverage orders for L and M?" I ask meekly.

I step up to the cash register and try to still my fumbling fingers. I switch through sequences of tasks, between cash payments and credit cards. I pray that no one wants to buy a "non-food" item like Vermont postcards, which changes everything on the cash register keys.

"That will be $13.60," I say to the gentleman.

"Is that with my senior discount?"

It isn't. Can I lie? *Of course, sir! That total does include your 10 percent off.* I look into his beady little eyes.

"You?? YOU are a senior citizen?! You're much too YOUNG!"

The old goat ain't buyin' it. I go through the laborious steps to void the ticket and make a new one, remembering to discount the pre-tax total.

Next up: Oh gawd, it's the apple pie lady. My anxiety over having to face her again and deal with this ever-lengthening line is now at a frenzy.

She takes a penny out of the "take a penny, leave a penny" tray and hands it to me.

My hand stops before I drop it into the pennies of the cash register.

"Ma'am," I announce, trying to hand it back to her. "This is a Canadian penny. It's foreign – I don't think I can accept it."

"BUT IT'S YOUR PENNY!" she cries, pointing out the obvious. She looks at me as if I'm deranged...

Yes. I am obsessing over a penny. It is the restaurant's penny. I am a total lunatic.

At the end of the night, after the customers have cleared out and the side work is done, we have to do the paperwork of totaling the checks that we handle, and reporting our tips.

"Be sure to tell Tom if you didn't have a meal; it's automatically deducted from your wages otherwise," Sherry tells me.

A *meal*? When would I have had time to eat? Nor did I ever drink water or go to the bathroom. It's as if my brain shut down every kind of physical need not related to waiting on tables.

"June, how, WHY have you done this so long..."

I'm giving her a lift to her home at 11:05 p.m. She doesn't drive. Even though her house is just a few blocks away, she counts out $1.50 and plunks it on the tray of my dashboard. She'll always pay when one of us gives her a ride, she explains. I protest the cash, especially for such a short distance, but she insists.

"It's not negotiable," she says.

June tells me she started the job at the age of 16 and her own father told her she'd never last.

"I think you've proven yourself."

I negotiate the quiet neighborhood streets of northwest Rutland as June tells me the turns to make and we talk about the crew at Seward's.

"Wait till you meet Karen!" she says, describing Tom's wife in glowing terms and inadvertently making her sound like his opposite. Karen is in Oregon visiting a grown son, and customers ask about her — When is she coming back, they want to know. I think Karen Seward may be the most popular person on the planet.

June and I arrive at a pretty little white frame house with bannistered steps and a picket railing. A porch light casts a soft yellow glow and a big old orange and white cat sits, then gets on his feet and stretches as June gets out of my car. Her husband has heard us pull up and he opens their front door for her and the cat.

I am struck by pangs of home. Of a refuge at the end of a bad day, with comforting rituals and someone you love welcoming you home and a cat who sits and waits.

Back at Sue's house, I'm over my sentimental mood, shifting into mercenary glee. I'm in my bedroom, having pulled wads of cash from the pockets of the green apron and flung it on the bed. $68! In one day! I'm rich, I tell you, *rich*!

But can I survive the work it takes to be "rich"??

The exhausting afternoons and late nights bring an end to my long-time life as a morning person. I no longer spring from bed at 6 or 7 a.m. and I've abandoned my running. Because Sue works a late shift, too, we don't see each other before 9 or 10 a.m., and then we roost in her living room, wrapped in robes, drinking coffee and talking and letting the day unfold slowly.

This morning, I awake early to the sound of a lawn mower. The noise tears through the air, the grinding roar rising and falling, back and forth, loud, louder, loudest. It is 6:30. Danny is mowing the yard in an uncharacteristic binge of work. I get to my feet and go to the kitchen where Sue is standing, helpless and wordless.

"I have no comment," she says, finally explaining that Danny is angry.

Eventually, he cuts the lawn mower and stomps into the house. Sue calmly, patiently tries to reason with him.

"Danny," I say, cutting in. "Are you angry at *me*?" I am determined to make him understand that his tirade is spilling over onto innocent people.

"No. Should I be?" He enunciates each word flatly, defiantly.

"Your mowing woke me up. Why would you do that at 6:30 in the morning?"

"It had to be done! Sure you're going to hear it if your window is open. You close the window and you won't hear it. The grass has to be cut and I'm the one to do it and it has to be done. You close your window and it's air-tight and you won't hear it so I can't help it if it woke you up. It's time to mow the yard and I'm mowing the yard..."

On and on, he went, his mental circuitry feeding outrageous behavior with endless rhetoric that circles round and round.

I guess I should feel sorry for Danny – I've been trying to view him as a harmless Vermont character – but he is a loud-mouthed hick who manipulates Sue, and I can't stand him.

So I'm outta there, abandoning his vehement stream of ego, dressing quickly and adjourning to the Vermont Bagel Cafe.

A morning stop at the café has become another favorite routine. The nondescript glass-fronted shop is across from the Pine Tree Lodge (so sometimes when I finish my bagel and hazelnut coffee, I cross the street to say hello to Net and Thelma). The café's big windows catch lots of morning sunlight and glimpses of green mountains beyond the commerce of Woodstock Avenue.

If I'm early enough, I can still buy the New England edition of *The New York Times* from the racks just inside the front door. Today, being even earlier than usual, I pick up my copy of the *Times* and open it to a most chilling article: The state of Vermont is preparing for a fall tourism season in which the population will balloon from 600,000 to 4 million.

That means I am part of the service industry that will be dealing with the visitors. Seward's welcomes tour buses.

16 TRIUMPHS AND (T)ERRORS

Learning to be a good waitress is a lot like learning to type. If you think about pressing one key at a time, putting words on a page will take forever. You learn where to position your fingers on a keyboard, with each finger assigned several letters in the alphabet. You practice, and then it's pretty much continuous fluid motion. Waiting tables has become a similar process — grouped sequential actions that are now second-nature and I no longer have to think so hard.

Besides, I've got Dave and the boys helping me. The Counter Boys. Yes, I soon drew "Counter" in the rotating assignments of sections and it's a tough new world that promises to throw me off stride from time to time.

"You're new, aren't you?" said Dave, one of the half-dozen guys who drift in after work. He was friendly and chatty.

"Yes," I said. "I'm still learning, so you have to be patient with me."

Dumb.

"I'll take a Pine Float," Dave said.

Seward's is legendary for its desserts. With all its flavors of ice cream, pies and cakes, one whole menu is devoted to sweets.

I grabbed the red and white laminated list and scanned the names. Brownie Delight, Banana Split, Strawberry Shortcake...Where could it be? Pine Float, Pine Float...

"I can't seem to find that on here," I finally admitted. "What is it?"

"It's a toothpick in water," Dave said, and his buddies laughed heartily.

But Dave is nice and full of empathy; his wife is a waitress. He left me two kinds of tips that first day: a buck fifty on his glass of iced tea, and this advice: "SMILE. That's the most important thing."

Karen Seward has returned from Oregon and she lives up to the build-up. She is my age but blonde, petite and still cheerleader-cute. She also has become my good-natured coach. The day I got my first order for a real dessert – Seward's infamous "Pig's Dinner" – I fled to her in an attack of anxiety.

"Karen, I have two customers who tell me they grew up in Rutland and are back in town for a visit. Their favorite thing is a Pig's Dinner. Not only do I have to learn how to make it, it's going to have to stand up to nostalgic memory!"

Karen led me to the deli and helped me pull together all the ingredients: the customers' choice of four kinds of ice cream and four toppings. These get arranged in a "dish" that is actually a short wooden trough.

"Now you take a banana and you cut it into quarters," Karen explained, arranging the banana slices in the four corners of the trough. "These are the pig's ears."

Completing the decadent mess are whipped cream, nuts and a cherry.

It was a triumph. The couple told me it was the best Pig's Dinner they've ever had.

They were among the mostly nice, appreciative customers. At the other end of the scale there was a Counter Boy who parked his butt at the counter almost daily and generally remained silent. He was not pleasant and the first time he had anything to say to me it was to complain that I had shorted him on a dip of chocolate ice cream.

"*This* is a dip?" he said.

I was torn between the business point of view and what Tom had shown me as a "serving," versus the other employees' practice of dipping, packing and heaping over-sized globes. Seward's isn't their business and they ward off complaints and possibly enhance their gratuity with this generous definition of a "scoop."

"In all fairness, if you feel you are being short-changed, I will get you some more," I said, returning to the dessert room and re-doing the man's order more amply. I returned with one large dip of chocolate ice cream and set it down before him.

He refused it. "I was not born yesterday!" he snarled.

It took me a while to think about what he meant by that remark. Egads, he thought I sabotaged him! We have all heard the stories – such as waiters who spit in the food of bad customers, although I never witnessed anything like that in thought, word or deed at Seward's.

I smiled and tried to lighten things up.

"I think that whoever's been serving your ice cream has spoiled you!" I said.

He pushed the ice cream away, slammed down his napkin and spoon and rose to his feet.

"I do not need to sit here and be insulted by a *waitress*," he said, storming out of the restaurant.

I turned to Karen for comfort and reassurance, which she is quick to give.

"You're doing a great job," she says this time and many times. June and the customers are right; she is incredibly warm and outgoing, with a caring word for anyone who needs it – employees or customers.

Karen's qualities in tandem with Tom's care and diligence toward the business surely explain some of their success. It's such a hard business – do people in small towns know what they have in a *family*-owned restaurant? I have a sad sense that it's another "American way" that is taken for granted and is slipping away as corporations buy up and re-blend the culture for a numbing national sameness.

It is my first day off, granted by Ralph after six grueling 3-11 p.m. shifts. The time off is unimaginably precious. I spend the morning with Sue's friend Patty, who has typed up my draft of a preamble to the petition to get rid of the abandoned house on Woodstock Avenue. We troupe in and out of restaurants, stores and offices, and some people sign the petition but others are afraid to put their name down. I myself am definitely losing interest in the project. My new job is my cause and my passion and my usurper of energy.

Having done my civic duty, I devote the warm afternoon to myself and my aesthetic notions of Vermont. I load my camp chair into the Honda and take the road that passes near the house. I look for a spot that is one with the land, the mountain vistas, the clear streams and unending groves of tree that are about to burst into a full palette of fall colors. The search itself is divine; the road curves through old settlements with general stores, farms with roadside signs offering maple syrup for sale, clapboard houses and historic cemeteries.

Eventually I find Chittenden Dam and an idyllic setting for writing. I set up the camp chair on a broad rock at a high point above the lake. With summer over, only a few canoeists and dog walkers show up to wander along the shore or venture into chilly waters.

On this September day, it occurs to me that it is also Sara's move-in day at the condo. I'm not in the mood to write or do much more than gaze at Vermont's beauty, so I dial my Hurst number. She answers.

"Hi! I'm just calling to say welcome and to see if you need anything." She did.

"Liz, I'm going to have to have this place cleaned. It's filthy."

I'm caught by surprise. Carolyn has been in and out a lot, and Martha had visited and befriended Lisa. Last April in the overlapping week before my trip began, I saw a young woman who was neat and orderly. Surely someone would have mentioned this kind of deterioration.

"What do you mean exactly, Sara?"

"I have found some people who can come in and clean and do what needs to be done for $150," she said, suggesting that we deduct that amount from her move-in charges.

"What *exactly* is wrong, Sara? Can you be more specific about what you find 'filthy'?"

Specifically, the bathtub needs to be cleaned as well as the refrigerator and the oven, which happens to be self cleaning. She spells all this out coolly, crisply. I tell her that she needs to send me some written quotes and I'll take care of it, or I'll consider $75 off her deposit. She backs off a little, and tells me not to worry about it.

A few days later, the happy surprise of a hand-addressed envelope for me arrives in Sue's mail. It is a letter from Carolyn, who has seen some serious lifetime changes in recent weeks. Her mother's long life came to an end this summer, and now Carolyn and Vernon are getting serious about a future together after nine years of dating.

Hi, Liz!

How's it going up there in Vermont? I check the weather section in the paper every day. The closest they come to Rutland is Burlington. But it gives me an idea of what your weather is like. Our weather has been brutally hot this summer and then we had some fall weather a couple of days last week.

Vernon and I are looking for a house right now. We have been doing some serious talking and making some plans. The 'M' word is being discussed pretty seriously. I think it's just a matter of when and where. He said, 'Ask Liz if we can come to Vermont and get married in her restaurant.' But I think that's a little too far from home.

Lisa called me last Sunday morning to say good-bye. She spent Saturday night with her friends before leaving for Chicago. She seems really excited about her new job. I hope it works out for her.

Vernon and I went up to visit Sara one evening last week and took canned cat food and Chow for Minnie and Bigelow. He put the closet door back on the track. Sara seems to be very nice. I couldn't believe it, though, when she said she thought Lisa kept a filthy house. It was always neat when I went up there.

I'll make this short. It's almost bedtime and I have a lot of errands to do tomorrow.

Our neighbors Nancy Smith and Marliese said to tell you hello. I gave them a copy of your Web site update that Lisa printed out for me.

Take care of yourself and don't work too hard.

Love,
Carolyn

I make a mental note of the Sara comment and just as quickly set it aside. I'm also struck by the fact that life is changing at home in Texas — it's not supposed to. I expect it to be the exact same place I left last spring when I return next spring.

But that's not to be. Within a week, Carolyn calls me to say that she and Vernon have set a November wedding date and they've found a house. She will be leaving the condos.

They want me to come home for the wedding and they'll book my flights to get me there. How can I say no?!

"November the 9th!?!" Karen Seward exclaims when I tell her that's probably my last day at Seward's. "Well then, go to Texas but come back. Spend Christmas with us! We have such a wonderful time."

I have completed the breakfast shift today and Karen and I are in her BMW tooling along a winding, two-lane road that will get us to an antiques store where she's spied a table and chairs she wants to buy. She drives with a rather heavy foot, but she knows the roads well, and speed seems normal for the situation.

Somehow I can't imagine Tom Seward and Christmas – just even taking the time off, much less caroling with the family 'round the Christmas tree. I look at Karen sideways but keep the thought to myself.

"Come back and I'll teach you to ski!" she adds.

"I can't – but it's tempting," I say, and mean it. After all, yet another uncertain time looms when my turn with Vermont is over.

I love it here. I love New England and the way Vermont clings stubbornly to its rural and rugged individualism, almost as if it is a separate nation. There's a type of Vermont hillbilly here – one of them is a Counter Boy who calls me Toots and Honey – and there are the rich who actually commute to executive jobs in Boston. In between, there is the unexpected. One day I made assumptions about a customer, a large man with a missing hand, with the look of a hard, working-class life. And then I learned he was the mayor of Rutland, a charismatic charmer with a special commitment to the cause of homelessness.

I love the friends I've made; they've created such a warm place for me that I feel I've known them a very long time.

And surprisingly, I love my job! It continues to feel desperately chaotic sometimes, but maybe it's that kick of adrenaline I need.

Just when I think I've mastered the most wicked balancing acts on a busy night, something happens to deflate my ego. One night, another waitress and I served six adults from a singles group whose orders ranged from breakfast (served all day) to ice cream desserts to coffee-only, all on separate checks. They arrived late, so the rush was over, but it took great effort and concentration to keep up with them.

Suddenly, two men in a booth near the group stood up and walked.

"We're sorry if we're too much trouble for you," one of the men said to me, and then they stopped and talked to Tom and brusquely exited out the front door.

"Liz," he said quietly. "Was booth W yours?"

I looked at the back booth where two menus lay on the table. Chills shot up my spine.

"Uh…yes."

"What happened? They said they never got served and now they're going to the Midway Diner."

Oh. Two men. Sat down at W and I delivered menus to them and then I …never went back. I forgot them, that's what happened. It's as if they were in some sort of blind spot – I forgot them and then I simply didn't see them because I was so busy with the group of six.

"I can't believe it," I stammered. "I don't know why...I'm sooo sorry."

Tom was livid.

"They said it's not the first time that's happened in here! That CAN NOT happen. Their business is gone now and who can blame them. You have got to watch your tables, you have got to keep up..."

I've never seen him so angry – 'round and 'round he went in circles of low thunderous scolding, reiterating my errors and the customers' parting words and the lost business to *Midway Diner*, our rival across town. I was mortified, but there was no convincing him of my remorse and my commitment to understand what happened and to not let it happen again. It was several more minutes before he ran out of steam.

Booth W continued to be tricky, but at least I knew it and learned to glance at the back table often, whether there were customers or not. The phenomenon also made me a more understanding customer when servers seem to overlook me. Basically, there are tables that are in a poor line of sight – maybe it's an odd angle or reduced lighting or a whimsical and mischievous secret about the order of the cosmos – but now I know, a server's scarcity is probably not personal.

At home in bed, my quick journey into a late night's sleep has suddenly stopped in its tracks.

Danny's shouts in the kitchen are barely muffled by my closed door. He is yelling at Sue, and while I don't quite hear all the words, two ring out over and over again: "You lie!! YOU LIE!!!"

"Shush...Please, keep your voice down..." she says.

This time I am truly frightened for her and I lie still, monitoring the rise and fall of Danny's senseless ranting. Once again, he is offended and aggrieved, not so much by anything real – I've watched Sue's patience and her help past the Nth degree – but by the workings of his own tormented mind. This time I'm wondering if he's so far off the deep end that he'll hit her, and then what do we do?

The drama may have been the last straw for Sue. The next morning, she raised the idea of taking her still-low-functioning car to an auto repair shop she's heard about in Rutland.

"You make the appointment to take it in and I'll follow you and give you a ride," I offered.

"I told Danny I don't want him here until he gets some professional help."

Whether this sticks or not, it's an important step for Sue. Not only do I wish for her to be rid of Danny, but that she'll start enjoying some success with self-reliance.

I'm still on a roll here. Later in the morning, I get a call from Jim Simonds, the zoning guy with the City of Rutland. He tells me that the abandoned house may be coming down quickly. A demolition team working on another building down the street has made the owner an attractive offer to bulldoze the house as well. I've generally forgotten my early project of city beautification, but now I feel triumphant, even if the action is more because of random and coincidental events, not any real torch bearing on my part.

At work, my roll stops.

"We had a $9,000 over-ring on the cash register last night," Tom Seward said quietly to me. I'd worked the cash register during the time in question, and it was easy enough for him to spot who made the mistake of somehow entering a bunch of zeros.

"Gee," I said. "I thought I did unusually well on tips; now we know why."

Tom did not laugh. But he didn't go berserk on me either, like the forgotten-customers incident. Soon he was working and making his usual tuneless whistling sounds which seems to signal his return to a neutral mood.

Today, I was cutting a wedge of pie and suddenly became aware of Lou the cook. He was standing nearby, idle, looking around furtively. Other waitresses were off at their sections, and Ralph was making soup in the kitchen.

"I was noticing on the schedule," Lou said, "that we both have the same day off on Sunday. I was wondering if you'd like to meet for breakfast or coffee or something."

Lou, the angry, Christmas-hating cook, was asking me out.

I've come to like Lou and to respect him greatly. He's a good cook and lately has taken to insisting on many days that he make me something special for lunch: "If you're just having a salad, at least let me grill some chicken for it."

I also admired Lou the day he fired back at a young waitress who was trying to change his personality to be more in tune with her silly, inane self. She didn't see anything wrong with humoring someone who does not wish to be humored. Having enough of the heckling chatter, Lou suddenly turned from the grill to face her and said, "Vickie, let's get one thing straight. I am not your friend."

'Course, the girl got on my nerves as well. One of the new hires brought in to help meet the fall tourism demand, she was lazy and flighty and got other people to do her work for her. She was also prone to obscenity-laced tantrums, and once stormed off the job in the middle of her shift, only to make a contrite return an hour later. Ralph lobbied to let her stay gone, but Tom let her back in. After all, the 4 million tourists are arriving by the bus load every day.

On Sunday, I met Lou at Sugar & Spice for breakfast. Arriving ahead of the crowd, we sat upstairs at a corner table and exchanged life stories quietly and succinctly, without a lot of elaboration.

"My parents moved us around a lot and then I became a hippie," he said. "Not the peace-and-love kind either, but a hippie freak, and I did all kinds of drugs."

That's when the parents and son parted ways and things have stayed that way ever since. He said nothing of wives and children and I didn't ask, so Lou remains an enigma. Less vague are his feelings about working at Seward's. He hates it.

Another reason I asked Lou to make the date early was so that I can go to Woodstock. I've learned to use my days off to see Vermont – an easy thing to do in such a small state. Sue and Eva and I have had a few fun day trips together to Manchester and Dorset and Weston. We've shopped at outlets and country stores and visited historic sites and shuffled through the leaves and taken pictures and sipped wine at lovely inns.

It's another precious day off and I get to be on my own. After a 40-minute drive, I arrive at Woodstock, an exquisite little town that serves up one of the richer balances of natural beauty, historic preservation and tasteful shops. It is an elegant package wrapped in the colors of autumn, fragrant with the smells of wood and vaguely of smoke and the baked goods of the shops and the expensive perfume of ladies who drift about the Woodstock Inn. 'Course, such perfection comes at a price, from linen-clothed restaurants to the art in the galleries – and it comes in the terrific hassles of tourism. Lines of people spill out of the bakeries and the apothecary shop. These folks are the lucky ones; they managed to find a parking place.

I find a parking place, but then I am at a loss. Suddenly, I am tired and I'm in one of my occasional funks about leaving "the good life." I had a customer the other day who reminded me of the days of disposable income and genteel choices. She was about my age, Dressed for Success, and we chatted about her new town house between my runs to fetch her coffee and BLT and then the check. I told her what I'm doing and she arched an eyebrow. She didn't tip very well.

So here I am, AGAIN pressing my nose to the window of affluent lives. I lose interest in aimless wandering on quaint streets. Then, as I cross the village green to return to my car, a procession of people and dogs on leashes and cats in carriers appears, led by the Rev. William Gallagher. He is about to begin the Woodstock community's annual Blessing of the Animals.

I fall in stride beside him and ask, "Can you bless my two cats in absentia?"

"Attend the service and go home and love them and they will be blessed," he says.

Good enough, although I can't, of course, go home to Texas right away.

So we all gather on the grassy Common as the reverend stands on a step. I sit among my fellow pet lovers, picking a spot near cats, most of whom peer sourly through wire doors, although one unusually self-possessed feline wanders on a leash and actually sits at the feet of the minister. The cat tilts its head upward as he invokes, "Almighty God, we come together to thank you for the beauty and glory of your creation...."

The dogs smile their dog-smiles, wag their tails, sniff each other, pant, pee and just generally find the whole thing an incredibly wonderful and exciting social occasion.

We sing a song, "All Creatures of Our God and King," and intone the Prayer of St. Francis. It is the perfect thing to do this October afternoon. Suddenly, I am no longer brooding, but happy and at peace with the animals and a spiritual side to the world in a beautiful place that no longer belongs to tourists and rich people and material cravings, but to God.

I slept well last night. I had lots of dreams, and while I don't remember the specifics, they were happy.

But I arise to another gray, rainy, cold day. Autumn in all her finery of yellows, orange, blazing reds and rich bronze, simply went away. She slipped out one night, taking her friends, the tourists, with her. They turned out the lights behind them. Vermont seems dark.

At the Vermont Bagel Cafe, the woman who serves me believes this kind of weather is good for her business.

"People come in on rainy days," she says. "It's a take-care-of-yourself thing."

At Seward's, Tom seems to fret about business, somehow forgetting the madhouse of the past few weeks, and not thinking about ski season just around the corner. I'm thankful for the slowdown, although I can handle just about any crowd now. Dave, the Counter Boy, says I'm their best waitress. Not better than the veteran June of course, or the vibrant and fun-loving Karen, who pitches in when one of the other girls quits or fails to show up.

At the café, I eat the bagel and cream cheese, sip the coffee, read the *Times*, and then it's time for some phone calls home.

First up, my dad. He's excited these days about his granddaughter's wedding next spring in Memphis. Tori calls him regularly and shares details of what is already shaping up to be quite a production.

"She's getting some weird advice," he says.

Apparently, she's using a professional wedding planner, something that was unheard of in southeast Kansas when we three Smith kids were planning weddings in the 1960s and '70s.

This wedding planner, an *outsider*, he said, "will take advantage of a kid like that!"

My niece is 30 years old and a lawyer.

Less amusing was Daddy's report on Mother. Yes, things are still going well with her in the nursing home. He visits and has lunch with her every day and brings her home to the farm house many weekends. Tomorrow he will drive her to a doctor's appointment in Topeka.

"I'm hoping the doctor will say she's well enough to come home to stay."

Note to self: Call back tomorrow.

My second call was to Sara. Having asked to pay her rent late because of special and unforeseen circumstances, she's missed the agreed-upon date.

I have to leave a message, but Sara returns the call five minutes later.

"I forgot," she said.

"Sara, are we going to have problems with the rent?"

"No. We are not. I would say more, but I'm sure you're not interested in my problems right now." As usual, her voice is casual, even and cool.

In the next call, I tell Carolyn that my confidence in Sara is a little shaky.

"I think she's OK," Carolyn says. "She seems nice and your condo looks good the few times I've been up there. She's been organizing a trip to Shreveport, putting up a notice at the mailboxes about a chartered bus."

Texans go to Shreveport, La., to play at the casinos, so apparently she can afford a social life.

On a brighter note, Carolyn tells me my flights have been booked for my trip to Texas for her wedding. Thoughts of the trip to HOME-home – all the way to sunny Texas and familiar things and people – brighten the day instantly. I'll also be able to meet Sara in person. Maybe we've just gotten off on the wrong foot, with the long-distance communications and all.

Back at my Vermont home, Sue is up and working on her projects, including a grant application she's writing to support a crafts program she has created for patients at the hospital.

"Sue, I'm afraid I won't have warm enough clothes to finish out my days here."

"I have things in my closet...," she offers.

Sue has already given me clothes just for fun, including shirts and socks. We're the same size and have similar tastes. But I've become curious about what a thrift store can do to tide me over. I over-packed on all my clothes, especially the ones for warmer weather, but still come up short on cold-weather items. I'm heading south for the winter, but not before New Year's.

"Every day on my way to work, I pass the Salvation Army store..."

"Let's go shopping, then!"

She didn't really have the time – we both had our late-day shifts looming ahead – but she knew I wanted her company and I was grateful for that.

The store, neatly and appealingly arranged, was a true *Eureka!* experience. Or as Homer Simpson would say, "D'oh!" And so I say, "D'oh! Why am I hauling around 80 pounds of clothes stuffed in my trunk when I could simply buy a new wardrobe in each town, suitable to its climate, then leave it behind when I move on?"

At Rutland's Salvation Army store, I paid a total of $15 for a pair of black jeans, navy pants, navy wool slacks, a red wool sweater, a black turtleneck, red and blue print turtleneck, and a Vermont souvenir sweatshirt advertising a little town's Bicentennial celebration (so I look like a native!) Talk about yer cheap thrill, the clothes are just great and I have the feeling of indulging myself in a wild shopping spree.

My sister says she can use T-shirts to make rags for use in her art classes, so I bundle up eight shirts and on my way to work, stop by the post office to mail them back to Martha in Texas.

As my shift begins at Seward's, Ralph greets me with a smile and an offer.

"I owe you," he said. "How would you like Monday off for a three-day weekend?"

Wheee! I haven't even had TWO days off together, feeling obliged as a short-timer to work any arrangement Seward's needs.

So what do I do with a three-day weekend? Why, get in the car of course, and take the Honda east across Vermont, then New Hampshire, and to my 24th state. There it is! Catching sight of the sign alone, "Welcome to Maine," and a grand bridge at Kittery, is thrilling.

And disastrous for the lobsters. I want them. My stomach rumbles and my mouth waters. If I had a child, I would sell it for a lobster. It is an eye-glazing, primordial craving, a seismic event of nature that sends a message ripping through Atlantic waters: *Run, you guys! Run for your lives! Liz is here and you will die for her.*

It's enough to make me abandon my good manners, for I am on my way to a town near Portland to visit friends and I'm running late. I promised Norma an early afternoon arrival. But a lust for lobster knocks out any care I've ever had for friends or family or the downtrodden or world peace. I call Norma and mumble an excuse about the drive taking a little longer than expected.

The State of Maine makes it extremely easy to find lobsters. The official blue "Food-Gas-Lodging" signs on I-95 offer this additional guidance: "Lobsters Available." It's as important as the big white H for "Hospital."

I select the exit to Kennebunkport, the summer hangout of President Bush, so I decide to go see what the fuss is all about. Indeed, the streets are filled with traffic and pedestrians, all looking definitely Republican.

In the heart of town is a restaurant called Alison's. Alas, there is a waiting list.

"We have a bar," the hostess offers helpfully.

Yes, the bar! I lurched in like a thirsty drunk and climbed up on a stool.

Soon, my lobster roll arrives – thick bread piled high and spilling over with cold pink meat.

From Alison's, I followed Norma's directions carefully to arrive at her house and two days of blissful hospitality. Norma escorted me on a magnificent tour of the best of Maine – beginning with her own backyard and her wonderful ceramics studio. (But isn't it cold to work out there in the winter?)

We saw high tide on the rocky coast and the "Portland Headlight," a lighthouse. We drove around the industrious, gritty city of Portland (which reminded me of Astoria, Ore.) We watched big ships on distant horizons. I saw tiny islands and wondered how people managed winter out there. When we wandered near the lighthouse, the temperature was 35 degrees with winds gusting at 24 mph and it's only the end of October.

Norma's food fave is clam chowder at Gilbert's in Portland so naturally, I had CHOWDAH (which I believe is actually better than "chowder") with my second lobster roll.

In the evening I enjoyed one more food high when Norma's husband Bob took us to the Bean Hole Dinner at the Blue Point Congregational Church. Two kinds of beans, cooked in a pit, were served with ham. All of this was polished off with homemade brownies and ice cream served up by the ladies and gentlemen of the church.

Church dinners are big in this part of the world, not that I had to be introduced. I've long maintained that they offer the very best food in America, plus there are no corkage fees or waiters with attitude and you get to go home with a little halo over your head.

I had to be back at work at Seward's by 3 p.m. Sunday, so I left Scarborough by 9, in plenty of time. About 30 minutes into my trip, the weather changed.

Why look at that, I thought. *It's spitting snow.*

Tiny leisurely flakes became flurries. They didn't stop and in fact flew faster and heavier and soon I noticed there was enough snow to swirl around on the highway. Then I needed my windshield wipers. By the time I stopped for gas in Contoocook, N.H., the world was turning white.

Returning to my car at the Mobil station, a man parked next to me was scraping his windshield.

"I see your Texas plates," he said. "Welcome to New Hampshire! This is typical – but early!"

The snow got heavier, and soon after leaving Contoocook, I found myself in a line of cars creeping behind a sand truck. To the left and to the right, cars were off the road. One big new Chevy Suburban was completely upside down. What is this, Dallas? Aren't these people supposed to know how to drive in this stuff?

The Honda, having made trips to Kansas and experienced a few winter storms in Texas, knew what to do and carried me safely back to Rutland.

My last week in Rutland was very full. There was Sue's 50th birthday – I taped a note to the bathroom mirror that said, "You don't LOOK 50!" and then Thelma and I took her out for a grand breakfast at Clem's. Eva took me out for a good-bye dinner, and I prepared for good-byes at Seward's, buying a large box of pens for the wait staff (we could never find a pen when we needed it) and Hershey's kisses that I tied in little bundles to dole out to customers. One of the Counter Boys took his and said to me, "I'd rather put my tongue down your throat." And so it goes – maybe I WON'T miss this place that much.

As I worked the cash register, one of my favorite customers stepped up to pay his bill. I call him "The Terrible Man," because he lumbers in almost every night, large and unsmiling. "How are you?" we ask, and he always responds, "Terrible." But he's not terrible at all, just a pleasant regular who never complains. He goes with the flow of whatever is happening – and sometimes that's chaos with a short staff and a long wait and problems on the line.

"I'll miss you, Mr. T," I said. "This is my last night."

"Yes I know," he said. And then he produced a lime-green envelope and handed it to me. It contained a good-bye card with rollicking cartoon figures and a $20 bill tucked inside.

Karen showed up with a Seward's ice cream carton wrapped in a big pink bow. It contained Vermont souvenirs and a menu autographed by everybody.

And Tom? What would he have to say at the end of the night? I walked into the kitchen where he was scrubbing away vigorously on stainless steel.

"I guess this is it," I said. "I'm ready to go."

"Happy trails," he said, barely looking up. "Keep smilin.'"

"I really did enjoy working here."

"Yeah, right," he said.

Yeah, Tom! RIGHT!!

17 THANKSGIVING DAY INVITATION

The Honda has carried me over 12,800 miles in 26 states.

I'm traveling again today, but time, distance and conveyance are fast-forwarding me to my next destination on this early November day. I'm going home to Texas on a plane.

But not to stay! I'm going to see my friends Carolyn Raynes and Vernon Walton get serious about their nine-year romance and be married. My car is parked in Boston.

Vernon booked the flight and surprised me with first-class accommodation. I'm unaccustomed to the luxury but adapt as quickly as possible. I accept without complaint a breakfast of French toast and fruit. Not a word against the hot towels, a roomy leather seat, having my coat hung up and being addressed by the flight attendant as "Ms. Moore."

By 9 a.m., the plane is descending at DFW Airport. I look out on the green and brown patchwork of Texas fields, Grapevine Lake glistening in full sunshine, row after row of suburban lots, and over it all, an immense blue sky that lifts my slight case of claustrophobia from mountain confines. My heart soars.

When Carolyn and I see each other in the terminal, we embrace without a word and bawl our eyes out. But soon enough, we're off to our old Mid-Cities neighborhood to run errands for the wedding, which will be held at her niece's house, and most importantly, to have Mexican food at Miguelito's on Bedford Road. These pathways are old, familiar and oh-so-comfortable. There's absolutely nothing for me to figure out, and in a friendship that goes back 16 years, no need to ingratiate myself.

But in a reminder of the changes I'll face when I return home to stay, Carolyn drove me over to the far north Fort Worth neighborhood and the new house she and Vernon have bought. How will Alameda Village – and I – manage without them?

They've been particularly helpful keeping an eye on the condo for me.

"I'm glad I'll meet Sara finally," I said. "We've had a little tension over the rent. In the first month she 'forgot' to make a payment."

"Sara plays bingo," Carolyn said, "so she has enough money to have fun."

In the afternoon, Carolyn deposited me at Martha and Paul's east Fort Worth house where I'll stay these five nights. It's another warm and familiar hive, its walls full of abstract art that my sister painted herself. I'm not generally an art lover, but I think her paintings are great and I never tire of looking at them. I always thought she should produce more – Exhibit! Sell! Be famous! But her fulfillment is in teaching.

This will be an "art night." Martha has tickets for the three of us to attend a members' night party at the Kimbell Art Museum. I've brought the two-piece black and turquoise dress I splurged on in Manchester in the early days of feeling flush with money from my waitressing job. It will double as my wedding outfit and now I don't like it, especially as Martha steps out ready to go, tres chic as usual in a French ensemble purchased in Paris.

The insecurity over my road-worn looks continues at the museum. I am among the women primping in a ladies room mirror, lamenting that my lipstick doesn't last very long.

"Have you tried Chanel?" a mirror mate asks.

Here I am, 72 hours off of my waitressing job and applying a little sample shade I bought for 25 cents at the Vermont State Fair. But I've also just flown in first class from Boston.

Do I have a great life or what?! Or is it just a weird life.

The wide, pale, marbled foyer of the Kimbell is full of patrons chatting a little stiffly while glancing about to see and be seen. Me, I head for the food tables, hoping for real hors' d'oeuvres among the cheese cubes and bread. My buddy in managing to stay out of actual museum galleries is my brother-in-law Paul. So while Martha strolls with friends into the featured exhibit (I forget what it was), Paul and I find the bartenders and stake out one of the few small tables not anchored by dowagers and gents.

The wedding was the next day. Martha entrusted me with her Mercedes and I drove to the south Arlington residence where Carolyn's niece and friends had made the most of a modest setting to celebrate a grand occasion. The ranch-style house was decorated with flowers, crepe paper and lots of balloons and while nothing could be done about the pool table that dominated the family room, an altar and seating for 30 was created around it.

The wedding of my dear friends was all that a wedding should be: personal, happy, and efficient. Carolyn wore a graceful, accessorized dress of dark red, having declared that she wouldn't "dress up." Vernon felt a little differently about that and wore a tux. They love Colorado, and so instead of "The Wedding March," John Denver's recording of "Rocky Mountain High" was played as the couple walked into the room together. There were the usual, minor, endearing little problems – Vernon's granddaughter fell off her chair and yowled – and then, after the pastor's jarring declaration that "woman" was created out of Adam's rib, the Waltons became husband and wife.

I decided to go easy on the cake and punch – even a sugar rush might be dangerous at the wheel of Martha's car – and I returned to Fort Worth. Paul drove us downtown to our beloved Irish bar, the Blarney Stone, just like Saturday nights of yore. At home later, we turned on the K-State-Nebraska football game, which was excruciatingly close before K-State finally won. Martha served some good chili. It was the perfect evening to close out a perfect day.

It's very odd to ring the doorbell to one's own house.

"Sara?"

"Come on in," she said, opening the outer patio door and stepping back on the red brick tiles.

I shook her hand and Martha said, "Hello again."

Short of age 60, Sara has a sturdy, mature look and a dignity that is reassuring. She smiles, but not widely, speaks, but not loudly.

I must say, my condo may look even better than when it was my space. My eclectic wall art of urban photographs, brass and copper objects and a sand casting have been removed. I see framed photos of smiling family members and one of Sara herself on a Las Vegas vacation. They line the fireplace mantel that I kept bare, but otherwise, the living room looks less cluttered, and flickering candles add a glow and a soft fragrance.

Even in this mid-afternoon, Sara wore a bathrobe and slippers and she sat curled up in her oversized chair.

Martha and I sat on the sofa and the three of us made conversation. I described Carolyn and Vernon's wedding. Sara talked about the care she's taking toward housekeeping. Martha inquired politely about her family. Very soon, the conversation ran out of steam.

"I don't think she felt well," Martha said later.

After going back and forth with myself over the issue, I did seek out my babies Bigelow and Minnie. Because a door knock signals just one thing to the gray tabby – the presence of a stranger who may well kill her and chop her up into little pieces – Minnie dove under the bed. Bigelow, who seems to know she's a lot smarter than him and wise to the ways of the world, always follows suit. But my pale yellow guy also likes people and gets bored in hiding – I'd like to think he knew me – and I coaxed him out to be petted. Into one pink ear I whispered assurances that I will be home some day.

I imagine Sara was very glad when we stood up to leave. She handed me a large stack of mail that we'd agreed didn't need to be forwarded, but I will enjoy the weekly church newsletters and then pitch the junk mail.

On the way out, I hugged her even though I felt a little chilled and off-center for reasons I couldn't put my finger on.

"I'm glad you're here," I said. By saying so, I *am* glad she's here.

The rest of my time in North Texas was spent catching up with friends and getting some reassuring offers related to life at home again next spring. My Arc colleague Jim, who spun off the post-Arc business, reminded me that free office space and the chance of taking on some freelance work await.

"Remember," he said. "I've got your old desk and it's yours rent-free to write or do freelance or job hunt or whatever."

Sometimes, I do think about that inevitable day of ending the trip and returning home. Then what? But I don't contemplate for long. The end is still four or five months away.

I dropped by the office of Doris, the friend who knows Sara and brought us together for the condo setup.

"Are you sure it's working out OK, Liz?" she asked. She was nervous, but Doris is almost painfully shy, a worrier I've known for nearly 20 years who agonizes about doing the right thing. "She was terrified when you warned her that there better not be problems with the rent, and thought you might even look for somebody else while you're here."

"I think we're just fine, Doris. I'm sorry if I might have given her a sleepless night or two over that thought, but maybe it's good to knock some sense in her head if she plays bingo with rent money."

With the Texas rounds over, my next travel horizon forms around Thanksgiving a week and a half from now. My journalist friend Kitty has extended her sister's invitation to include me for a family dinner. Gina Frieden lives in Nashville, Tenn. The state of Tennessee – or Kentucky or Missouri – offer attractive options for a November-December life. And then it's back to the Kansas farm for Christmas, and New York City for New Year's Eve.

The plane made a hard landing on Boston's Logan Airport runway. And it was a hard landing on the realization that the comforts of Texas were far behind me, and I was about to pick up the journey again with all its unknowns.

This road is a particularly rough one: I-95 and the toll roads where every hour is rush hour from Boston to Washington, D.C. Negotiating Boston traffic to get headed south, the Honda and I cling to the right lane as cars suddenly appear out of nowhere, whipping past on the shoulder. Routinely! Even on Dallas-Fort Worth freeways, only the most reckless desperadoes pull a stunt like that.

I get to make a detour to Portsmouth, R.I., where old friends from my Arc days have told me I'm welcome for a night or longer. Art and Edna are retired teachers who bought their home close to water's edge in the 1960s. It's my own little lighthouse of blessed relief, having been badly frightened by Boston traffic, frustrated by wrong turns, and thwarted by bad road signs. I even needed a figurative tug boat to bring me in – responding to my telephoned SOS, Art drove to the point where I had become hopelessly lost and blind in the November darkness to lead me back the few miles to the house.

All was well when Edna produced a chilled bottle of wine to go with a tray of appetizers, and after that, LOBSTER with drawn butter, scallops, green beans with almonds and apple crisp for dessert. THIS is a port in a storm.

There was a news story a couple of years ago about a giant whale carcass decomposing on a Rhode Island shore. I remember the incident, because it caused quite a stink, so to speak, and nobody seemed to know what to do with the whale, but people swarmed around it and an international array of news media wrote about it and photographed the whole problematic mess. I never heard how things worked out, although I did manage to move on with my life.

Today I saw the whale.

"You can still smell it a little bit," said the ticket taker at the Whaling Museum of New Bedford, Mass.

Now *that's* an attraction, so I paid admission for Art and me to learn the story of KOBO (King Of the Blue Ocean), a 65-foot long 4-year-old male that tangled with a ship's propeller and was dragged into Narragansett Bay in 1998. As the whale decomposed on shore, somebody suggested taking it to the New Bedford landfill. Then a group of whale body enthusiasts, of a nobler spirit than I, volunteered to remove the flesh from bones and begin the process of preserving the skeleton for study and display.

Magnificently, KOBO now hangs suspended from one corner to another above the museum's main floor, and while I was disappointed that I couldn't detect the odor, KOBO drew me into the world of whales and whaling for a couple of fascinating hours.

Art then drove me to downtown Providence to meet up with Edna at the end of her day as a docent at the Rhode Island School of Design Museum of Art, which I understand has more conventional kinds of art not likely to emit odors. However, there is on this day a showing of carpet squares by an artist named Jim Isermann.

I was a few hours early and used the time to walk around the city's downtown, enjoying the leisure to varying degrees. At one end were the Statehouse and a mall and the Westin Hotel's cool Library Bar. I wrote in my journal there and drank a beer and eavesdropped on the conversation of two fat-cat businessmen that began with one of them saying, "My wife asked me for a divorce today." They also talked about their girlfriends.

My ears are always open, even as my eyes appear to look elsewhere. While walking on a downtown block not yet touched by redevelopment, I stared straight ahead and quickened my footsteps as some guy asked me for a cigarette.

"Fucking dyke," he said when I didn't respond.

I love Rhode Island, as long as I can take my time getting around. Spaces are small and I keep bumping into the other states, Massachusetts and Connecticut, or the sea, which cuts into the jagged coastline, then turns still and tranquil between inlet walls. The sight of sailboats is fresh and bright.

But my thoughts turn to Tennessee or Kentucky or Missouri. I'm ready for the next section of the country.

"How can I get to Washington, D.C., without going through New York City?" I ask my hosts.

It is Saturday, and I've purposely waited for a day free of commuter traffic. A longtime colleague at The Arc who made the move to Washington has invited me to "stop by" and spend a night or two.

"It's very easy," Art assures me. Edna and I stopped by a AAA office yesterday to pick up maps, and now we have them open before us.

"Before you get to New York you'll come to Hwy. 287. Turn west there and drop down through New Jersey," he said.

I have a beautiful day for such a big drive. It begins with what I view as the last of bucolic New England as I make my way to I-95 over the majestic skyward sweep of the Newport Bridge and 30 miles of twisty two-lane road. The straight-line driving through Connecticut turns fast and aggressive till I finally have to give it a rest and pull into McDonald's for a Coke and a phone call to Lisa.

"Are you there??" I said, surprised that my former condo caretaker answers.

"I am here!"

"I'm on my way to Washington, D.C., today and wondered how close you might be to I-95. Maybe we can meet?"

"Absolutely!" she said. "When do you think you'll get here?"

There are two special topics I'd like to take up with Lisa. First, she has described an anti-poverty program in Kentucky I might be interested in. I've decided I want to pursue a meaty volunteer project next time around, having earned enough in wages to not be concerned about a job before the holidays. The other topic is the enigmatic Sara. What are Lisa's impressions of her? Their tenancies overlapped a week so maybe she has some insights.

Entering the state of New York, my fear of somehow winding up in an NYC traffic hell was averted when I spotted the turn described by my hosts. I crossed the Tappan Zee Bridge to New Jersey. I LOVE that name, to say it out loud anyway – Tappan-Zee. It's a tap dance for the tongue: TAPpan-Zee TAPpan-Zee TAPpan-Zee.

New Jersey nickel-and-dimed me to death. Pretty highway, but toll booths sprang up willy-nilly for a cross-state trip that was stop-and-go.

As I approached Philadelphia, Lisa and I talked a couple more times, but between her unfamiliarity with the route I was on, and the approach of evening and my desire to reach my friend's home before dark, I gave up on the idea. We were too much like space ships trying unsuccessfully to dock.

So I swept on through Delaware and into Maryland and found Suzette's apartment in Silver Spring with no trouble. She stood in the parking lot, ready to direct me to a visitor's space and let me into the locked building.

Suzette and I go back 18 years – she's been with The Arc even longer than I was – and we share many secrets and rich stories of office life. Until recently when she bought a new car, we even drove the exact same color and model of Honda Civic, and we formed the BITCH Club – Broads In Tan Cool Hondas.

She's on one of her occasional diets, but a simple meal of tuna sandwiches and raw vegetables is fine with me.

We go nowhere virtually the entire weekend, and I am grateful for the down time.

Generally, except for a lunch rendezvous in Bethesda with another old colleague, we spend hours curled up in the living room, rehashing office war stories, erupting in cackles and whoops and pounding on throw pillows. I struggle not to talk much about the organization's present, because in recalling the good years, my former employer becomes much like a former lover. No matter how amicable the separation, there is a touch of jealousy and little resentments, as the breakup is a little too recent.

"Hey!" I said. "Meet me in New York City for New Year's Eve!"

"I've always wanted to go there!" Suzette responds.

I describe the annual trek that Martha and Paul and I make up to the city to participate in the New Year's Eve Midnight Run of the New York Road Runners Club. This year will be no different, despite my travels. The Midnight Run is less known, but every bit as festive – and a lot more fun – as standing around in Times Square waiting for the ball to drop. The event is in Central Park and attracts thousands of people.

I've already worked out holiday logistics, planning Christmas in Kansas, staying with my father until Dec. 29. Then I'll fly to New York and meet my sister and brother-in-law for our traditional holiday week at the Olcott. I booked the flights during my visit to Texas.

Suzette agrees to meet us for a couple of days and I'm thrilled to have an additional fun friend join the party. On the day Suzette leaves Jan. 2, Sue Rowe will arrive on the train from Rutland. In addition to being pals to romp with in the city, they will help me bear the week's financial load of lodging, a consideration this year!

On Monday morning, it is time to leave and I make a stupid decision. I drive up Silver Spring's Colesville Road to meet up with I-495, the infamous Capital Beltway, at 8 o'clock in the morning. From that point I must drive about a quarter of the circumference of the loop to get to I-66 and turn toward Roanoke, Va.

I will do anything to avoid stop-and-go traffic but this time I'm stuck. There is no other way, except trying to make a dive through D.C. Still, horrified at the traffic converging on a stoplight on

Colesville Road, I keep driving north, stopping at a gas station to ask about alternatives.

How long will the traffic be backed up like that?" I asked the attendant.

Till 9 or 9:30, but sometimes it's that way all day," he said.

Defeated, I doubled back and eased into the lanes of cars, trucks and buses, trying to think about something other than the on-and-off brake lights ahead of me, so I found National Public Radio. That helped to keep me mostly sane, although I did imagine the grotesque enlargement of my left leg created by a massive growth of calf muscle from managing the clutch. Getting around that relatively short piece of loop, a distance of 17 miles, took 2 hours.

Resuming normal speed, I was already tired and bored. Twelve more miles down the road I stopped for a second breakfast in Manassas. A few more miles and a gas stop. And then a rest room break. Roanoke became the big goal, but the drive through mountains and snow flurries turned picturesque and I finally hit my groove. I whipped past Roanoke and sought the Tennessee line.

And so I stopped in Bristol, which straddles the line, and I found an over-the-hill chain motel with a nearby Mexican restaurant whose parking lot was mostly full.

This was laundry night. After dinner, I drove around, peering through darkness at signs and retail strips until I finally spied a laundromat. It was attached to a tiny convenience store on a side street off the main drag, and it wasn't until I had parked and hauled out my cardboard box full of clothes from the trunk that I realized I was the only middle-aged white lady around. Good. I'm ready to shake off the effects of all-white Vermont, where the rare black customer at Seward's caused me to stop and stare in wonderment. *Wow, dark skin. How pretty!*

The next morning, I got back on the road and discovered many newer motels out on the highway, if I'd just driven a bit farther. But I would have paid more money for a bland experience and missed out on a Monday evening's neighborhood life in Bristol, Tenn.

To ease today's boredom, I stopped at a Cracker Barrel and chose an audio tape on – get this – career success. Stuff like time management and motivating employees. Think I might be giving some thought to my "real" future? I knew everything taught on the tape but I had trouble relating to it. The advice about behavior and office life sounded as relevant as rocks and little green men on Mars. However, I guess they both have their systems.

A mere 300 scenic miles were demanded of me today, and a country music station and the homespun "honeys" and "dears" of a cashier at an Arby's heralded "Nashville!" I had enough energy left over to navigate the city's strange wheel-and-spoke-like layout correctly, using a map to find Gina's pretty house, which is red brick with shutters the color of the tall trees shading the property.

"Hello-Hello!!"

I've stepped in the door and in one sweeping glance, thrill to the sight of 64 years in "friend years." Kitty and Phil Shook and I all met as cub reporters at the *Abilene Reporter-News* in Texas 26 years ago. In fact, Kitty and Phil met each other there, married, and now I include their 12-year-old daughter Beth in the continuous friendship timeline.

Even though I left journalism, I enjoy it vicariously through Kitty's tales of chasing Texas stories out of the *Houston Chronicle* newsroom. Phil now writes popular books about fly fishing. It's typical that this afternoon, they've been glued to news events reported by CNN. Kitty quickly reintroduces me to her sister.

"Liz, remember Gina?"

The willowy blonde busy in the kitchen looked very much the way she did in April 1978. That one and only time I was around Gina, we wore identical green bridesmaid dresses and walked down a church aisle ahead of the nervous bride, her big sister.

"You were barely out of kid-dom," I recalled.

"I remember you as being very calm – and working hard to calm Kitty down," Gina said.

I heard about Gina over the years, of her marriage, divorce, and career as a psychologist, but I guess I was still expecting the shy girl in green voile. Today she exudes hospitality and fun.

"Martini?" she offered.

"And then I want you to tell me what you think of this kitchen counter top," she said, waving a hand at the just-remodeled kitchen. "It was installed today and I've come home and the guy put in the wrong thing – it's not what I picked out."

I loved the counter top, but maybe I would have felt differently if it had been mine. It was black granite with little gold flecks that wink and flash in light – more like what you'd find in a Las Vegas kitchen, or Rio de Janeiro. It suits the grown-up Gina and her lively confidence and this whole wonderful time of spending Thanksgiving with old friends, which I suppose doesn't sound particularly relevant.

She took us all out to a restaurant and during dinner, said I'm welcome to stay as long as I want. I do like Tennessee, and I have only about three weeks before I'll need to make my way to the farm for Christmas. But it always feels like I'm cheating the scheme to stay with somebody I know.

Actually, I don't know Gina, do I. She regaled us with a story about 18 therapists in her house for a party and I started to wonder, is she one of those crazy psychologists who enter the field *because* they're crazy?

The next day, with our hostess off to teach her class at Vanderbilt, I drove the Shook family to the mall where a tremendous amount of time was spent shoe shopping for Beth in one store. At first, I looked at shoes myself, then made ever widening circles beyond the shoe department until I discovered Santa Claus out in the mall's center.

Yes, it's still a day short of Thanksgiving but Santa was set up in garish red, green and gold staging, seated on an over-sized throne with a towering canopy. With nothing else to do, I stood at the rail on the level above the scene and scrutinized from afar. He's one of these "natural" Santas, of the right age with a real-looking beard. But the suit was heavily padded and lumpy – either that or he was wearing a bullet-proof vest.

I'm pretty sure this Santa doesn't like kids. He fussed with his robe and looked bored, not even smiling very much when the photo elves plopped a little girl on his knee. Santa sort of looked at her sideways and probably said something like, "Whadda ya want, kid, a dolly?" He could not care less about this gig.

"This mall has a problem Santa," I announced to the group as we *finally* left with shoes. "It may be my mission in Nashville to keep an eye on him."

"Maybe he's warming up to the job," Kitty said.

I guess I'm warming up to the idea of taking Gina up on her invitation to hang around. We had such a fun Thanksgiving, all of us buying and fixing our favorite foods. For the big meal, a friend of Gina's named John joined our group, a 50-ish man with a long gray pony tail and the gentle, laid-back nature of an old hippie.

He asked me many questions about my cross-country adventure.

"I began this trip with the idea of living in *small* towns," I told him.

"Nashville IS a small town," John said.

With everybody else turning dithery and helpless, I wound up with the job of carving the turkey. Now, in my childhood home, this was my father's role of course. But not at the table – in the kitchen, where he dispatched the bird on a wooden board, wielding a screaming electric knife that scared me with its spectacular, double-bladed blood-gushing potential. I could never relate to the magisterial scene of TV shows, movies and American advertising of the family patriarch slicing with graceful precision.

But I was a good sport today. I took up the large carving knife and, beginning the process with some grace, sought to slice nice even pieces of meat. When that didn't work, I started hacking, sawing and chopping as John helpfully speared the carcass with a fork so it wouldn't skid off the plate. We got the job done.

The Shooks had to leave the very next day to return to the demands of Houston journalism and book writing. With the house emptied of guests, I weighed time and opportunity. I can have a bedroom and bathroom all to myself at the opposite end of the house from my hostess' "suite," and we'll still rattle around in the spaciousness. There's even a beautiful sweet cat named Ghandi.

I also decided Gina wasn't crazy. On the other hand, what else can you say about a woman who puts up with the dreaded...*THANKSGIVING GUEST WHO STAYED.*

18 "IT'S OVER"

"Daddy, I'll be in Nashville until Christmas," I announced in a phone call to Kansas. "Then my plan is to drive to the farm and stay with you a week until my New Year's trip to New York with Martha and Paul."

"Good! I'll have Mother at home while you all are here."

I can relax. A month ago, this discussion would not have been about my mother's visit, but a permanent return, a release from the nursing home. Both my parents seem to have adjusted to the new reality in recent weeks. Mother accepted it quickly in fact, according to their housekeeper Pam, who helps my dad at the house and reads to my mother in her room. Along with my brother and sister-in-law, Pam offers helpful, third-party reports to corroborate what's going on.

"Are you weighing yourself these days, Daddy?"

This is another check-up type of thing that bears watching. Now that he's given up the arduous care of Mother, and through some shepherding to the doctor by Ed and Sharron, he's had time to address his own health issues. These include some heart problems, and he's under orders to keep his weight down and take his medicine.

"My weight is fine."

Pick your battles, I decide. Right now, this can't be one of them.

I have gained 7 pounds on my trip, not counting Thanksgiving dinner. Nashville and its climate look pretty comfortable for running, so today, Saturday, is the first day of the rest of my healthy life. I lace up the Asics shoes, still clean even though I bought them way back in Iowa. And then I run for 25 minutes, discovering a lack of sidewalks in this neighborhood, and short streets that keep intersecting with busy streets. I'll have to work on finding my route.

The rest of the day, Gina and I change the sheets on the beds and put away holiday dishes, veer off to do our own personal stuff – I write Northeast host thank-you notes – then get back together to find a movie, dinner and more time to get acquainted about things beyond Kitty and my trip. I am fascinated by her carefree ways with such a demanding professional life, but she truly seems to love her work with the intricacies of the human mind. Even the movie gave her an idea for a lesson plan for one of her college classes.

Another morning, another run. Early Sunday is much lighter on traffic, and the clouds and cool mist blend perfect conditions for running.

Normally, in strange cities I don't get terribly lost, being able to memorize turns and straight-aways and keeping track of street names, or having a good sense of direction. But today, I get caught up in the wonders of one street leading to another street leading to...Belle Meade Boulevard. With four lanes divided by a landscaped median, Belle Meade is lined with mansions atop sweeping hillside lots. I run and gawk for a long way.

Suddenly, I realize I have gone too far to retrace my steps, and I have no idea where I am. I don't have my phone with me, and there is no 7-11 or any other public place in sight.

"Excuse me."

I have made eye contact with a man out for a fast walk. We passed each other earlier and exchanged good-mornings, and he has reappeared, perhaps on his return trip home.

"I'm afraid I'm hopelessly lost."

"Where do you want to be?"

I tell him the street and ask if there is a shortcut back to it without going all the way around the path that got me there.

"I know that street and you are a long way," he said. "If it wouldn't make you uncomfortable, I can drive you back."

I definitely want the run to be over, and in such a posh neighborhood, this man who has introduced himself as "Bill" must be a regular. I accept his kind offer.

Bill is exactly my age and we have a lot in common. As we walk toward his house, we talk easily over a range of baby boomer subjects: politics, work, exercise and aging parents. I'm curious where we'll wind up in this rich neighborhood. Sure enough, we approach the end of a street and a great big house.

But we don't go to that house. Bill leads me up a small road beside it, where nothing but thick woods is in sight.

"Don't get nervous," Bill said. "This leads to my house."

The road curves, and suddenly an enormous "castle" rises before us.

"My wife and I saw this in Europe and had it built here," Bill said, probably hearing me stifle an impolite gasp.

At the front door, I enter dark, serene, fragrant, decorated perfection. I'm so awed that I take no further steps, feeling like a dirty, penniless street urchin. The space could be a grand hotel lobby, with a massive Christmas tree two stories tall and dozens of gorgeously wrapped presents piled around its base. It's only three days after Thanksgiving!

Bill disappears into a room somewhere off to the side, and I hear murmuring.

"She's LOST??!!" his wife says loudly, shrilly.

He returns and I am attempting to look discreet and nonchalant by turning my back and looking out the window. But my eyes must have that popped-out look.

"I have one of those wonderful wives who has the Christmas decorating and shopping done by the day after Thanksgiving," Bill said, escorting me to an impossibly clean garage and a shiny SUV.

When I arrive back at the house, I can't wait to tell Gina, but she isn't around. By now, I am in a rush to clean up and get myself to church. I've spotted a lovely, steepled one, probably having a big congregation where I can disappear as an anonymous visitor.

It's a toney institution all right – "high church," with readings and sing-song responses and a homily delivered from an elevated pulpit by a scholarly reverend who nearly puts me to sleep.

And now comes communion...and I am jolted awake. One of the people delivering the elements is none other than BILL. He's going to think I'm following him around! Unless he serves other pews and doesn't see me – oops, here he comes. He sees me and blinks.

When the service ends, Bill makes his way over to me with a gorgeous woman in tow.

"I can't believe it," he says, introducing his wife. "This is eerie."

Mrs. Bill is all dazzling, smiling perfection, with not a hint of the skepticism I overheard in their house.

"Perfect, eh?" Gina says, when I regale her with the crazy story an hour later. She is amazed and amused. "Ah, how I'd love to know about the cracks."

It is Monday, the start of a work week, and I do want to work in these scant weeks before I head over to Kansas. Time to join some human orchestra working in concert for a product, service or cause.

In fact, I'd like to be a bell ringer collecting money for The Salvation Army. Thanks to the lucrative weeks of waiting tables in Vermont, I don't feel compelled to pursue wages, and I've caught the holiday spirit.

At 10 a.m., I am steering the Honda across Nashville, negotiating the crazy slant-pattern streets and curvy freeways. Last night, Gina got out the phone book and helped me find the address and a route to get there. I zigzag through Nashville's prosperous downtown, cross the Cumberland River and pass the Titans' football stadium. Nearby is a huge warehouse marked with "The Salvation Army Angel Tree" on a white banner hung over one corner of the building.

Inside, I find an enormous drafty space with rows of metal folding chairs in the center and a series of small sparsely-furnished offices on the side. I can't wait to get my assignment to a bell and a kettle out at some nice mall – maybe even the mall with the surly Santa I want to keep my eye on.

The volunteer coordinator introduces herself as Myra and seems happy to see me.

"You've got me until December 22nd and I can work 40-hour weeks," I tell her.

"That's – wonderful. When can you start?"

I tell her "right away," but then notice that she seems a little uncertain about where to place me. I'm not going to mention the bell ringing, because I want to do the job *they* need done. But I sure hope it's bell ringing.

Myra offers a tour of the operation, beginning with an explanation that the folding chairs I see are empty because the application process for individuals and families to sign up for gifts is generally complete. She guides me into the next room, and there is the most fantastic sight: A football field-sized wonderland of piles of packages and a growing corral of bicycles.

There are also many people bringing order to the scene. Right now, the opposite side of the building is open to a loading dock and a truck has backed up to it. Young people with the national AmeriCorps volunteer program scramble to unload the delivery of gifts gathered from Angel Tree locations across the city, where contributors plucked paper angels from Christmas trees and fulfilled the wish lists of children and adults in need. The program will provide for more than 14,500 Nashville citizens this year.

Myra explains a numbering system that overlays everything and invites me to start helping with the distribution, counting, labeling and checking of the thousands of toys that are laid out in a grid pattern on the vast floor.

There are many people helping today – and only so many arrivals of trucks, so there is some dead time and by mid-afternoon, there's not much for me to do.

"I wonder..." Myra says to me, "if you could do some data entry for us. Nobody seems to want to do that."

My holiday spirit of Ho-Ho-Ho deflates to Ho Ho-Hum. But OK. That's the reality of volunteer service, and I am here to serve. Tomorrow I will return to sit in one of the little offices at a computer keyboard. Dang it. The AmeriCorps kids have the cool job.

I am feeling a little nervous about Texas again. Two days into December and there's no sign of the rent payment. I talked to Sara last week about an unrelated matter and she didn't mention a problem. Twice in the last three months she at least asked permission to pay late.

When we spoke, Sara was in a terrible mood.

"Is there anything wrong?" I asked.

"Just my mother. She's a bitch."

Sara once told me her mother is 90 years old.

The condo situation is becoming a distraction to the fun times Gina and I are having out and about in Nashville. She is introducing me to her many friends, we've been shopping and attended a lecture, and we've dined and bar-hopped across the "Music City U.S.A." My favorite attraction so far is the famous Bluebird Cafe, where many famous country music performers got their start and many more hope to be discovered. Opened as a casual cafe in 1982, "The 'Bird" has become a music club first, restaurant second. On the night we were there, four young hopefuls had survived an audition to sing and play original songs. They may have included the next Garth Brooks and Faith Hill.

Or not.

"Who was your favorite?" Gina asked me.

"I'm not sure. I DIDN'T like the singer of endless weepy ballads."

"She's depressed," Gina said.

"Are you *always* working?"

On my next day of work at The Salvation Army, the weather was cold and windy and so the warehouse was particularly drafty. If I had to sit still at a computer, I was glad to at least get to sit in one of the offices off to the side. It was enclosed and mostly protected against the constant opening and closing of the main entry door.

I was introduced to Susan, the woman I will work for in the Adopt A Family program. She conducts interviews and verifies the authenticity of need. Her desk faces the door, and I am on the other end of the small narrow room at a table, seated in one of the metal folding chairs brought in from the big room outside. I can also look through a window and today, people are arriving to pick up the gifts donated for their families' Christmas.

Virtually without exception, the expressions on the faces of the moms and dads are radiant. It's as if they can't believe their luck and all this goodness. They have great armloads of packages, and many are guiding a bicycle out to their cars and old pickup trucks.

I overhear Susan, gentle and low-keyed, interviewing a woman who has been admitted for an interview. The woman also speaks quietly, politely.

"You say you are working at Captain D's right now?" Susan says.

"Yes ma'am, I just started."

"I see your list of needs – what do you *want* for Christmas?"

"Just – the food. Some underwear for the kids."

"I understand that," Susan said. "But isn't there something you'd like to have beyond necessities?"

"Maybe some gloves. Red ones? A hot plate, or one of those little toaster ovens. That's about it really."

After the interview was completed, I told Susan what a surprise it was to hear someone having such a short list when invited to express her wishes.

"That's not uncommon at all," Susan said. "Most of the people I see are having such a struggle, or they're in such a crisis, they can't think beyond basic needs."

Referrals from hospitals, social service agencies, domestic violence, prisons and witness protection programs all come through here. At one point, Susan took a call from a hospital social worker who conveyed the story of a female patient with two young children who was in a car wreck a few days ago. One of the children had been with her in the car, and the child died, but the mother does not yet know this.

Meanwhile, I am working with a list of names of prisoners who have filed needs for wives and children.

"That can get tricky to check out," Susan said. "Sometimes the children are those of more than one wife, or there is a girlfriend, and the women don't know about each other. We have to be careful."

"What about cons?" I asked.

Oh yes, she said, but the screening process makes it difficult for someone to lie and get away with it. There is also the occasional "extraordinary" request, like the family that asked for five video cameras and a carpet shampooer.

Bell ringing would not expose me to such rich stories, and I've become grateful for such an extraordinary place to work. I've always admired The Salvation Army, seeing the organization come through for people in terrible straits – of their own making or not – when other agencies have fallen away or thrown up barriers to helping because the people or situation was so undesirable.

And now I find myself in my own undesirable situation. In my bedroom at the house, it is time for a phone call to Texas, and on the evening of Dec. 6, I dial the condo.

"Sara?" I try to contain my angry fears. "Sara, where is the rent?"

Seconds of silence, and then she responds very calmly, "I deposited the rent."

"It doesn't show in my account, and your five-day grace period has ended."

"Then the bank made a mistake."

"I rather doubt that," I reply, losing my battle to contain my feelings.

"Are you calling me a liar?"

"I don't call people names but you can think whatever you like."

And then, she offers up the name of the teller who processed the deposit. At that point, tiny doubt pricks my indignation. Ending the conversation quickly, I allow myself to feel some hope, because why would she give me the teller's name if she knows I will check it out? She sounds *so* indignant. Banks do make mistakes – I was a teller myself many years ago.

At work the next day, I stare at the names I am matching with ID codes, but the mental processing just isn't there.

"Susan, I need to go make a call. I'll be back in a few minutes."

It is mid-morning, and I step out of the little office and sit in the back row of the metal chairs, away from people who are coming and going. The spot still isn't quiet, with all sounds echoing in the cavernous space. The chair is cold and my fingers are shaky.

Fortunately, I don't have to work through a bank's phone menu and I get a live person right away. I ask to speak to the teller, enunciating her name carefully.

"She is out of the office today."

"Today? Can you tell me if she was there on Monday? This concerns a transaction on my account."

"No, she's on vacation this week. Can someone else help you?"

At that moment, I freeze, with a sick lump in my stomach and a numbness slipping down the sides of my face and over my ears. My cheeks are burning.

Sara did indeed lie to me. And, well, I have to face up to a huge flaw in my planning for this year, for there is more than rent at stake here – the condo's telephone bill and electricity remain in my name.

I dial TXU Electric. I am grateful for the anonymity of the menu this time.

The sum of the voice-recorded numbers stuns me: "Two. Hundred. Seventy-Four. Dollars."

Nothing has been paid since Lisa moved out and Sara moved in three months ago.

I dial the phone company.

"Four. Hundred. Sixty-Three. Dollars." That's 20 times my monthly phone bill.

I snap the phone closed and just sit, absorbing the fact that Sara is using me for a free ride. Finally, I rise from the metal chair.

My apologies to Susan and Myra were swift. Deeply embarrassed, I explained that I must leave and I can't return and I'm so, so sorry.

And then I called Gina.

"It's over. My trip is over. I have to go home, if not tonight, first thing in the morning."

19 BETRAYAL

I didn't sleep, of course. Gina talked me out of a same-day departure. We went out for a drink at a neighborhood bar, meeting another friend of hers, and we all dissected the situation, analyzing the consequences and implications.

"Do you have a lawyer?" was one of the questions.

Not really. I did my will through one a decade ago, but no, I don't "have" a lawyer. I have lawyer relatives and lawyer friends.

One of the friends lives near the condo in the Hurst-Euless neighborhood where I ran regularly at 5:30 a.m. everyday. Dwayne and his wife Diane, who works in his office, walk the same route. After years of pre-dawn hellos and good-mornings, we eventually got acquainted.

At 5:30 this morning, I am packed, dressed and sitting on the edge of the bed, waiting for the sun to rise, mentally tracing my friends' morning walking routine, and calculating the time of their return to their house. I can't wait for office hours.

Dwayne answers the phone. I tell the sad tale.

"I am feeling very stupid right now. Can you help me get her out of the condo?"

Dwayne should be annoyed by my intrusive call and my stumbling recitation of events, but most of all, he should be astounded by my stupidity. He shows none of these things. He is cool, calm, efficient with a few questions, and then he says magical words that become my new favorite phrase in the English language:

"I'll take care of this for you."

Gina continues to help me stay calm and thinking rationally as I hastily pack my car.

And then I am off and making it home, hell-bent for Texas, stopping only to fax the condo contract to Dwayne from a convenience store.

The Honda and I dive down the western half of Tennessee toward Arkansas. I am so preoccupied I don't even play the radio or a book tape, preferring to re-gather my wits and think about next steps and the weeks ahead. At least this is the holiday season and I have no big plans. I'll spend Christmas in Kansas and welcome the new year of 2001 in New York.

I have looked forward to finishing my year with winter homes in the South, completing a tidy circuit that has swung from the Southwest to the Northwest, Midwest and Northeast. *Maybe* the final three months of the adventure I want can still happen, but how? How can I find somebody else to trust with my home?

No, that's not the essential question today. It's more troubling than that – How can I trust myself, my judgment.

I'm barely aware of gas stops and food breaks and the setting sun as I break my rule to not drive after dark. (Again, where is my good judgment?)

On the interstate in Arkansas, the blackness of a December early evening wraps me and my thoughts in the rocketing Honda. I get a call, and I grope around in my purse without taking my eyes off the road, scrambling to find the phone before the ringing stops.

"Liz, this is Sara."

I regret the effort. Has Dwayne done something already? Does Sara know what's afoot?

"I was surprised to come home and find a notice to vacate."

"I suppose you were."

"As you should know, according to the contract I have until the tenth day of the month, and if I have not paid, you can impose a late charge."

I am amazed at her cool. If I came home to an eviction notice on my door I'd be freaking out – if I were innocent, that is. It's interesting, too, that she's let go of the bank deposit story. It's almost as if she's been through this sort of thing before.

"Sara, I do not want to discuss this now. I'm driving home to Texas and I will talk to you when I get there."

She probably thinks she can talk her way out of her dilemma. I like that idea; it's certainly preferable to the one in which she reacts with rage and revenge, trashing my place, or doing something to Minnie and Bigelow.

I reach the state line at 8 p.m. and pick out a motel in Texarkana. I call Dwayne to tell him about Sara's call and to find out about the legal plan.

"Diane and I went over there this afternoon and posted the notice," he said. "She has five days to get out."

Bless you, bless you, bless you forever, Dwayne and Diane.

Wearily, I steer the Honda into my sister's driveway, trying not to think of her concerns about this trip a year ago. Fortunately, she's not an "I-told-you-so" type, and anyway, who would have thought of this situation? Ironically, it wasn't trouble on the road that yanked me home – accident, illness, or anything else "out there" – but trouble over things that were easily within my control.

At least it is one of those dazzlingly sunny-and-60 December days found often in a Fort Worth winter. It is an enormous relief for me to have a soft place to land, and I lug a couple of suitcases into the house, leaving as much in the car as possible because I'll be moving back into the condo VERY soon.

"Hi!" Martha says, steady and non-judgmental as ever, as if it's just another Saturday and I've come over to go shopping with her.

I don't know why I felt so calm about it, but going over to the condo later that afternoon for a sit-down chat with Sara seemed perfectly natural. In fact, she greets me at the door – not happily, of course, but accepting of the situation that we've got a problem. And, my hunch is correct. She thinks she can still negotiate and avoid eviction.

"Here's what I want to know, Sara. You have a good job, you're a mature person with no one else to take care of; what's more important than shelter in your financial life?"

I have settled onto the sofa and she is in her big chair, glaring at me.

"I don't make as much as you may think," she says. "And, I have a 92-year-old mother to help out..."

Ah, the mother. The one she called "a bitch" a few nights ago.

"I just don't think you keep your priorities straight," I say. "I've heard that you play bingo a couple of nights a week. That doesn't seem smart when you can't pay the rent."

She ignores my lesson in Personal Finance 101.

She hauls out the bigger emotional ammunition: "Cancer isn't cheap."

I recall the "cancer-free" T-shirt and declarations to the neighbors that she's well. And anyway, doesn't she have health insurance? But like my observation of the turnabout words on dear old Mom, I don't comment.

"Well Sara, here's the thing. I've learned that in addition to the rent problems, you've paid nothing on the bills. I cannot afford to support you and this situation."

Suddenly, she gets it. Caught, she gasps and flails an arm and cries out, "Well that's IT, isn't it." Tears flow. "You do want me OUT of here, out on the streets at Christmas time."

I am unmoved; in fact, she has quite the opposite effect on me. *Show's over.* I stand up, ready to leave.

"Yes, that's it. Leave the keys on the mantel. Don't forget to leave the mailbox key."

Over the next four days, we talk on the phone a couple more times and Sara seems resigned. She actually vows to "to make it up" to me and pay back the lost funds. I tell her I suspect she has a problem and needs help...

"Oh yes," she agrees, "I do have a..."

"Gambling problem. I think you're addicted to gambling, Sara."

I have reached this conclusion in speculation with Carolyn as we try to put pieces together. She told me that Sara once posted flyers on the bulletin board of the Alameda Village clubhouse, inviting people to join bus charter trips to the Louisiana gambling meccas of Shreveport and Bossier City. Including the bingo games and the Las Vegas photo, her interest seems more than casual.

Sara has no comment on my theory.

Short of marking big black "X"es on a calendar, I count the days and the hours until I can have my home back. I see friends, even attending a Christmas party of Arc ex-employees, who gather at my colleague Jim's big office where, as promised, my old furniture and computer stand ready for me.

"Andy and I are going to do the Jog 'R Egg Nogger in Dallas," my friend Al announces. "Are you ready to run a 5K?"

In many ways, there seems to be a place for me to resettle easily into my old life – minus the job – and this is somewhat reassuring. But I feel as if I climbed to an exciting new place in the world, and suddenly, somebody put a big foot on my head and sent me plunging down a long chute. I've landed unceremoniously right on my butt.

"Liz, I am sooo sorry. I knew that Sara had some problems but I didn't know she would do this," said Doris, my long-time friend who has known Sara four years. "She even tried to borrow money from me to pay you. I loaned her some money once and it took forever to get it back, but she did pay me. She's had depression and some other things."

Slowly, Sara's days to vacate passed. My home is mine again, and I am standing in it. Sara has removed all of her possessions, and if she took anything of mine, it's not readily apparent. Beyond that issue, my home is spotless throughout – the living room and den, the little galley kitchen, the baths and the bedroom.

"It will be clean," she asserted in one of the recent phone calls. She always bragged about her housekeeping; it was a huge point of pride. Perhaps that quality was one well she could still dip into for the dignity she otherwise lost to her deadbeat, sponging, out-of-control, financially ruinous ways.

And the cats? Not in sight.

Beside the bed, I get down on my knees and lift the dust ruffle to peer into their low dark sanctuary. Two glowing pairs of eyes, very close together, stare back at me as they huddle against yet another change in their household.

"MOMMY'S HOME!" I screech in my high-pitched "cat voice." They stay put. All is normal.

I have guessed right, that trashing my place and hurting my pets were not in the realm of Sara's disorders.

As requested, the condo door keys have been left on the fireplace mantel. The mailbox key is not there, and my ire rises again. I will NEVER be rid of the woman. I don't want to see her or talk to her ever again. Yet now I'm going to have to hound her to return the key I need to gain access to my own mail.

Screw that. I grab the Yellow Pages and find a locksmith two blocks away.

"I have just evicted a tenant and I want to change all of my locks. I also need a way to get into my mailbox and change that lock because she may be trying to keep the key."

I wonder if all locksmiths work like 911. Dave arrived with his tools within the hour and he almost seemed to know me. He may have thought he did, too, because he's made so many runs to Alameda Village. He moved about the condo in a familiar way, working fast, making keys, and then he made the final change at the bank of mailboxes at the complex's clubhouse.

The final bill to change all the locks was $109, worth every penny, but now the costs of simply dis-inviting Sara from my life are over $1,100. I paid the electricity and phone bills right away, reckoning that those things were in my name to begin with and I'm just stuck.

I get into the mailbox and it yields mail that's mostly not mine, including a bright green flyer addressed to Sara from "Touso Ishto, Chickasaw Indian Gaming Center" in Thackerville, Okla.

Another envelope is from Spiegel, but it is addressed to Elizabeth Moore, which is odd because I've never been on their mailing list. I slide my thumb under the corner of the flap, tear the edge open and pull out the letter, which has a plastic card attached...

"We welcome you as a Spiegel Charge customer."

I didn't know companies still sent unsolicited credit cards in the mail...

And then a pain shot through me like a lightning bolt, a realization that was so stunning and so frightening that I could not walk or talk or think. I just stood there, the mailbox door gaping, and I stared at the blue plastic with the raised imprint of an account number and my name – "Thank you for opening a Spiegel Charge...use your new card soon and use it often...."

Back at the condo, I nearly yelled into the phone, "DORIS, WHAT do you really know about your friend Sara??!" I was crazy with shock and foreboding.

"I'll be right over."

Doris arrived quickly, her eyes wide.

"Liz, what..."

I handed her the letter.

Doris took it, read the page the card was attached to, and when she absorbed the implication, she shrieked.

"No, no, Liz, she wouldn't..."

With Doris still there, I dialed the customer service number and asked about the new credit card issued to Elizabeth Moore.

"We show that you have ordered merchandise in the amount of $670. It has been shipped and should arrive via U.S. Postal Service within the next few days."

At that point, I just asked Doris not to worry, and to leave and return to her own day, for she was even more panicked than I, rocked by a friend's betrayal. Two messed-up heads weren't better than one in this situation. I opened the front door and we stepped out onto the patio into the cool air.

"Let's go have lunch together tomorrow," I said, wanting to reassure her that I don't hold her responsible for the actions of her friend.

"I'm sorry, Liz…oh I am sorry."

After she left, I called Dwayne, and that's when I just really lost it, becoming short of breath and crying.

Again, he was cool.

"Come over to the office," he said. "There are very specific steps you'll need to take, starting with a call to the credit bureaus, and I'll draft a letter for you."

At Dwayne's office later in the afternoon, I was greeted warmly as an adventurer coming home, not a hapless victim of identity theft.

"We're having our holiday 'Italian party' December 29th. Why don't you come!" Diane said.

Upbeat and matter-of-fact, Dwayne described the steps I need to take as if I'm the hundredth client he's counseled and maybe I am. ID theft is the fastest growing crime in America.

But how many victims make it so easy for the thief? Sara had access to my mail, my home telephone and, with just the least bit of rummaging, Social Security number, birth certificate, credit card accounts, bank checks and savings accounts.

"What I'm afraid of," I said, "is, what's ahead? There's no clear ending to this thing. The very first time I opened my mailbox, I drew out a new credit card – how many others are out there? Has she already opened accounts in my name that she's using?"

"Start with the credit bureaus," Dwayne said. "Make those calls and put an alert on your accounts."

At home, I suddenly grabbed cleaning fluids and the vacuum cleaner and furiously went to work. I poured Lysol over everything, scouring sinks and toilets with a vengeance, running the vacuum across the floors over and over again, tearing off bedding and just taking it all, pillows and everything, to the dumpster. I scrubbed doorknobs and anything else she might have touched and I obliterated every hair, fingerprint and dead skin cell of her evil presence.

20 PUTTING LIFE BACK TOGETHER

"Hi, Jim."

"Welcome!!" He stood up from behind his desk as I walked across the wide-open space of Soffar Distribution on my first day of "work," lugging my briefcase that is already growing wide with papers.

My footsteps are strangely but nicely springy; when the previous tenancy was a big dance and gymnastics studio, the floor had been covered in a layer of some kind of cushioning topped with soft industrial carpeting. Makes it rather fun to walk on, and it's enough to muffle sound in the otherwise cavernous space.

Overhead, a heater rumbles on, sending an enveloping wave of warm air, another comfort, and all around are the working reminders of our old office, desks and computers, rows of file cabinets, shelving that holds stacks of The Arc's publications, and there's even the fully decorated Christmas tree that had been put up year after year in the Resource Development Department. It all looks so out of place. I'm going to have to get used to it.

"Want some coffee? I just made it," Jim said.

"Thanks. I also need a phone, the Internet, a printer and a fax machine."

"Help yourself."

I have canceled my existing credit cards and changed my checking account. I've placed fraud alerts with all three credit bureaus, Trans Union, Experion and Equifax. However, it's not a simple matter of making a few phone calls or tapping out some emails – I have to maintain a laborious paper record, putting events in writing, filling out forms and maintaining a running log of every discovery and response. I track names, instructions and confirming numbers given to me over the phone. I certify my mailings for proof to support the record. When I received and filled out a fraud affidavit from Spiegel, I stopped by my bank to get it notarized ("$6 please").

Sara ordered a second phone line and a computer support package in my name. She also opened additional phone service accounts with two more companies.

Other people in the circle are putting two and two together to discover that they were victims of Sara's deeds. My tenant No. 1, Lisa, was sent an unordered box of clothing that arrived in Chicago. She was in the process of moving at the time, and her stay in the condo had overlapped with Sara's about a week, a time when Lisa was traveling and simply hadn't moved her things out yet. Luckily, although Sara had some kind of currency of Lisa's, nothing more happened beyond the disappearance of a few favorite household items.

"Sara was extremely rude to me as I was in the process of moving out," Lisa added. "On the night before I was completely out of your condo and Sara was in, I slept on the sofa but I almost slept in my car, she was so hostile. And I have no idea why."

Lisa never mentioned this episode, and I wonder, if we had been able to meet up on my swing down the East Coast in mid-November...it might have come out over a face-to-face lunch.

And then there's poor Doris, for whom some mysterious occurrences were starting to be understood.

"Liz," she said, "something really awful happened to me. It was months ago, maybe even a year."

Doris looked down, away from me. And then she described the evening she was driving in Fort Worth and suddenly saw police lights spinning in her rearview mirror. She pulled over, perplexed, because she hadn't been speeding, nor had she broken any obvious traffic rules.

"I was handcuffed and taken to jail," Doris said quietly, almost in a whisper. "I had been sent some blank checks and they were in my house, but I had never used them. I was wanted for check forgery – 'Somebody' got those checks and used them. I hadn't even known they were missing."

On another day, Doris and Sara met for lunch, and $50 was taken from Doris's purse while she was away from the table in the ladies room. She didn't realize the theft right away, and certainly hadn't connected it to a friend.

"Sara offered to cat-sit for me," Carolyn told me. "I'm sure glad I didn't take her up on it."

Sara was sweet as pie to Carolyn and Vernon.

"She'd say, 'Come by for a glass of wine' if I ran into her on the sidewalk," Vernon said, who told a very odd story about a safe.

Sara turned up with the safe, a heavy little block that was loaded in her Jeep.

"I asked her if she needed help moving it somewhere, and she said no, but did I know how she might get into it. There was no key. She said she'd bought the safe, but that's why it was such a bargain – the key had been lost."

Sara duped our mail carrier.

At the Hurst Post Office, I met with two postal officials who listened intently as I got set up to receive (and return) the Spiegel merchandise.

"She taped what amounts to five names, in big black lettering, to the edge of the mailbox," I told them. "There's my last name, three different last names for her, and the name of my neighbor's home-based business, the ABC corporation."

I had noticed the ABC and was able to make that connection, because Tom's mailbox was right above mine, and I had poked his misplaced deliveries under his door several times. Sara must have received something lucrative and simply added the business name to her many other address names – a fast-moving letter carrier wouldn't notice the difference and she could continue to get at least some of Tom's mail.

Bang, another form to fill out, for the U.S. Postal Inspection Service, Southwest Division.

I tried to be philosophical about this whole turn of events and focused on just straightening everything out. The detail work helped me to avoid thinking about the awfulness of it all, and otherwise, I worked to resume old habits and pleasant pastimes of living in North Texas.

But for the first time since struggling with depression 25 years ago, I had anxiety attacks. With friends Al and Andy, I rode over to Dallas on a cloudy December Saturday to do the Jog 'R Egg Nogger, a holiday 5-kilometer run that should have been fun and festive and a happy time with friends. Halfway through the 3.1-mile race along White Rock Lake, I simply shut down. I was short of breath and couldn't run any more. I walked, with other runners breezing by like cars on the freeway passing the roadside flat tire. *Breathe, stand tall, look up*, I told myself. *Breathe deeply and keep walking.*

One of the sources of my distress over the Sara mess is the apathy I've felt from the agencies I'm dealing with.

"Identity theft is extremely common and hard to prosecute."

This shrugging comment is from the Hurst police officer I meet with. He's impossibly young and skinny, with a croaky voice.

"You'll need more than this to have a case," Officer Timmy tells me, reading over my report paperwork.

"But in most ID thefts, the person doing it isn't known!" I exclaim. "Here's her license plate number, here's her BUSINESS card, for crying out loud. Can't you just go get her?!"

"If more things turn up, let me know. Then we'll assign a detective."

I'm starting to feel naive, stupid really, like somebody who has watched too many cop shows and believes their tidy stories: Crime Doesn't Pay.

One more thing about Sara that I haven't mentioned: She's a former veteran cop with the Corpus Christi police department. It's another winning detail on her résumé that impressed me about her.

I'm realizing that Sara knows how to fly just below radar. She's spread her victimizing around, not hitting any one person too much to be noticed and dealt with.

In fact, I'm sensing that my rip-offs are finite. I'm less apprehensive about opening my mailbox, and my diligence with the paperwork is holding up. I'm also finding that the process of scrubbing the dirt off my name amounts to a few clicks on a keyboard – if the person at that company finds me and my paperwork credible.

As always, crazy luck plays a role, too.

One day, I was on the phone with one of Sara's three telephone service providers. It was the company of the $400 bill that I had paid, because the account was in my name to begin with. I had decided to eat the basic service costs that she had run up, but I was negotiating the rest, pointing out that the second phone line and other goodies "were fraudulently obtained."

I had steeled myself for the call, keeping the lengthy billing statement in front of me to address line by line: "I shouldn't be charged this amount because..."

To my amazement, the customer service representative is surprisingly agreeable. It takes virtually no argument to get the charges erased. Line by line, she replies, "OK."

We're now ready to conclude the call.

"Thanks for your patience, Ms. Moore," she said. "If I sound a little distracted, it's because there's a SWAT team on our building."

In a Dallas murder case this week, the police believed they had their suspects cornered in a hotel across the street from the phone company. It's dumb, bizarre luck for me. My customer service rep needed to get rid of a customer and return to her own drama.

My problems with Sara seem to be under control, for now. The condo has more of the feel of home, and the cats are out from under the bed. In fact, I felt a corner had been turned when I suddenly noticed the skittish Minnie one evening, sitting in the middle of the living room floor, gazing up at me and smiling in that contented way you see in cats with expressive faces.

Christmas week has arrived and I get to return to the road — sort of.

It's not my car, but it's a Honda, my brother-in-law Paul's roomy van. Martha and I hand him the last of our suitcases and our shopping bags bulging with wrapped gifts. My nephew has driven up from Austin to go with us.

Just over 8 hours and 500 miles later, we all arrive in Kansas' Osage County on roads illuminated by little on a dark night, although if you look at the sky, you can see thousands of stars.

Positively ablaze is my parents' house, with every room light on and a modest strand of multi-colored bulbs lining the eaves above the porch. The Christmas tree is lit in the picture window of the living room, and framing the glass are the famous trout lights. I gave these to Daddy many years ago (perhaps in the same year I gave him a fish tie for Father's Day) after finding them in an eclectic shop on New York's Columbus Avenue. Now, of course, you can find just about everything in a novelty light string — fish, frogs, jack-o-lanterns, chili peppers, flowers, you-name-it.

"Hello-hello!" my dad calls out, opening the door wide to our clomping footsteps. At the same time, we haul as many gifts and suitcases as we can manage, not wanting to return to the winter night from the warmth of the house.

However, my dad grabs his puffy green jacket and cap from the coat rack in the hallway.

"I'm going to run into town and pick up some fried chicken for supper," he announces with a jingle of car keys. "We'll have that with pie and the ice cream I've made."

Quite the homemaker he's become. When Mother had to stop cooking, he seemed to decide he hasn't had enough dessert in his life. So hey! If he has to do meals, he might as well make things he likes. Those foods include homemade ice cream and made-from-scratch pies. Aunt Lugene gave him the recipe for the crust. The pies are always a hit at church dinners and community potlucks.

Mother is "home" for the holidays, brought here from the nursing home for the duration of our visit. Martha and I agree to stay with her, as well as to find some green things to add to the meal, while Daddy, Paul and Matt run into Lyndon for the chicken. Let the festivities begin!

The next day, my brother and sister-in-law arrive from Ottawa to join the family gathering. However, my brother is still smarting from a wounding encounter with Daddy. Ed and Sharron have been worried about my dad's health issues and risk-taking, particularly in this month's siege of bad weather. On a recent Sunday morning of 7 degrees and snow on the ground, Ed called to check up on Daddy and ask about his plans. Our dad informed Ed that he intended to make church, then pick up Mother in Osage and take her to Lyndon for lunch and back to the farm for an overnight stay.

"I asked him whether he really thought that was wise and he asked why not," Ed had told us in an e-mail. "Ultimately I told him that I really didn't think it was a good idea and he said he was acceding to my judgment."

And then our dad asked Ed a question that was drenched in sarcasm – whether Edwin thought it would be OK if he brought Mother home for Christmas "to be in her house with the family."

I'm realizing that being so far away, Martha and I can revel in the good news we hear. With Mother safe and cared for in the nursing home, Daddy has been able to resume old freedoms to zig-zag the county on errands during the day and have a social life at night, with bridge games and dominoes in the homes of friends. We've focused on that kind of information, avoiding thoughts of falls and car accidents on ice, downplaying a doctor's warning that the cold weather is not good for our dad's heart.

The only front-and-center sadness for us is that Daddy is about to lose "his" church. Lyndon's 130-year-old First Presbyterian is closing. My dad mentions matter-of-factly that two services remain before the doors are locked Dec. 31.

The news rocks us. Four generations of the Smith family have been members, occupying the bare wooden pews of this spiritual house, its dark red bricks stacking up as one of the town's more impressive buildings. Like a good piece of furniture in a room full of scuffed bargains, it anchors a shady corner lot quietly, steadfastly. It's so much a part of Smith family history and life, its east windows are etched with our ancestors' names as memorials.

"What's to become of it?" we ask our father.

Still stoic, resigned, he recounts the deliberations of the Session, the tiny church's governing body which finally had to come to grips with the fact that eight or 10 aging attendees at a typical service can't support such an edifice. I can only imagine the pain of discussing options like turning the place into a warehouse, or attracting a trendy restaurant business, or even tearing it down. Finally, it appears that another church, one of the upstart "fringe" groups that nonetheless has youth and energy to go with its audio-visual equipment, is interested in buying the building. At least it will remain a church, but for non-Presbyterians for the first time since 1870!

On Sunday, Daddy and the guys stayed home with Mother as Martha and I went to church to pay last respects. We treasured every creak of the floorboards, the labored sermon, the greetings and hand-shakes of the few hearty souls willing to stay to the end of a piece of very personal history. We all would have mangled the hymns if our voices had been louder. On the other hand, "What A Friend We Have In Jesus" lives on, doesn't it.

The actual holiday of Christmas was abbreviated. Eight of us demolished the pile of gifts, sending up crackling clouds of paper and yards of ribbon until someone finally fetched a big black trash bag. We all pitched in to stuff the wrappings and clear some space to at least walk through the living room and provide a pathway for Mother's wheelchair so that we could move her to the kitchen for dinner.

The usual Smith Scavenger Hunt had to be abandoned due to the weather. This is a raucous tradition of recent years when my dad rises early on Dec. 25th, wraps his gifts in aluminum foil and three colors of bows, takes them to his truck and drives to all parts of the property to place the presents on tree limbs and fence posts, barbed wire and prairie grass. Later, as he drives with Mother in warmth, the rest of us ride in the bed of the truck, eyes peeled for our color of ribbon – red for the Gordons, white for me, green for Ed's crew. It takes a real love for the game and a dose of sheer greed to brace us against the piercing blasts of wintry air and bone-rattling ride of the bounding pickup, which we manage to stop only with shouts of "RED!" "GREEN – OURS" "WHITE – THAT'S MINE."

The weather, in fact, was bad everywhere at Christmas. A huge storm front was invading the heartland, threatening to glaze Kansas and Oklahoma roads with ice. With my nephew having to get back to Austin for work, and the Gordons and I having a New York-bound plane to meet, we couldn't risk being stuck an extra couple of days. Early on Christmas afternoon, we said our good-byes and scrambled into the van for a slow, dark trek back to Texas.

Caution and the skills of my brother-in-law, a former driver's ed teacher, got us safely back to Fort Worth. Let out at the condo, I dropped suitcases and gifts, glanced at the phone for a blinking message light – there was none – and rushed to the mailboxes. No surprises there either.

It's time to be thankful for a good Christmas, a safe return to Texas, quiet on the Sara front, and now the prospect of life on the upswing, starting with the annual fabulousness of New York at New Year's. After that, maybe, just *maybe* I can think about a way to return to the road. Lisa knows a nice seminary student who might be interested in the condo arrangement. With FBI-like thoroughness, maybe I could investigate him, remove my phone line this time, install hidden cameras, get his driver's license, fingerprints and a DNA sample....

Officer Timmy finally called me this week to give me a case number. Wow, I've won "case status"! All it took was a filled-out police report, the Spiegel fraud affidavit, a copy of letters to the phone companies, the report to the Postmaster, and a list of new theft discoveries – chief among them being the blue pig. A possession since my 16th birthday, the giant plastic bank was so heavy with coins that it sat, immovable, on the floor of my bedroom closet.

At Dwayne and Diane's Italian party, I contribute a platter of antipasti, and drift through rooms full of interesting people. But I am distracted. On this night before our flight to New York, I am all packed and ready to go, but there are weather reports of a massive winter storm bearing down on the Northeast.

The next morning, Martha and I get phone calls from our airline that LaGuardia is closed and our flight is canceled. New York is shut down by a foot of snow.

"I can't believe this," I say to Martha.

I am on my cell phone, waiting for breakfast. It is mid-morning on a beautiful day, and at sudden, dispiriting loose ends, I've decided to at least eat out.

"What have you heard about the weather up there?" I ask.

Martha sighs heavily.

"Same as you – nothing good."

I guess somehow I thought my older smarter sister could produce an idea, news, something more hopeful, information I did not have – like maybe she's learned of the sudden reopening of the damn airport.

"What about Suzette?" Martha asks, remembering my Maryland friend traveling to the city to meet us.

"I haven't talked to her yet. Surely she's canceled."

Finally realizing that we're truly stuck, I give up on answers from Martha and start spearing pancakes. At least the waitresses aren't their slightly surly selves this morning; they've decided to favor me with coffee refills. I try to read the *Star-Telegram*, but none of the news of the day, not even the comics and Dear Abby, are registering.

"Suzette? It's Liz. Where are you?"

"On the way to the hotel."

"You're kidding. How? Our flight has been canceled."

Washington, D.C., was completely spared. Suzette boarded Amtrak at Union Station and made it up to the city just fine.

"Why don't you see if you can fly to Washington and take a train up?"

And in a light-bulb moment, the trip is back on.

My brother-in-law agreed — not real heartily on a day perfect for golf — but he did say he will go along with whatever Martha and I decided. We rebooked for Washington, and with 24 hours to spare before New Year's Eve, the three of us were on our way to Reagan National Airport. Martha and I may have forgotten one tiny detail in selling Paul on the quick-change rerouting: The next train to New York is not scheduled until 3 a.m.

The plane landed at 10:30 p.m., so the cab ride was swift and enjoyable as we passed the Jefferson and Washington monuments, softly illuminated in the night, and the Capitol dome in all its magnificence (if one did not think too hard about the politics within). Grandest of all was Union Station, its arches and marble facade inviting adventure, a portal to our true destination. But to get to the City That Never Sleeps, we appeared to be in a city snoozing soundly — nothing was open in the hushed halls and we bought our tickets from a machine.

The 3 a.m. train was on time and by then, a good-sized crowd, perhaps fellow revelers who had also discovered Plan B, filled the waiting room. We boarded silently.

As Amtrak rolled across barren landscape, it was hard to imagine the snowfall; depths up to 20 inches in some parts of New Jersey were being reported. I needed to sleep, but I was wound up for travel like a little kid. I kept peeking out the window. Soon, like monstrous ghosts in the night, the snow began to appear — lengthening, deepening blankets of it in towns where nothing moved, with cars still buried in it, and signs and features so obscured, the scenes were timeless; we could be in another century.

At 7 a.m. in Penn Station, the last day of the year was well under way. Travelers poured through either coming or going. *We*, New York, are arrivals! Ridiculous, fool-hardy fun seekers! So bring on the fun!

With streets a mess, we stayed underground, taking the subway to the Upper West Side. We checked into the Olcott, collected my roommate, and minutes later, the four of us filled a booth at Utopia and dug into hot platters of eggs and toast and hash browns.

You would think I'd be tired by now. Martha and Paul returned to the hotel to get some rest. I couldn't wait to plunge Suzette into the sights and the buzz of the city. Wearing our most serious winter boots, coats and scarves, we plowed across Central Park where half the city, it seemed, had turned out to play. Children and grownups were the same, frolicking and shrieking, and I half-expected everyone to break into song. There was a perfect Currier and Ives moment of snow and sleds, running and snowball fights, people spilling over the hillsides without a care in the world. New Yorkers use their park so very well.

When cold nipped our feet and ears, we ducked into a Park Avenue cafe and deli, taking our time with steaming lattes and eyeing foods to carry back to the hotel for the post-run New Year's party. We picked out some cheeses and flat breads, then headed over to the New York Road Runners Club to pick up everybody's packets containing our paper numbers, T-shirts, course maps, instructions and freebies.

The city is rapidly digging out although I took pictures of cars completely buried by the snowfall itself and by more piles pushed and blown to the side by removal equipment. On Fifth Avenue, car "mounds" wrapped in white matched the lines of the swirling architectural design of the nearby Guggenheim Museum.

Food and hot drinks continued to fuel our day concluding with a soothing Thai meal on Amsterdam Avenue that brought my excitement level down so that I could rest in the hours before the run. Settled in our rooms, we all waited as late as possible before going out, given the weather conditions to be endured in running clothes without coats – if you over-dress, you get too hot during the race. At 11:15, we stood in the hotel lobby, bracing ourselves, then barged out onto 72nd Street and walked briskly down the block and into the park to a point near Bethesda Fountain.

The crowd of 5,000 pulsed with the beat of fire-you-up music and the sheer electricity of the night. It was like a New Year's Carnivale, with part of the pre-event entertainment a parade of runners in costume prancing in a circle in the glare of klieg lights. People, lights, music and excitement thawed the fierce cold as we pressed toward the start line. There was a countdown of the year's final seconds, and at midnight, the first blaze of fireworks splashed the sky, and the pops and booms provided a thunderous cadence to pounding feet. Happy 2001, New York City!

Martha and Paul and Suzette chose to walk the snow-packed streets and trails, so I ran by myself, wanting to knock out four miles in less time. It took me about 50 minutes to complete the course, and then it was hopeless to try to find everybody, much less wait for them as my sweaty clothes turned cold and clammy, so I walked back to the hotel and plunged into a hot bubble bath. Dry jeans and the new, long-sleeved Midnight Run T-shirt always feel so good afterwards!

Given 48 hours of little sleep, the after-run party in the Gordons' room was short. A glass of champagne, bits of cheese and crackers, "Happy New Year!" – we're done. Good-night, World; Hello, Mr. Sandman.

We've slept late into the morning, and have now pulled ourselves together quickly for the next tradition: a meal in Chinatown. While the rest of Manhattan recovers slowly and quietly, Jan. 1 is just another busy day in this neighborhood – the Chinese New Year is still weeks away. The narrow sidewalks are filled with people and commerce, offering an antidote to the holiday's "party's-over" letdown.

My friend Karen has joined us for lunch, arriving by subway and by cell phone, which we used to call and finally spot each other in the jostling crowds of Mott Street. We've all agreed on Sun Lok Kee and are seated at a round table a little too big for five, but good for sharing foods, each of us taking turns selecting something. We also take our time. It is brutally cold outside.

A long slow bus ride back uptown is a good "indoors-New York" thing to do on a day like this. Karen rides with us, exiting near her street. The rest of us decide to hop off in Times Square and investigate theater offerings at the TKTS windows.

Today, the show choices have to be good, with the discount all the way to 50 percent off – not just 25 – and the line of same-day ticket seekers not *horrendously* long. We peer at the list, look at the line, and keep moving. We decide to go back to the hotel, rest a couple of hours, and then take on the city again to enjoy the theater of the streets or another dinner out.

Back on the block of our hotel, we stop by a news stand, load up on junk reading material – I love the tabloids with their screaming headlines –

and return to our rooms. I read and doze lightly, tired but eager to go back out again. I lay in the dark and listen to Manhattan's unique noise concerto of sirens and horns and voices, mentally scanning a list of things we all might agree upon. Dinner at Niko's? Back to Times Square? A martini at a swank hotel?

Suddenly, my cell phone plays its little nameless tune.

"Liz. This is Tori."

My niece rarely calls me; we're more likely to do e-mail. She sounds small and far away, farther than Mississippi where she lives and works as an attorney.

Tori? What -"

"It's Grandpapa..."

I don't remember her exact words after that. First I had to translate the relationship and then absorb the rest of the sentence. Grandpapa was dead. My father was dead.

In that instant, I saw him in his old faded jeans, a plaid shirt tucked in. He was smiling, as if he'd just heard something funny that was about to crack him up completely.

That's not like him. He wouldn't do that. He would never leave us like that.

21 GRIEF IN WINTER

The last seat open on the first Kansas City flight available the next day is 3A. I settle in, and the flight attendant asks if she can bring me a beverage. The opportunity to right now order a Scotch on the rocks is worth the price of the First Class ticket. The drink arrives quickly, a big glass tumbler glowing with ice and swirling amber. I close my eyes.

"They" – Daddy's housekeeper, my brother and sister-in-law, the doctor, the sheriff…believe he went to bed three nights earlier, on Dec. 29, and died sometime in his sleep. Heart attack. He had phoned my brother that evening to say that he would be picking up Mother at the nursing home the next day to spend the holiday weekend at the farm.

A couple of days later, Ed began a series of phone calls to check in with Daddy, but each call, beginning with the unanswered ring at the house, raised his level of alarm another notch. *Why no,* the nursing home employee told him; *Rodney never showed up. Jane was here all weekend.*

The plane hummed, skimming above clouds.

"Mother?"

From the New York hotel room, Martha and I had called her. Ed and Sharron had arrived at the nursing home straight from the farm to deliver the news. I envisioned our mother in her wheelchair in her room. I could imagine my brother putting the phone to

Mother's ear and making sure she had a good grip on the receiver, despite the tremors of Parkinson's.

She also had a grip on the news. She was more lucid than I've heard in months.

"I can't believe it," she said. "This is just terrible. It's the worst thing that could happen."

I wished that Mother had the checklist of what we do now and could be in charge. Instead, everyone flailed about in confusion.

The Gordons immediately booked return flights to Texas. Then we planned to unpack from New York, re-pack and drive to Kansas and then ride up with the Gordons, but my brother had caught up with me in a call I answered at LaGuardia as we waited for the flight to DFW.

"You and Martha have got to get up here right now, *today*. I need help with these funeral arrangements."

I looked at my watch at 5 o'clock, 20 minutes before landing. My eyes searched for the flight attendant, who appears magically in about two seconds.

"Excuse me. Do I have time for another…"

She flashes a smile as bright as the late afternoon sun: "Of course!"

What a good fine competent, really really fine excellent fine good competent professional she is. A credit to American Airlines. Give that woman a raise.

The second drink not only ceased to soothe, it washed away everything that covered and contained terrible sadness. Suddenly, I didn't have the strength to do anything, and the thought of just pulling my suitcase out of the overhead bin was too much. I asked the man next to me for help, an unthinkable request for this self-sufficient woman.

If my brother had known they'd have to pour me off the plane, he might have sent a different chauffeur. Ed's friend and colleague, District Judge Thomas Sachse, kindly offered to drive the 65 miles from Ottawa to the Kansas City airport to pick up any arriving Smith family members or friends. Judge Sachse was totally cool about having to deal with Edwin's inebriated sister, loading me and my luggage into his car and making comfortably easy small talk all the way to Ottawa.

I spent the night at my brother's house. The next day, our little family group widened as grandchildren arrived – Tori brought her fiancé Jeff – and then Martha and Paul and Matt. Countless details moved from the sad – finishing up funeral details and calling relatives and friends – to the surreal, having meetings with the lawyer and the banker to handle immediate issues of the will. As sure as the harshness of January in Kansas, one deals with the business of death, even before the funeral.

We've caravanned the 30 miles west to Osage County and arrived at the farm. We are out of our cars and huddled in the driveway, not wanting to enter the house.

Inside, we move around quickly, nervously. We find the Christmas decorations still in place, which is not surprising because it is a family superstition that one invites bad luck by taking down the tree before Jan. 1. (For anyone who shares this belief, it has now been disproved.) The rest of the house – dishes on the kitchen table, a plastic-wrapped ball of pie dough in the refrigerator, papers scattered on the open, drop-leaf desk – was that of a man who expected to open his eyes and get out of bed the next day, and the next.

My sister's family and I moved into the upstairs bedrooms. Another nephew, Ed's son Ramey, set up camp in the living room where he would spend three nights not sleeping very much. Once, I awoke at 4:15 a.m. and padded downstairs to the bathroom. The living room lights were ablaze and the television was on and Ramey was huddled under a blanket on the recliner. My other nephew Matt slept on the floor beside his grandfather's desk.

There was, at least, sweet cosmic justice in the fact that the officers of the Lyndon Presbyterian Church still held the keys to the front door. Of course my father's service was held there, as were his mother's and father's, and on Jan. 4, sunlight filtered brilliantly through the colored glass windows.

I sat with Mother, Ed and Martha on the front pew, aware and comforted by a wall of people around us and warmed by the beauty of flowers and prisms of light. I stared at the short-shag threads of the red carpet, in a direction well away from the casket, and listened to Rev. Freitag relay the string of stories I had shared with him when he was preparing the eulogy.

The day included a simple luncheon prepared by women of the church. It was served to 25 or 30 of us who sat at long tables in Lyndon's community center.

Shortly after my last spoonful of potato soup, my cell phone rings.

"Liz? Where are you?"

It is Doris.

"I'm in Kansas. You wouldn't know, but my dad..."

"Liz, Sara is in the hospital, really really sick."

Apparently, Sara wasn't lying when she laid the cancer story on me in my living room a month ago. Doris has severed contact with her former friend, but a mutual friend of theirs has told her that the disease is back with a vengeance.

There is an awful layer of irony to the already-unfortunate timing of this call. If I had not been forced home by Sara's deeds, I would have been with my father in the days leading up to his death. I would have been with him on Dec. 29, his last day alive. Perhaps with just the two of us in the house, I would have seen more clearly the acuteness of his health problems, and taken him to a doctor.

In hearing about Sara's hospitalization, my heart is stone-cold.

Friends and relatives who filled the house that night were both a comfort and a bother. The good ones left us alone and didn't hover. Others – well, I felt inanely like a party hostess for them, chatting and making sure they had food and drink and everything else needed for a pleasant evening. The worst was a visitor I'll call "Barbara Stanwyck." That's the name of one of those early-day actresses who, in the latter years of her career in the 1950s and '60s played strong-woman roles, especially in a TV show called "The Big Valley." She was the matriarch of a clan of ranchers and was always standing tall, planting her feet and scowling into the horizon and saying something stern and brave about how things were to be there in The Big Valley and therefore scaring the bad guys away and dispelling any other threats to the American way.

Our Barbara Stanwyck decided it was her place to stiffen our spines – never mind that she had no idea whether Martha and Ed and I needed "backbone" or not – and doling heavy-handed advice about organizing my parents' property, from managing the business side of the estate to going through all the photos and records and other personal effects of the household.

"Your parents had to do it for their parents and I had to do it for my parents and now it's YOUR turn," Miss Stanwyck said sternly. "It's a phase of life and we all have to go through it." On and on she went until I just wanted to punch her lights out.

Of course, she left the next day to continue her appointed rounds of telling the world the facts of life. The Smiths meanwhile – children, grandchildren and spouses – stayed another day, pouring all thought, action and energy into formidable tasks. We dismantled the Christmas decorations and hauled trash. There was a sofa and a so-called "cat's chair" that needed to go to the landfill. The basement was a mess of water-damaged goods and papers and mouse droppings, and as we climbed up and down stairs with stuff, valuable and not, I regretted all the years of Christmas afternoons spent napping instead of helping my parents lighten and downsize and streamline their 63-year accumulation of possessions. ("Hey, everybody, I know what let's do! Let's clean out the basement!") Naagh, I guess that wasn't likely.

Before leaving New York, I remembered to call Sue Rowe before she boarded Amtrak to ride down from Rutland to meet me in the city. She understood all too well from her experiences of losing a husband and twin brother.

"From now on," she told me, "your life is going to go hour to hour for a while."

She was right, although the haze was beginning to lift. I had found peace and comfort in the fact that Daddy's death was as charmed as his life – he waltzed out quickly, with affairs in reasonable order.

The funeral was planned, executed and over. Friends had eased out the door and into their cars with promises to call. It was time for us to go, too, back to homes and jobs and plans in Ottawa, Kansas, and Fort Worth, Texas, and Oxford, Mississippi.

There was just one thing. The farm. A big old house and garage and barns and equipment and land, with nobody to protect it from marauding, criminal opportunists, some of whom ply their trade through perusal of obituaries in rural newspapers.

Already, hunters weren't even slowing down as they entered the drive and zoomed past the house and up the lane. Some my dad knew, others not. We learned that on the very New Year's afternoon that he was found, with my brother and the sheriff and the doctor and the undertaker at the house, somebody breezed by in a pickup, with a cheery little wave and a touch of the foot on the accelerator as he hurried on around the parked vehicles and sailed through the gate.

There was also the specter of other intruders – bored kids or worse – who could easily learn that some of the five entrances to the house didn't even have secure locks. What a place for a party!

And finally, quiet, isolated Kansas farm houses are notorious fronts for the manufacture, sale and use of methamphetamine drugs. Ed and Martha and I had already discussed the hazards of renting to keep the house occupied; we could see a piece of the action happening without a contract. Bad people slipping into my parents' house and taking it over, pawing, violating, stealing, vandalizing, destroying? Horrifying. Unthinkable.

The day after the funeral, I woke up in the antique bed that belonged to my grandfather Hal Smith. I stared at the sloped ceiling of the west bedroom and reached a decision, which I announced later at the breakfast table.

"I think I'd better stay."

"I was afraid you'd decide that," Martha said.

22 KANSAS

Everybody departed for their homes on Saturday, two days after the funeral. I called my neighbor and asked if she would mind extending the cat-sitting duty a while longer. Martha promised to ship my computer along with some boots for trudging through snow. Otherwise, my suitcase that was filled with clothing for a week in New York City is surprisingly compatible with my new, rural environment. I have jeans, sweaters, an extra-heavy winter coat, hats, scarves and gloves.

Why did we think we could override Mother Nature that day? There was a reason we weren't supposed to fly to New York...

When the last car drove off, I left, spending the day away from the house and putting off the moment of being alone in it for the first time in my life. My brother and sister-in-law helped delay that point by inviting me to bring Mother over for dinner. The trip to Ottawa killed the last half of the day, but even after I returned Mother to the nursing home in the evening, I lingered in its dining room talking to two aides who were having a late supper.

Oh how I dreaded going home and facing that first night alone! Unlike my little condo, the two-story, four-bedroom house was spread-out and rambling, so that someone could pop through a window in the basement, or the ground-level utility room, or an upstairs bedroom adjacent to a crawl-worthy part of the roof, and depending on where my little self might be in the house, I would most likely not even hear it. There were two shotguns in a closet, but I had no idea how to use them.

I tried not to think of *In Cold Blood*, the 1960s book by Truman Capote that described in chilling, matter-of-fact detail the deaths of

Herbert Clutter, his wife and two children on their farm near Holcomb, Kansas. One night in 1959, their house was entered by a duo named Smith (no relation!) and Hickok, drifters who had heard that Clutter was rich and kept his money in a safe at home. There was no safe, and so they killed Herbert first, and then went from room to room executing the others. My aunt Lugene had known the Clutters, and my college journalism advisor, Bill Brown, had been the newspaper editor who covered the case and witnessed administration of the death penalty through the hangings of Smith and Hickok. How could I NOT think of *In Cold Blood*?

Sometimes, faith is all there is. God is here.

I finally left the nursing home and steered the car over the four and a half graveled miles, Whitey's headlights piercing the inky darkness to sweep the road and the snow piles and the occasional scurrying shape or glowing eyes of a small animal. At home, the lights I had left on were the only illumination in my patch of the world.

At least the cats were there, the long-haired tortoise-colored Tertia, and Casey, the big, sweet adoptee who has now lost two people; my dad took him on a few years ago when an Osage City woman died. Tertia and Casey became reassuring anchors to the idea that the farm still has souls, even little ones encased in fur.

In the living room, I turned on the big Zenith cabinet TV in the corner and very quickly, "Saturday Night Live" was making me laugh. Suddenly my world was no longer about fear and sadness. I was wrapped in silly comedy and a cotton quilt and a big soft recliner and the illusion of being back in New York City where I was supposed to be this week. And then, because I was relaxed, I yielded to exhaustion and it was a very short trip to the upstairs bedroom and sleep.

One by one they came, knocking on the screen door, or calling me up, or sending their pitch via the U.S. Postal Service to the black metal mailbox on our slender roadside post, most with honorable and helpful intentions, others grabbing their gain from our loss, or *maybe* they were just slack-jawed idiots lacking the most rudimentary sense of decency and timing as they stumble about society. Three days after the funeral, we started getting sales letters, one addressed in hand-writing to "Mrs. Jane Smith," from the monument companies.

Like the graveyard headstone pitches, a young lady in Osage City didn't even bother with a "sorry-for-your-loss" type of opener in her phone call.

"Are you going to rent your house?" she asked me. "I'd really like a house in the country for me and my kids."

There were also the "Crops Man," Gregg Romine, and the "Hay Man," Bill Wiley, kind friends of my father who introduced us to the business operations of his life on the farm. Each arrived to explain their roles in planting the crops and harvesting the hay, tenants' activities described by Daddy many times as we paid scant attention. Now, my brother and I took notes on yellow legal pads, although five minutes of detail about the USDA and crop insurance and what fields were where was about all I could handle. Gregg was particularly, dutifully thorough, and I just had to leave the room and hope that Ed was paying attention and learning whatever it was we were supposed to know and that he would know what to do whenever we were supposed to do it.

We sat with Bill at the kitchen table and learned about the hay operation. More business, business, business. But when he stood up to leave, Bill told me, "There's a bunch of us that have coffee every morning at 9 at the A&L. There'll be a place at the table for you."

Now *that* was welcome information.

I started the A&L habit immediately. The café is in Lyndon, our "other" town; the farm sits halfway between Lyndon and Osage City. The buff stucco restaurant is among Lyndon's permanent, "heart-of-town," two-block string of low-rise buildings. They line both sides of U.S. Hwy. 75, also known as Topeka Avenue, depending on whether you're a Lyndonite familiar with the street names, or a passenger on a charter bus roaring north through town to get to the Indian casinoes on the other side of Topeka. The A&L has a choice location, catty-corner from the Texaco station and directly across the street from the only full grocery store in town, the D&A Market.

At 9 a.m. I found the group at the front end of the A&L's one long room. The café's paneled walls are mostly adorned with basic restaurant art, which in Kansas means perfunctory and straight forward. There is a wall calendar for an implement company, dusty faded prints of painted flowers and landscapes, a small framed copy of The Lord's Prayer, and somebody's craft project, which appears to be bits of costume jewelry glued in a Christmas tree shape onto black velvet.

More interesting to me is a sort of front alcove, where the gang sits. The wall decor there consists of two large framed wall maps, one of the world, the other the United States. I love looking at the U.S. map and visually tracing the route of my trip, from Texas to Kansas to Arizona to Oregon to Iowa to Vermont to Tennessee and home again. It didn't seem possible.

When I walked in and sat down, not really knowing anyone well, I wasn't worried about being accepted – that happened just by being Rodney Smith's daughter because everybody liked him.

"Oh your dad – he had stars in his crown," Harvey Wahlquist said to me that first morning. "The way he took care of your mother…"

I was also a fourth generation of Smiths joining a Lyndon, Kansas, table of coffee drinkers, although I doubt if my ancestors spent as much time in lolly-gagging chit-chat.

Actually, I think anyone could walk into the A&L and just plop down on the first available metal-framed orange vinyl chair, as long as hugs and how-are-yous are not expected. The group is suffused with a simple, basic Kansas goodness that everybody can and does take for granted. That means there's no showy, time-wasting exertion of hospitality – don't expect any big hello and huzzah and back slapping and special treatment. There's nary a twitch in anyone's facial expression as other coffee drinkers arrive, gradually merging into conversations about weather, basketball, cattle, and sometimes, more intriguing topics such as rumors of a full-grown cougar – make that cougars – prowling around nearby farm pastures.

The group spans nine decades, from Carl and Charlotte Manning's 7-year-old grandson to Virgie Sims, 94, who finally gave up on making the weekly dance not too long ago. Somewhere in the middle were the Sturdy men – yes, men named Sturdy – Clint and Rod and their father Darrell. Clint and Rod are 30-somethings, handsome and teasing and they lend the group a good dose of sex appeal.

I sat near the middle of the long table, next to the Mannings, because I knew them the best as fellow Lyndon Presbyterians. Charlotte helped serve soup and pie at the family luncheon held at the Community Center right before the funeral.

Because the table was long, there were two conversations under way. I tuned into the one about Wal-Mart.

"It is the ruin of small towns today," Lawrence Stadel was saying. "They come into a place with their low prices and lots of merchandise and the little stores in town can't compete. The little guys go outta business, and then Walmart raises their prices back up because they've got all the customers by then and no competition."

I hadn't intended to say anything on my first day but I couldn't resist.

"I hate Walmart," I said. "When I was touring the country, I saw what you're saying time and again, plus America's small towns are losing their distinctiveness. Too many of them have a Main Street that's just abandoned, because a big gray box and parking lot full of cars out on the edge of town are sucking the life out of it."

Boom. I'd made my first friend.

What I didn't say was that family friends Pam and Denis Hockett had invited me over for dinner and a "Walmart run" to Topeka one night this week. I rationalized that Walmart in a city is different – there is competition from a lot of other big boxes. Besides, right now my need for companionship superceded any benefits to my conscience from allegiance to principles.

Somebody changed the subject.

"Say, Lawrence, those are good-looking gloves ya got on today."

"Yeah, well, they're gettin' worn out. I'd sure like to find the same kind again."

Lawrence is a bright man, closer to being an intellectual than any of the rest of us, but he'd just walked right into the trap.

"I know I've seen that kind at Walmart!"

The table erupted in its first guffaw of the day. A little later that week, on Lawrence's birthday, a decorated sheet cake was brought in. Of course, the icing was blue with a yellow smiley face and the words, "Welcome to Walmart." Lawrence looked at it and folded his arms.

"I'm not eating that cake," he stated.

This group, this ritual of starting the day together, is a god-send for me. For at least an hour every day, there will be no loneliness and isolation. For this time at least, life is normal, with friends and fun. Managing the next couple of months alone on the farm won't be so bad after all – in fact, it's pretty much an extension of my trip. It's just one more adventure, and I FEEL GREAT! My dad's gone? Hey, he had a wonderful long life, and he went out peacefully.

Now I can go home and face all the tasks that need to be done and just do them!

Back from the A&L, I bounded into the house. There were dishes to load in the dishwasher, clothes and bath towels to launder, shopping lists to make. I needed to unpack for a longer stay, emptying my suitcases and hanging clothes in a closet and taking over a couple of dresser drawers. The Christmas decorations had been taken down, but needed to be boxed and stashed. Those sorts of tasks were easy enough to identify – less mindless were the thank-you notes for flowers and memorial gifts and food, supporting Martha's and Ed's responsibilities in rounding up assets and other concrete matters of the "the estate." And, we must decide what to do with all the stuff that fills every room of the house.

I loaded the dishwasher, venturing into the refrigerator as well to cast out old food. There on the bottom shelf was a ball of pie dough, with indentations made by my father's hands, encased in plastic wrap. I pushed it back more deeply on the shelf.

The laundry seemed like a better thing to tackle. In the upstairs bedrooms I pulled the sheets off the beds, rounded up my clothes, then headed back downstairs to the bathrooms for towels. In my parents' bathroom, I found a heap of clothes in a hamper, including Daddy's jeans and plaid shirt, probably what he had last worn Dec. 29. A nearly brand-new tube of Crest toothpaste, purchased in the long-lasting giant economy size, lay beside the sink.

I remembered the things I was pretending not to see, like his puffy green jacket and winter cap hanging on a hook in the hallway, ready for him to grab the next time he'd be running out the door. I walked past that hallway quickly, but my eyes fell on the hutch cabinet and the trout lights that lay there, a jumble of plastic fish and wire and electrical cord. They needed to be boxed up and put away until the very next holiday, perhaps Groundhog's Day, an idea that was no longer hilarious.

It was all too much. I was glad when the phone rang.

"Is Rodney there?" the caller asked brightly.

I did not respond. For a second, the voice of a friend, who obviously knew him well, seemed the true reality, that none of the past 10 days had happened, and that the phone woke me up from a dream. Hadn't the big tube of toothpaste proved that as well, and the hat and jacket? *Sure*, I would say, laying down the phone to call out in the direction of the workbench in the garage. *Daddy! Can you come to the phone?!*

"Who's calling please?" I said.

Larry Shepherd lived several counties over, and sometimes, at this time of year, he would get my dad's permission to drive over to hunt, or in the springtime bring a troop of Boy Scouts over to camp.

There was silence after my explanation of a new situation at the Smith farm. I hoped it wasn't just a wordless "damn" that we had shut off the hunting first thing. On the day after the funeral, my brother and nephew and I had scrambled to repair and padlock gates and to post larger, brighter "No Hunting" signs.

"I sure did like your father," Mr. Shepherd said, and I breathed a sigh of relief when the rest of the brief conversation did not go beyond condolences.

The day had turned dark and impossible so very quickly. I left the house.

"Hi, Mother."

I found her in the dining room of the nursing home, already wheeled up to the edge of her table, bib snapped in place. With four other companions, she was ready for dinner.

"Hi, Baby!" she said. Big smile. "You're still here? I thought you'd gone."

"To Texas? No, you get me another couple of months, remember?"

I had decided to take on the nursing home and find things to love about it. It couldn't be worse than the house this day.

Daddy hated this place. "It's full of old people," he'd complained, without a trace of humor. I tried not to smile. *Oh yeah. All those 80-year-olds. You're only 86.* But I knew what he meant.

Actually, on the darkest edge of his despair of having to place Mother, he suggested moving himself in as well. Everybody – his children, the A&L cronies, his friends at church, erupted over that idea. Please, do not do that, we all said.

I found a chair and pulled it up beside Mother's wheelchair.

"So!" I began on a gust of airy cheerfulness inhaled deeply to get the Happy Neurons going in my brain. "What's for dinner?" At that moment, a plate arrived in the hands of an aide. All the food was white. A dome of starch, perhaps mashed potatoes; white bread, cream gravy, and a flat thing that looked like tofu but was more likely meat.

"Mmm. What would you like to try first?"

"What is it?" Mother asked, not making a move toward her fork. She really cannot see very well so it was a fair question.

I put the Happy Neurons to work making each item sound delicious. The little pile of potato product became "creamy home-made mashed potatoes," the mystery meat: "I believe it's fresh chicken, Mother, very interesting and creative in the way they've fixed it."

She was not inspired, and I finally picked up the fork, loaded it halfway up the tines, and fed her. She liked to be fed and we were soon on our way through the meal.

Nobody at her table nor the other tables carried on conversation, save the presence of a few family members and employees helping to make sure plates were cleaned as much as possible before an inspecting nurse with a clipboard came around. It's as if the residents were all played out after too many years of social small talk. I can imagine that. There are certainly advantages to being old and seemingly out of it; you don't have to talk to people any more if you don't want to.

The man across the table, nicknamed "Cowboy," did talk, but in a low, incomprehensible mumble. I heard the words "judgment" and "come on." He would exit his wheelchair if he could, so a thick cushion had been placed on his lap, its sides lodged under the armrests of the chair. He pulled at the cushion, trying to free it, all the while carrying on the quiet but insistent exhortations.

I stopped working so hard at table talk myself. Silently I moved the fork from the plate to Mother's lips, trying not to worry about the woman nearby who had finished her meal and apparently wanted to move elsewhere. "Can somebody help me?" she asked in a strong, monotone voice. And then it became a sort of chant, "Can somebody help me Can somebody help me Can somebody help me." "In a minute, Meryl," said an aide who worked steadily through post-supper duties of table clearing and helping people get back to their rooms. Ah. Meryl had to wait her turn.

Suddenly, the aide was at the front door with another employee talking gently to Agnes.

"But I have to go out there," Agnes was saying. "My mother is waiting for me. She's over there and I have to go to her – she's waiting for me."

Agnes's mother has been gone for 30 years. Agnes also had no way of accomplishing the complexities of pressing a numbered code into a keypad beside the locked door. She was agitated.

"Agnes, your mother is not there – let's go back and finish dinner. You didn't finish your dessert!"

By this time, I was wheeling my mother back to her room. I sat beside her and we continued our silence. All I could think was, how can ordinary life be so sad? How is it that I find myself back in my old, anchoring "home" in Kansas, but not; I will return tonight to a house with no people, filled with the stuff of life with no purpose but to remind and replay happy scenes of 40 years ago, 25 years ago, last Christmas. How could Daddy have left us in this sorry predicament?! Mother said nothing and I said nothing until my head and shoulders were too heavy to hold upright. I leaned over and rested my head on Mother's lap. She touched my hair.

Suddenly, from the hallway, we heard, "GOD DAMN BASTARDS GET THE FUCK OUT OF MY WAY, ALL O' YA GOD DAMN YOU..."

An old man had erupted like Mount Vesuvius, spewing profanity and a general wrath that shocked me and yet – I laughed, is what I did. For he had pretty much summed it all up for me too. Life can sure suck. Well said, man! Yessss! Somebody in this place can still rail back and there's the hope for the rest of us. Life can be hell but we don't have to like it; we can shake a fist and cry out. I felt a tiny shot of adrenaline return and then the strength to get in the car and drive back to the house.

I said good-night to Mother and I drove home where I removed the hat and green jacket from the hallway hook. I boxed up the trout lights, too, and put them away, but not too far away so that they'll be available to brighten the next holiday.

23 FINDING MY WAY

At 8:45 a.m. I pulled Daddy's green jacket out of the dryer and put it on. It felt really good, warm and soft. I also wore the new jeans purchased on the Walmart run with Pam and Denis. I was all set to take on a frosty morning and drive into town for coffee at the A&L.

"There's Liz. She's got new jeans on!" Charlotte said when I walked in.

Gee, that's awfully observant. They're just jeans. How could she tell?

"You've still got the tags on 'em, Minnie Pearl."

Argh. I'd remembered to cut the tags attached with the plastic stems at the waist, but I forgot the sticky-backed paper plastered to one leg. Luckily, with Lawrence sitting there, "Walmart" was nowhere in sight.

I sat next to the solid little white-haired pint Virgie, the 94-year-old, who had a two-item agenda today. First, she'd cranked up her regular rant about her little apartment over on 10th Street.

"It's just too crowded," she said. "I've got to get me a bigger place."

Up to my eyebrows in stuff at the farm, I've recommitted myself to the religion of downsizing. The Smith house is all too typical of Americans' failure to keep possessions pared to their essential usefulness and/or standing of being loved and treasured.

"Virgie, have you thought about thinning things out? Wouldn't it be nice to not have so much stuff to take care of?"

Virgie said nothing, but if her level gaze had been an utterance, flames and claps of thunder surely would have been part of it. It's pretty obvious that others have told Virgie she should pare things down.

Now that I'm learning everybody's hot button, I was wishing I'd had the sticky-backed paper from the Walmart jeans pasted over my mouth. So then I changed the subject, an easy thing to do because Virgie was selling tickets to a Lyndon Lions Club soup supper at the high school.

"I'd like to go," I told her, reaching into my purse for my billfold. I fumbled and the wallet fell to the floor. I slid down from my chair and under the table to find it.

"Say! While you're down there..." Rod Sturdy said, saying no more but leering when I looked back up at him from just below his knees. Rod will say anything just to shock and tease and try to cover up the fact that he's a nice, hard-working Kansas boy. I scrambled back up to my chair and tried to hide my blushing face behind a big drink of water.

The Lions' soup supper was tonight. I bought two tickets from Virgie and I also gave her a ride to the school, which was buzzing with the social life of an entire community. Families lined up for chili and pie in the cafeteria, which had become over-heated on a cold night. A basketball game filled the nearby gymnasium, its sounds of cheerleader chants and yelling fans, the pounding of basketballs and the brass and drums of the band bouncing wildly. Careening between spaces were children and teen-agers in a frenetic race between the things that ruled their evening: Parents with money and permission to give, friends with secrets to share, soup and soda pop and, oh yes, the game.

Daddy had been a member of the Lyndon Lions Club. I found myself resentful of the fellows and women carrying on so industriously without him.

One gray day, I rode to the university town of Lawrence with Charlotte Manning, who had an upholstery client to see. I've started venturing into day trips to Lawrence, Topeka, Wichita and other big cities of Kansas. (Actually, there aren't any others – even Kansas City, the BIG Kansas City that most people are referring to, is in Missouri.)

We stopped for breakfast at a shopping center restaurant comfortably dotted with KU students who were studying or conversing or both.

I can tell that Charlotte has advice she'd like to offer, but generally keeps still unless I provide an opening by asking a pertinent question. Today, *she* asked the pertinent question.

"Liz, do you think you'll have an auction?""

I had a piece of toast in my hand and put it back down on the plate. I had just heard a very important question.

"An auction? At the house?"

"Because if that's what you guys want to do, you need to get on Wayne's calendar. Spring is coming and he gets booked up fast."

What else can we do?? We've got an eight-room house filled with the possessions of people who no longer live there. It's not my stuff, and I'm not taking it to Texas with me.

And I DO want to go home to Texas. Soon. When I checked the voice mail on my home phone the other day, a Hurst police detective had left a message saying he had been assigned my case. (What's to investigate, I wonder. Go out and *arrest* the woman!) Martha picks up my mail, and while there have been no new credit cards or other surprises, I'm feeling the need to be back in Hurst — permanently this time.

Wayne Wischropp is the local auctioneer and Charlotte is right. He'll soon be working every weekend, plunging into a seasonal frenzy that has unsettling elements: loss and avarice. All over the county the landscape of families and their stuff will shift, with homes and farms newly void of life, yet left with the detritus of those lives. From my new vantage point, auctions are a mix of the poignant and the mercenary, nostalgia and pragmatism, and of strangers pawing and discarding precious things.

I surprise myself by embracing the idea whole-heartedly. I pledge to confer with my sibling partners in this business of organizing our world post-Daddy. It makes me a little uneasy because we've started bickering, each of us in our grief and confusion reverting to childhood and respective roles. As the youngest, I've been the most helpless and weepy, looking to my older siblings to be in charge. In this phase of carrying out the will, Martha is the executor, but Ed with his law background and access to records is trying to help her, so sometimes they clash and one day my brother, the big bad judge, actually muttered, "Martha can be so bossy."

We're all doing our best. Martha takes on the business of stuff, organizing family lists so that everyone can choose what they want. Some things she puts on eBay, and for our own Kansas auction, will arrive at the farm a week early to help out during her spring break.

Ed wants no part of the auction. Go ahead with it, he says, but he'll pick up Mother on auction day and do something special with her — away from the farm.

I work on the lists and dig through closets, cabinets, drawers and an attic, seeking out the treasures that we want to sort and keep for the family, or advertise on the sale bill – old coins, glassware, furniture, jewelry. Some things are easy – old postcards and stacks of unidentified photographs – others are hard, like my dad's college letter sweater.

"And his caps! He has all of his 'gimmee' caps hung on nails, decorating the hallway," I told Rod Sturdy.

"I'll take 'em," he said.

"Would you do that??" It was just the kindest offer he could make.

"Sure! I have a collection. I'd be honored."

I can stand only so much of this house, this winter, this life. I'm trying to rope my friends into visiting me. Nancy Ogle, who goes back 25 years with me and now lives in Wichita, and her sister Kathleen from Seneca took me up on a weekend invitation to drive to the farm, go to a movie with me in Lawrence and shop at an Overbrook quilt store.

Heck, I wish my friends could just come and LIVE here. Being such a solitary thing, I never thought I would say that. But I also never thought I would find myself alone on all this empty farmland, with my nearest neighbor a half mile away. What fun it would be to fill this four-bedroom home and run a commune! Now THAT would be groovy.

"What about James? I hear you've been going around with him," Clint Sturdy deadpanned one morning at the A&L. Laughter rippled around the table.

James is a grizzled eccentric bachelor whose parents lived in the house across the road many years ago. James has some cattle on the property, but the house is dilapidated and he lives elsewhere, driving out in the daytime to do chores. He is notoriously tight-fisted about money, and supposedly he's abandoned the house and turned off the electricity and running water – even as he invests in the stock market.

"James has money," Clint said, running on despite my pleas to cease and desist. Actually, James is a good man, a nice, interesting, smart person who has always been helpful to our family and I like him. But I'm not about to stick my neck out and say *that* to the coffee crowd.

Here's my daily routine now:

The morning begins with a check of the bird feeder outside the kitchen window. When the feeder is full, it attracts redbirds – the most beautiful redbirds I've ever seen. I guess they're the ONLY redbirds I've ever seen, en masse and up close anyway. When I first discovered that the clear plastic cylinder was empty – it empties through holes to little side perches and a tray attached below – I went to the grocery store and bought a small box of bird feed.

That did not last long. So I went to the store and bought a bigger box of bird feed. That lasted longer – maybe a day.

Finally I went to the Dayhoff Elevator Co., the grain mill in Osage City. A worker loaded 50 pounds of grain into Whitey and I was in business to more conveniently refill the bird feeder every morning at 7:30.

After feeding the birds, I dress for a run in Lyndon where I sometimes use the high school track on the east edge of town. More often, I trace the town's streets, which generate 40-year-old memories. There is the old abandoned ice house on the southwest side, where Grandmother used to stop for Butter Brickle ice cream during my summer visits (Just to be clear, I didn't like Butter Brickle – she did.) Continuing north up Washington Street and toward the City Park, I can never look at the water tower and not think of a story about my dad and one of his pranks of childhood.

"We climbed up there with baby rabbits," he told me. "We put little parachutes on them and dropped them over the side."

Somehow the subject got changed when I asked what happened to the baby rabbits after they floated safely to the ground. (They DID float safely to the ground, right?)

The run ends by 9, in time to meet the crowd at the A&L.

This week it looks like we're without Virgie for a while. She's in Stormont-Vail Hospital in Topeka, although everybody agrees she's likely to be back among us soon, and selling tickets to something or campaigning for sympathy for getting a bigger apartment.

Then Rod announces that he's checked out my Web site and wasn't impressed: "It don't have nudie pictures on it!"

The A&L actually has two 9 o'clock coffee crowds. The other consists of women of my parents' generation whom I call "The Lyndon Ladies." Now you can guess why the groups sit separately. I happen to like the raucous fun of the front table, although sometimes I pay my respects to the back, dutifully responding to polite inquiries about my mother, not that any of these old friends ever visit her now.

Just as the coffee time begins promptly at 9 a.m., it ends by straight-up 10. Charlotte has to return to her custom upholstery business. Others go back to offices and farms.

Just a few of us who don't have jobs linger a bit. One day, Rod hangs back and when nobody is in earshot, says he wants to show me something.

"It's out in the truck," he says. "I'll go get it."

What in the world…

He returns with a file folder full of papers.

"I can see from your Web site that you can write," he mumbles. "Well, I do too – poems. I wonder if you'd look at 'em."

And so I did, and they were poems about lost love. We sat a while longer and talked about them and the woman they were about. She's gone now, moved to another state, although the two still talk in late-night phone calls.

"Does she know about these?" I asked Rod, thinking that she wouldn't be gone if she knew these things in his heart. Men. What bone-heads. But Rod would no more share these poems with her than he'd nail them to the walls of the A&L under spotlights.

Since it's late morning now, I drive straight from Lyndon to Osage City to read to Mother and have lunch with her. She's always surprised to see me, thinking I've gone home to Texas and not remembering my visit of the day or evening before. It's also not clear these days what she understands about my dad's death. Once, she was talking about him as if he was about to walk in the door.

"Mother, Daddy died a few weeks ago, remember?"

"Oh," she says. "I was afraid of that."

It was a funny thing to say, but my mother always had a quick dry wit, a good vocabulary, and a precise way of expressing herself.

One day I read to her a piece of mail from the son of one of Daddy's childhood friends in Lyndon.

"Lewis died, Mother – just the way Daddy did. He went to bed and didn't wake up."

"Well!" she said, "We'd better stop letting our fellows go to sleep!"

The hard part of the day is always to go home and try to sort through the 8,000 things that fill the house and garage. Sometimes Ed breezes over, scooping up the business papers I've pulled from the mail and the desk and the file cabinets, but he doesn't like to hang around the house. Sometimes we'll drive back into Osage then for ice cream sodas at Park's pharmacy.

So the afternoon is the hard part of the day and I give up easily on the daunting tasks of organizing. It's nap time before an hour of "Oprah," some reading, writing thank-you notes, or watching a movie rented from the D&A.

It's weird being in charge of my parents' house. I'm here alone and they're never coming back. Bring on the '60s and all the familiar things of home from those years. My favorite dinner is a hamburger pattie fried in the iron skillet, canned corn and instant pudding. I've dug out dusty old Montevani and Broadway show tunes, swept the newspapers and magazines off the top of the "hi-fi" and discovered that the record player still works. I've rediscovered the comforts of the Early American easy chair, fuzzy house slippers and "I Love Lucy."

I'm definitely feeling better. I finally got some auction-related advice to go out and pick up boxes. When I don't feel like photographing furniture, separating jewelry and sorting books, I can gather boxes – lots and lots of boxes. So that's what I do, driving from the D&A with its sturdy grocery cartons to the beer distributor in Osage City where the low cartons that held six-packs are the real prize. Wayne's helpers tell me that most small things will go in there for easy display on the backs of flat-bed trucks.

One day, for once I'm firing on all cylinders. I arise early to feed birds and run, staying out on the farm roads so that I can squeeze in some more early chores at the house. I'm also shooting pictures, working on the furniture listing, packing books, sorting through photographs, even folding clothes to take to Goodwill in Topeka later this afternoon.

So I arrive at the A&L later than usual. In fact, most of the gang has scattered already, although Lawrence Stadel and Harvey Walquist are still there. They're talking quietly when I take a seat at their table.

Then Lawrence says, "Virgie didn't make it."

"Died? But I thought she was doing so well, supposed to leave the hospital any day now."

"No."

I started to cry, and it was just the oddest thing. I didn't know Virgie that well, but I couldn't talk and I couldn't stop crying. Lawrence and Harvey reminisced for a minute about all the times Virgie had beaten cancer and worked hard jobs through tough years and then they steered the conversation on to other things. Because what else was there to say? But I just kept spilling tears that seemed to have no end in that void of nothing else to say.

I suppose this was some catch-up grief. It's a sneaky thing.

I'm slacking again, finding more excuses to escape the house. This is not good. I now have 71 empty boxes, and very few are filled relative to the goods available. I did go to the Dollar General Store in Osage and buy six large plastic bins. I've got to do something with the hundreds of good photos, letters and fragile papers on family history, including a Danish great-grandparent's naturalization papers. So I twisted arms to divide it all up for distribution among my brother, sister, niece, nephews and myself.

But the rest of it just sits around: furniture, appliances, lamps, dishware, books, games, decks of cards, record albums, pots and pans, crystal, knick-knacks, tools, table linens, quilts and blankets, framed pictures, stationery and notebooks, mops and brooms, canned food, rugs, calendars, pet supplies, telephones and telephone books, Christmas decorations, travel souvenirs, recipe boxes, fireplace accessories, shoes, hats, wrapping paper and greeting cards, unfinished sewing projects, costume jewelry. It's mostly untouched, not sorted or inventoried, and in fact I think it somehow grows and multiplies in the night because every time I return to the house, I step over and around more stuff.

And so I escape. One trip was to Marysville, 130 miles north and west of the farm, near the Nebraska border. I spent four wonderful years there as a reporter at *The Marysville Advocate*. Escape to a happier time and place.

"I'll come up mid-week, write something for you and help with the press run," I told my old boss, Howard Kessinger.

"Sharon and I would love to have you," he said. "Stay with us."

On the way to Marysville, I stopped in a tiny town that was my home for a year in the mid-1970s, pre-*Advocate* career. My mission: To look somebody up, peer from a discreet distance, see how he had changed in 25 years.

Some people would call it stalking I suppose. Too bad such a time-honored art has picked up such *negative* connotations. A few bad apples spoil it for the rest of us.

Anyway, back to the sneaking. Would I recognize him? Had he put on weight? Lost his hair? Did his face show wrinkles?

In 1976, after college and a stint in the Air Force in Abilene, Texas, Tom and I went back to his hometown so he could join the family business. That's when our relationship fell apart. I couldn't handle living there, although to be fair to that sweet little town and a fine fellow, it was hard to imagine living anywhere at that point.

My long-festering depression had come to a head, crippling my outlook and my judgment. I was a mess: lost, self-absorbed, despairing of ever having a *career*. A psychiatrist, who eventually helped me regain my equilibrium, put me on antidepressants that caused me to sleep all the time. When I eventually landed a job as a bank teller in a larger neighboring town, I slept when there were no customers, laying my head down in my teller's window and asking the other women to wake me if anybody came in the door. (That did not make me popular with the other employees.)

This is what Tom had to deal with and he was a trouper for as long as possible. He was everything I was not: calm, optimistic and stable. He was also utterly predictable in his interests and habits.

That's why I felt fairly certain that today, I would find him at lunchtime, walking from his Main Street office to his house.

I slid into town in Whitey, feeling conspicuous. Never mind that it's been 24 years since I darkened the sun here, I was ready with a partial disguise in case somebody recognized me and rang the bell for the villagers to rush into the streets shouting and waving flaming torches. Hat? Check. Big sunglasses? Check. And something to do while I waited. I had picked up a hamburger and a newspaper. At least I hadn't stooped so low as to bring binoculars. OK, so I forgot them.

I parked half a block away. Within 20 minutes, I spotted Tom walking up the street.

Quickly, I started the car and drove up the street where he walked along the curb (the town is too small even for sidewalks). I scrunched down slightly, as if I were a very short person, kept my head level, and slid the car past him. I could see that his hair was no longer sandy but dark, 'though not gray. He wore a dark coat and a scarf that draped over part of his face. The rest of his face looked exactly the same, maybe a little more serious and care-worn.

This is a man of great civic responsibility, willing to be on the city council or the school board or wherever called upon to serve. Such volunteer jobs in a tiny town are vastly different from big-city power politics. Often somebody has to be recruited to put their name on the ballot. I'm sure he's been everything there is to be and knows everyone and they know him.

He looked straight at me. He dare not ignore a lone lady passing slowly in the white Oldsmobile. Surely he knew me or discussed street improvements with me or perhaps I was a customer or a friend of his mother's.

He drew his hand out of his pocket and flipped his palm up in a little wave. Otherwise, his expression didn't change and in my rear-view window, I could see that the gait of his walk had not altered nor did he turn around to figure out who I was.

Well Tom, you just waved at your ex-wife. Heh, heh, heh.

On that Wednesday in Marysville, I arrived in time to actually contribute a little work at *The Marysville Advocate*, my employer of the late 1970s. The weekly is in a two-story brick building, with a basement where I used to work hurriedly in a photo dark room just as dank and claustrophobic as it sounds. But the graceful building itself echoes a bygone era – before housing the weekly newspaper operation, it was the work place of telephone operators who sat at a switchboard plugging wires and speaking into headsets, keeping the town's communications flowing. Many years later, the Kessingers managed to transform the building into a modern newspaper operation without sacrificing its history and the charm of big-windowed views on the park across the street.

It has been 20 years since my reporting days there, and I revisited those good times by writing a guest column, then joining the employees in the back for the loud and frenzied press run and the folding, stuffing and stacking of 5,000 newspapers.

"Over the next two weeks, we have to put together an expanded edition with a special section – why don't you stay and help us?" Sharon said.

It is soooo tempting.

"I just can't. My sister arrives on Sunday and the auction is next week. I think I'm finally able to make the last big push and get myself home. I want to go home – *Texas*-home. I want my 21st century life back."

On March 17 I woke up and said a prayer.

It is auction day, and its success is now up to others. I feel woefully unprepared. *Lord help me. Make the sun shine. Bring the people. Clear out this stuff. Let me have my life back. Help me make it home.*

Last night, Wayne Wischropp & company brought the farm equipment into the yard, and their flat-bed trucks stand ready to hold goods. There's even a small trailer available to sell snacks and lunch to workers and bidders.

All the household goods are clustered and ready to move out onto the flat-beds. Still, who will do all that? Will anyone, who has said they'd help, show up?

There's also the matter of remaining Smith family residents – Casey and Tertia. *And Lord, the cats need a home.*

There is banging on the front door. Charlotte and Carl Manning walk in quickly as I fiddle with the coffee pot. They are all business.

"Come in here boys!" They have brought three strong teen-agers, and Charlotte becomes a no-nonsense field marshal, ordering them to start the heavy lifting and toting to set up for the auction. As the furniture and boxes are carried out, a team is in the basement wrestling a deep freeze and dismantling an old iron stove.

I am tremendously relieved. The sun is even shining.

"I'm ready for that first fall of the gavel!" my sister exclaims.

"What do you think this is, Sotheby's? This ain't no Manhattan auction house, Martha," I tell her.

"Oh. Well I've never been to an auction."

Soon, the house is literally turned inside out. A refrigerator and microwave, beds and bedding, tables and linens, lamps and recliners line the driveway. The flat-bed trucks hold books and all the little things – dishes, games, tools, toys of children and grandchildren. People arrive and start shuffling around slowly, sizing up the dining room set, the hi-fi, the living room chairs. Serious buyers stake out the tractors and the auction display cases holding silver dollars and antique glass.

It surely sounds sad, but I'm not. I'm realizing that 90 percent of it all hasn't been used in a long time. Now these things can be important again – functional or decorative or simply loved – in thriving households, including those of my family's friends. I focus on the pleasure people derive from being the winning bidder.

Where are the cats? Tertia is somewhere in the house – I wonder what she's thinking, not finding a soft bed to curl up on.

And big Casey, with his funny crooked face but a winning personality – well, he's working the crowd. I spy him strolling here and there, finally winding up on a picnic table trying to engage the man sitting there with a free hand available to pet him. I watch the man try to ignore him. Casey pokes his nose under the hand, which finally draws up and over his pale yellow fur.

The auctioneers plowed through it all as quickly and systematically as a combine cuts wheat. The yard was beginning to empty out, and people were loading their buys into cars and pickups that lined the road.

"Miss Moore?"

A man who had been preparing to leave with his bounty walked back toward me. He handed me a small sterling silver spoon covered in good-luck symbols, four-leaf clovers and horsehoes.

"Turn it over," he said. "You may want to keep that.'

The spoon was engraved: "Jane Blaney. July 15, 1915." He was returning my mother's baby spoon.

Meanwhile, back at the picnic table...

"You like him? He's on the auction block too, but we'll make you a swell deal," I said.

The man with the lazy hand has become Casey's best buddy. The cat has stayed put, lolling around on the tabletop, content to stop working the rest of the crowd.

"I was just tellin' my wife that's a nice cat."

Just then, the man's wife appears and starts petting the cat, and soon they leave – with Casey. He has a new farm home with, I understand, a number of feline brothers and sisters.

When the auction ended, the yard swiftly emptied of people and Smith family possessions as if swept by a Kansas cyclone. Oh, there were a few odd things that people either forgot to take away or decided to leave behind, but a cyclone always leaves debris.

Today, history blew away. Ancient history to me. I've saved the few remnants I care to have as links – a wooden rocker, an antique clock, metal cookie cutters in Christmas shapes – but the rest resides in photographs now and I have no trouble letting go of the other, tangible forms. The people it all belonged to were important; the things themselves mean little.

Martha and Paul and I did not linger to contemplate all these meanings. In the late afternoon, we loaded my belongings – which now include Tertia the cat – and my sister's chosen keepsakes, packing every square inch of their van. We locked up the house, climbed in the car and peeled out scattering gravel, for we were in desperate agreement that we wanted to head south and drive as fast and as far as we could toward Texas.

And so my big idea, my grand tour, has come to an end this way, not in the state of Kansas or Texas, but in a Land of Irony. The freedom I thought I was embracing never really existed.

When I started out, I'd contemplated the idea of being forced home by unforeseen problems – and indeed, Sara caused that to happen – but then to go to the state of my birth, to the place that made my whole life possible at all, is ironic and humbling. In the large scheme of things, the parents who always encouraged my independence had drawn me home, but certainly not by intent or design. Credit for that plan surely goes to God, although if He sent me out on my grand tour just to set up my availability to take care of the farm this winter, His methods certainly seem convoluted.

Other things impinge on true freedom to move around. On a practical level, I worried about health insurance, and eventually bought a modest policy. Its premium costs grew by leaps and bounds, certainly out-pacing the wages of little jobs, and my thoughts return to the yoke of professional life with a salary and benefits. I hope and believe that I flexed some new muscles on all the different roads I explored, giving me skills and strengths for the work place and a renewed confidence in the adage that we mustn't sweat the small stuff in life.

I also never imagined the role that people would play in supporting my adventures. I looked forward to traveling and settling into my destinations alone, making them home-like, and answerable to no one on the decisions I made. I was conceited enough to think that it was mostly up to me to make this the year I wanted it to be. But time after time, I was astounded by the willingness of people to help me, with little to go on but blind trust and their own sense of goodness.

Remember how I bragged about living with all my worldly possessions fitting into a car? Obviously, there's more to moving around in the world than that. We all carry lots of baggage all the time. Most of it is good – I'd never give up my sense of responsibility and adventure and a good work ethic – but the material possessions we think we can't live without too often weigh us down and cut us off from life. Stuff is OK if you want to stay home and look at it and take care of it and saddle your heirs with it, but it's the people, the sights and the sensory pleasures of the world that supply life's wealth. The spirit is sustained by love and friendship, a soul by the experiences of seeing and learning, whether the landscape is right around you or far away.

I can't wait to get home to Texas, to resume life pretty much the way it was, with some predictable routine again and a good job. But if that doesn't happen, I now know there are a lot of other routes to happiness, and other ways to feel "at home."

AFTERWORD

Sara is dead.

"How do you really know that?" my brother Ed probed.

As a lawyer and a judge familiar with the ways of criminals, Ed questioned my evidence, but I had proof. I heard about Sara's death, caused by cancer, from her friend Doris who learned about it from another friend. Sara died in an Arlington, Texas, hospital mere weeks after my return home from Kansas. I found the newspaper obituary online.

In the previous December, when I confronted her and she tearfully talked about her cancer, I thought she was the girl who cried wolf.

I don't know if that hastened my forgiveness, but I quickly got over her deeds. Besides, she could have done a lot more damage, and I think she struggled mightily against the thievery and other demons in her head. When I moved back into my Hurst condo, there was a strange decal stuck on the headboard of my bed that said, "No Hate In My Heart." So I took that idea on myself.

It's now been ten years since my turn-of-the-millennium tour.

It's not surprising that many of my loved ones who figured prominently in this tale are now gone – my mother, my aunt Lugene, Carolyn Walton, my sweet cat Bigelow….

You don't expect PLACES to go away, but those passings sadden me as well. Greensburg, Kansas. The World Trade Center. Lyndon's A&L Café, which was in an old decrepit building that was demolished. And one day, on a 2004 trip to New York City, I was informed upon checkout at the Olcott that the hotel was closing and being converted into apartments.

It's silly to equate people and places in the same way, isn't it? After the tornado hit Greensburg, it was described as "gone," but now it is being rebuilt. The A&L was razed, and in better economic times, something else will probably be built there, too. Yet I grieved the changes at the Olcott as if "she" were a person turning me out.

Another inanimate object of sentimental attachment: the old Honda, which I sold in 2002. I know it wound up in Dallas and was possibly involved in a life of crime; a ticket was forwarded to me when the car dealer didn't get the paperwork changed promptly.

My year as a runaway left its mark on me, changing the course of my life by introducing new influences, and resurfacing old ones. "Dropping out" for a year didn't seem to hurt my career, and what else would a wanderer get into next but work related to transportation? I returned to communication management, first with the Fort Worth Transportation Authority and later for Easter Seals Inc. and a federal project that's about transportation. I moved to Northern Virginia and commuted daily into Washington, D.C.

Five years in Washington finally ended my infatuation with cities. Life on the bustling East Coast was exciting at first, but the novelty quickly wore off. All the hassles of just getting around, of driving on streets and highways dense with traffic, navigating crowds at events and grocery stores, the tyranny of public transit schedules and delays – all leave little time for a meaningful life outside the work day.

Another reason I detested Washington was its values. Too many people believe in their own self-importance. I would love to see some of them try my experiment and find out just how tenuous that hold on power and "influence" really is.

And so, I have returned to small-town life. After 36 years of being away, in 2008 I moved back to my hometown of Independence, Kansas. The only things I miss are restaurant choices and theatres showing independent films. Otherwise, it's a far richer life for me. I've joined organizations and causes, and rekindled friendships with childhood friends, many of whom have returned to care for aging parents. Every place I go in town is between 1 and 7 minutes away.

New friends mix with the old in my life, and there are new family members in the generation of my niece and nephews. And I'm still a traveler – fascinating destinations are a mere car- or plane-ride away.

But for day-to-day life, I'm really glad I've made it home.

ABOUT THE AUTHOR

Born in Independence, Kansas, Liz Moore is a journalism graduate of Kansas State University. She is a former reporter, editor and photographer for newspapers in Kansas and in Texas. She was the national communications director for The Arc of the United States in Arlington, Texas, and served as a communication and marketing manager for the Fort Worth Transportation Authority and for federal transportation projects of Easter Seals Inc. in Washington, D.C. Now a resident again of Independence, she is the  site director for the Little House on the Prairie Museum. *Making It Home* is her first book.

(Photo by John Koschin)